Bailey

ROBERT J. MARZANO

DEBRA J. PICKERING

with TAMMY HEFLEBOWER

The Highly Engaged Classroom

Marzano Research Laboratory
Powered by Solution Tree

THE **CLASSROOM** STRATEGIES **SERIES**

555 North Morton Street
Bloomington, IN 47404

888.849.0851
FAX: 866.801.1447

email: info@marzanoresearch.com
marzanoresearch.com

Visit **marzanoresearch.com/classroomstrategies** to download the reproducibles in this book.

Printed in the United States of America

Library of Congress Control Number: 2010909217

ISBN: 978-0-9822592-4-5 (paperback)

978-0-9822592-5-2 (library binding)

14   13   12   11   5

FSC
Mixed Sources
Product group from well-managed
forests and other controlled sources

Cert no. SW-COC-002283
www.fsc.org
© 1996 Forest Stewardship Council

Vice President of Production: Gretchen Knapp

Managing Production Editor: Caroline Wise

Copy Editor: Sarah Payne-Mills

Proofreader: Elisabeth Abrams

Text Designer: Raven Bongiani

Cover Designer: Amy Shock

MARZANO RESEARCH LABORATORY DEVELOPMENT TEAM

Staff Writer

Lindsay A. Carleton

Marzano Research Laboratory Associates

Bev Clemens

Jane K. Doty Fischer

Maria C. Foseid

Mark P. Foseid

Tammy Heflebower

Mitzi Hoback

Jan Hoegh

Edie Holcomb

Sharon Kramer

David Livingston

Beatrice McGarvey

Margaret McInteer

Diane E. Paynter

Debra Pickering

Salle Quackenboss

Tom Roy

Phil Warrick

ACKNOWLEDGMENTS

Marzano Research Laboratory would like to thank the following reviewers:

Abbigail Armstrong
Assistant Professor, Department of Curriculum
  and Instruction
Winthrop University
Rock Hill, South Carolina

Margaret Ferrara
Associate Professor, Department of Curriculum,
  Teaching, and Learning
University of Nevada, Reno
Reno, Nevada

Lee Freeman
Clinical Assistant Professor, Department of
  Curriculum and Instruction
University of Alabama
Tuscaloosa, Alabama

Jacey Morrill
Eighth-Grade Mathematics and Science Teacher
Greely Middle School
Cumberland, Maine

Michelle Switala
Mathematics Teacher
Pine-Richland High School
Gibsonia, Pennsylvania

CONTENTS

Italicized entries indicate reproducible pages.

CHAPTER 3

CHAPTER 4

CHAPTER 5

CAN I DO THIS?

CHAPTER 6

PLANNING FOR HIGH ENGAGEMENT

ABOUT THE AUTHORS

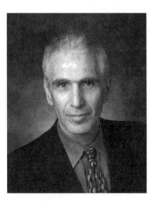 Dr. Robert J. Marzano is the cofounder and CEO of Marzano Research Laboratory in Denver, Colorado. Throughout his forty years in the field of education, he has become a speaker, trainer, and author of more than thirty books and 150 articles on topics such as instruction, assessment, writing and implementing standards, cognition, effective leadership, and school intervention. His books include: *The Art and Science of Teaching: A Comprehensive Framework for Effective Instruction*, *Making Standards Useful in the Classroom*, *District Leadership That Works: Striking the Right Balance*, *Designing and Teaching Learning Goals and Objectives*, *Formative Assessment and Standards-Based Grading*, *On Excellence in Teaching*, and *Vocabulary Games for the Classroom*. His practical translations of the most current research and theory into classroom strategies are internationally known and widely practiced by both teachers and administrators. He received a bachelor's degree from Iona College in New York, a master's degree from Seattle University, and a doctorate from the University of Washington.

 Dr. Debra Pickering consults with schools and districts nationally and internationally as a senior scholar for Marzano Research Laboratory. Throughout her educational career, Dr. Pickering has gained practical experience as a classroom teacher, building leader, and district administrator. For many years, she has used this experience to provide training and support to K–12 teachers and administrators as they seek to continually improve student learning.In addition to her work with schools, Dr. Pickering has coauthored (with Dr. Robert Marzano) educational books and manuals, including *Dimensions of Learning*, *Classroom Instruction That Works: Research-Based Strategies for Increasing Student Achievement*, *Classroom Management That Works: Research-Based Strategies for Every Teacher*, and *Building Academic Vocabulary*. With a combination of theoretical grounding and over three decades of practical experience, Dr. Pickering has worked with educators to translate theory into practice. Her work continues to focus on the study of learning and the development of resources for curriculum, instruction, and assessment to help all educators meet the needs of all students. Dr. Pickering has a master's degree in school administration and a doctorate in curriculum and instruction, with an emphasis in cognitive psychology.

Tammy Heflebower, EdD, is vice president of Marzano Research Laboratory in Denver, Colorado. She is a consultant with experience in urban, rural, and suburban districts throughout North America. Dr. Heflebower has served as a classroom teacher, building-level leader, district leader, regional professional development director, and national trainer. She has also been an adjunct professor of curriculum, instruction, and assessment courses at several universities. Dr. Heflebower began her teaching career in Kansas City, Kansas, and later moved to Nebraska, where she received the District Distinguished Teacher Award. She has worked as a national educational trainer for the National Resource and Training Center at Girls and Boys Town in Nebraska. A prominent member of numerous educational organizations, Dr. Heflebower has served as president of the Nebraska Association for Supervision and Curriculum Development and president-elect for the Professional Development Organization for Nebraska Educational Service Units. She was president-elect of the Colorado Association of Education Specialists and legislative liaison for the Colorado Association of School Executives. Her articles have been featured in the monthly newsletter *Nebraska Council of School Administrators Today*, and she is a contributor to *The Teacher as Assessment Leader* and *The Principal as Assessment Leader*.

Dr. Heflebower holds a bachelor of arts from Hastings College in Hastings, Nebraska, a master of arts from the University of Nebraska at Omaha, and an educational administrative endorsement from the University of Nebraska-Lincoln. She also earned a doctor of education in educational administration from the University of Nebraska-Lincoln.

ABOUT MARZANO RESEARCH LABORATORY

Marzano Research Laboratory (MRL) is a joint venture between Solution Tree and Dr. Robert J. Marzano. MRL combines Dr. Marzano's forty years of educational research with continuous action research in all major areas of schooling in order to provide effective and accessible instructional strategies, leadership strategies, and classroom assessment strategies that are always at the forefront of best practice. By providing such an all-inclusive research-into-practice resource center, MRL provides teachers and principals the tools they need to effect profound and immediate improvement in student achievement.

INTRODUCTION

The Highly Engaged Classroom is part of the series of books collectively referred to as *The Classroom Strategies Series*. The purpose of this series is to provide teachers as well as building and district administrators with an in-depth treatment of research-based instructional strategies that can be used in the classroom to enhance student achievement. Many of the strategies addressed in this series have been covered in other works such as *The Art and Science of Teaching* (Marzano, 2007), *Classroom Management That Works* (Marzano, 2003), and *Classroom Instruction That Works* (Marzano, Pickering, & Pollock, 2001). Although those works devoted a chapter or part of a chapter to particular strategies, *The Classroom Strategies Series* devotes an entire book to an instructional strategy or set of related strategies.

Engagement is obviously a central aspect of effective teaching. If students are not engaged, there is little, if any, chance that they will learn what is being addressed in class. A basic premise of this book is that student engagement happens as a result of a teacher's careful planning and execution of specific strategies. In other words, student engagement is not serendipitous. Of course, no teacher will have all students engaged at high levels all of the time; however, using the suggestions presented in this book, every teacher can create a classroom environment in which engagement is the norm instead of the exception.

We begin with a brief but inclusive chapter that reviews the research and theory on engagement. Although you could skip this chapter and move right into those that provide recommendations for classroom practice, you are strongly encouraged to examine the research and theory, as they are the foundation for the entire book. Indeed, a basic purpose of *The Highly Engaged Classroom* and others in *The Classroom Strategies Series* is to present the most useful instructional strategies based on the strongest research and theory available.

Because research and theory can provide only a general direction for classroom practice, *The Highly Engaged Classroom* (and each book in the series) goes one step further to translate that research into applications for the classroom. Specifically, it addresses four emblematic questions students ask themselves, the answers to which determine how involved students are in classroom activities.

The first question, "How do I feel?," addresses the affective side of learning. The second question, "Am I interested?," deals with the extent to which classroom activities intrigue students. These first two questions combined constitute what we refer to as *attention* (as opposed to *engagement*). Attention is a short-term phenomenon that ranges from a few seconds to a few minutes. Emblematic questions three and four deal with engagement—a more long-term phenomenon lasting beyond the parameters of a single class period. Question three, "Is this important?," addresses the extent to which students perceive classroom goals as related to their personal goals. Question four, "Can I do this?," deals with the extent to which students have or cultivate a sense of self-efficacy. For each of these four emblematic questions, specific classroom strategies are provided in chapters 2 through 5.

How to Use This Book

The Highly Engaged Classroom was designed as a self-study text that provides an in-depth understanding of how to generate high levels of attention and engagement. As you progress through the chapters, you will encounter exercises. It is important to complete these exercises and then compare your answers with those in the back of the text. Such interaction provides a review of the content and allows you to examine how clearly you understand it.

Teams of teachers or entire faculties that wish to examine the topic of engagement in-depth may also use *The Highly Engaged Classroom*. When this is the case, teacher teams should do the exercises independently and then compare their answers in small-group and large-group settings.

Chapter 1

RESEARCH AND THEORY

Student engagement has long been recognized as the core of effective schooling. In the book *Engaging Schools*, the National Research Council's Committee on Increasing High School Students' Engagement and Motivation to Learn (2004) explains that "research on motivation and engagement is essential to understanding some of the most fundamental and vexing challenges of school reform" (p. 14).

Despite its obvious importance to teaching and learning, engagement is not an easily defined construct. As Ellen Skinner, Thomas Kindermann, James Connell, and James Wellborn (2009) stated, "There is, of course, no single correct definition of *engagement*" (p. 224). They noted that a variety of constructs seem to overlap in meaning and use—specifically *motivation, engagement, attention, interest, effort, enthusiasm, participation*, and *involvement*. Because our audience is the classroom teacher as opposed to researchers and theorists, we do not attempt to reconcile differences among researchers and theorists regarding Skinner and her colleagues' constructs. Rather, our attempt is to articulate an internally consistent perspective on engagement that K–12 classroom teachers can use to plan and execute specific strategies that enhance student engagement. We first examine the four topics that constitute our model of attention and engagement and are typical aspects of any engagement discussion: (1) emotions, (2) interest, (3) perceived importance, and (4) perceptions of efficacy.

Emotions: How Do I Feel?

With every new situation, feelings affect human behavior. In a sense, we ask the question "How do I feel?" If our emotions are negative in that moment, we are less likely to engage in new activities or challenging tasks. Skinner et al. (2009) associated the following emotions with engagement:

- Enthusiasm

- Interest

- Enjoyment

- Satisfaction

- Pride

- Vitality

- Zest (p. 227)

In addition, they associated the following emotions with a lack of engagement, or "disaffection" as they referred to it:

- Boredom

- Disinterest

- Frustration

- Anger

- Sadness

- Worry/Anxiety

- Shame

- Self-blame (p. 227)

It is certainly true that the first set of emotions can be considered effects of high engagement—when students are engaged, they tend to experience enthusiasm, enjoyment, and the like. However, teachers can also think of these emotions as affective states that set the stage for engagement—when students feel enthusiastic or zestful, they are more disposed to engage in new behaviors and tasks.

In his review of the research on motivation, Reinhard Pekrun (2009) explained that emotions affect a wide variety of human behaviors, one of which is engagement. Indeed, Gary Ladd, Sarah Herald-Brown, and Karen Kochel (2009) identified emotional engagement as one of a number of types of engagement (others include cognitive engagement and behavioral engagement). The classroom certainly influences many aspects of emotional engagement. Here we consider three: (1) students' energy levels, (2) a teacher's positive demeanor, and (3) students' perceptions of acceptance.

Students' Energy Levels

One primary factor in how students answer the question "How do I feel?" is the level of activity in the classroom (National Research Council, 2004). The activity in a classroom affects students' energy, or what some psychologists refer to as *arousal*. Elizabeth Styles (1997) explained arousal in the following way:

> [It] is rather like a limited power supply: if you turn on the rings of a gas cooker, and the central heating boiler fires up, the height of the gas jets in the cooker rings goes down. There is only a limited supply of gas to these two appliances, and the demand from the boiler reduces the amount of fuel available to the cooker. (p. 140)

Styles's characterization indicates that any classroom task that raises the level of activity in the classroom can help heighten students' energy levels. Maintaining a lively pace can help keep energy high. Edmund Emmer and Mary Claire Gerwels (2006) explain that "the teacher needs to keep the activity moving and avoid interruptions to the activity flow by using good pacing" (p. 423). Pacing is key when transitioning from one activity to another. Poorly orchestrated transitions can waste time and create a lull in classroom activity, making it difficult for students to stay engaged (Arlin, 1979). Efficient transitions that teachers have practiced in class allow students to quickly respond to brief signals.

Another classroom factor related to energy level is the amount and type of physical movement that occurs within the classroom. Eric Jensen (2005) cited a number of studies that connect physical activity to enhanced engagement (Dwyer, Blizzard, & Dean, 1996; Dwyer, Sallis, Blizzard, Lazarus, & Dean, 2001). Jensen (2005) explained this connection in terms of oxygen: "Oxygen is essential for brain function, and enhanced blood flow increases the amount of oxygen transported to the brain. Physical activity is a reliable way to increase blood flow, and hence oxygen, to the brain" (p. 62). Jensen (2005) also noted, "Amazingly, the part of the brain that processes movement is the same part of the brain that processes learning" (p. 61).

Supporting Jensen's assertions is the fact that regular physical exercise has been associated with improved cognitive functioning (Colcombe & Kramer, 2003). Physical activity seems to have a particularly beneficial effect on executive functioning. According to Sabine Kubesch et al. (2009), executive functioning affects a wide variety of cognitive processes such as planning, decision making, and recognizing and correcting errors. As it relates to student engagement, physical exercise has been shown to enhance students' abilities to attend to classroom activity—even in the face of distraction. Specifically, Kubesch et al. (2009) examined the effects of a single thirty-minute exercise program with thirteen- and fourteen-year-old students. They reported their findings as follows: "In our study, we showed that a single PE program of 30 min leads to an improvement in the maintenance of on-task attention in the face of distraction. This, in turn, may support students' selective, sustained, and focused attention processes" (p. 240).

A Teacher's Positive Demeanor

A positive demeanor on the part of the teacher is the second and most general influence on emotional engagement. The teacher can communicate a positive demeanor in a number of ways, one of which is through demonstrating enthusiasm and intensity, both of which have been associated with student engagement and achievement (Bettencourt, Gillett, Gall, & Hull, 1983; Armento, 1978; McConnell, 1977). Barak Rosenshine (1970) surmised that teacher enthusiasm facilitates student achievement "because animated behavior arouses the attending behavior of pupils" (p. 510). Other studies support this notion (Coats & Smidchens, 1966; Land, 1980; Mastin, 1963; Williams & Ware, 1976, 1977; Wyckoff, 1973).

Thomas Good and Jere Brophy (2003) described intensity and enthusiasm in the following way:

> An intense presentation will begin with a direct statement of the importance of the message ("I am going to show you how to invert fractions—now pay close attention and make sure you understand these procedures"). Then, the message itself is presented using verbal and nonverbal public speaking techniques that convey intensity and cue enthusiasm: a slow-paced, step-by-step presentation during which key words are emphasized; unusual voice modulations or exaggerated gestures that focus attention on key terms or procedural steps; and intense scanning of the group following each step to look for signs of understanding or confusion (and to allow anyone with a question to ask it immediately). In addition to the words being spoken, *everything about the teacher's tone and manner communicates to the student that what is being said is important* and that they should give it full attention and ask questions about anything they do not understand. (p. 238)

Brophy (2004) emphasized that teachers should be enthusiastic regularly and intense selectively. About enthusiasm he says:

Students take cues from the teacher about how to respond to school activities. If you present a topic or assignment with enthusiasm . . . your students are likely to adopt this same attitude. . . . *Projecting enthusiasm does not mean pep talks or phony theatrics.* . . . You can use dramatics or forceful salesmanship if you are comfortable with these techniques, but if not, low-key but sincere statements of the value that you place on a topic or activity will be just as effective. (pp. 274–275)

Brophy (2004) explained that intensity is communicated through timing, verbal and nonverbal expressions, and gestures that tell students the material is important and deserves close attention. Often, intensity is first signaled by statements like "I'm going to show you how to balance this type of equation. This is important, and I need you to pay close attention." Brophy (2004) cautioned, "Pick your spots for using such an intense communication style. You cannot be so intense all the time, and even if you could, your students would adjust to it so that it would lose much of its effectiveness" (p. 276).

A teacher's positive demeanor is also communicated by using humor. In the book *Laughing and Learning*, Peter Jonas (2010) summarized the research on the relationship between humor and student achievement and engagement. He noted that "using humor to improve classroom instruction is not only supported by research, but it has proven to be successful" (p. 27). Jonas's positive findings for using humor in the classroom included the following:

- Humor was associated with a 40 percentile point gain in instructional effectiveness.
- Humor can change the culture of a classroom.
- Humor is associated with enhanced productivity.
- Humor reduces stress in students.
- Humor promotes creative thinking.

Students' Perceptions of Acceptance

Students' perceptions of acceptance is the third determiner of how they feel about themselves and the classroom environment. Stated differently, if students sense that they are not welcome, accepted, or supported in the classroom, it is unlikely that they will engage in classroom activities. Certainly, the relationship teachers have with students is one of the most powerful determiners of how a student answers the question "How do I feel?" Carol Goodenow (1993) found teacher support was consistently the strongest predictor of motivation among students in sixth through eighth grades. Kathryn Wentzel (2009) explained the importance of the relationship teachers have with students in the following way:

Secure relationships are believed to foster children's curiosity and exploration of the environment, positive coping skills, and a mental representation of oneself as being worthy of love and of others being trustworthy. In contrast, insecure attachments are believed to result in either wary or inappropriately risky behavior, difficulty in regulating stress in new settings, and negative self-concepts. (p. 302)

Ladd et al. (2009) explained that peer relationships are equally as important as teacher-student relationships:

> When peers dislike persons within their group they tend to act in rejecting
> ways toward these children (e.g., ignoring, excluding them from activities),
> and these behaviors become observable indicators of rejection not only for
> rejected children but for the larger peer group. (p. 327)

One might make a case that peer relationships have an even stronger effect on students than their relationships with teachers. For example, a study by Ladd et al. (2009) found that the longer students were rejected by their peers, the less likely they were to participate in classroom activities. However, when students moved out of rejection status, they tended to re-engage. They noted that the most profound cases of disengagement were observed in students whose peers continually rejected them throughout grade school.

Clearly the relationships students have with the teacher and with their peers have a profound effect on their perceptions of being welcomed, accepted, and supported, which, in turn, help establish an affective tone that either promotes or discourages student engagement. A teacher can take concrete steps to foster accepting and supportive teacher-student and peer relationships, thus increasing the probability that students will respond positively to the emblematic question "How do I feel?" We consider many of those strategies in chapter 2.

Interest: Am I Interested?

A second emblematic question that influences engagement is "Am I interested?" Even if an individual is engaged emotionally (responds positively to the question "How do I feel?"), he or she may still fail to engage in a new activity simply because he or she doesn't perceive it as interesting.

Ulrich Schiefele (2009) summarized much of the research on interest and made a distinction between *situational interest* and *individual interest*. According to Schiefele, "Situational interest describes a short-term psychological state that involves focused attention, increased cognitive function, persistence, enjoyment or affective involvement, and curiosity" (p. 198). A student paying particular attention to a science teacher's demonstration because it appears to defy the laws of gravity is an example of situational interest. The situation captures the student's attention. Individual interest, on the other hand, is more of a long-term phenomenon, and represents one's general disposition toward a specific topic. For example, an individual's personal interest in hockey lasts well beyond a specific situation. In this section, we focus on situational interest. The topic of individual interest is more germane to the next section on perceived importance.

Suzanne Hidi and William Baird (1986) and Mathew Mitchell (1993) distinguished between two forms of situational interest. *Triggered situational interest* involves capturing a student's attention. *Maintained situational interest* involves holding a student's interest over time. Both of these types of situational interest are important to the classroom teacher, who must catch and then hold attention. How does this happen? To answer this question, we begin with a model of the interaction between three types of memory: *sensory memory*, *working memory*, and *permanent memory* (fig. 1.1).

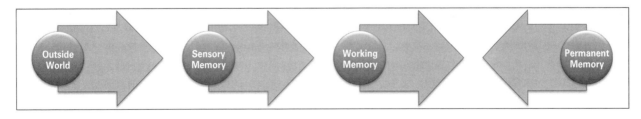

Figure 1.1: Model of interaction between three types of memory.

Sensory memory addresses temporary storage of data from the senses. As indicated in figure 1.1 (page 7), it is the conduit from the outside world. John Anderson (1995) described sensory memory in the following way:

> Sensory memory is capable of storing more or less complete records of what has been encountered for brief periods of time, during which people can note relationships among the elements and encode the elements in a more permanent memory. If the information in sensory memory is not encoded in the brief time before it decays, it is lost. What subjects encode depends on what they are paying attention to. The environment typically offers much more information at one time than we can attend to and encode. Therefore, much of what enters our sensory system results in no permanent record. (p. 160)

At any moment in time, then, a myriad of stimuli bombard an individual's senses and not all the stimuli are attended to. More specifically, only those that reach working memory become part of a person's conscious attention.

As its name implies, working memory is where data are actively processed. As illustrated in figure 1.1 (page 7), working memory can receive data from the outside world through sensory memory or from permanent memory. Even though working memory can hold only small amounts of information for a single situation, there is no theoretical limit to the amount of time information can reside there. As long as an individual focuses conscious attention on the data in working memory, those data stay active. To this extent, working memory is the seat of consciousness. A person's experience of consciousness is actually his or her experience of what is being processed in working memory (Dennett, 1969, 1991).

Permanent memory contains all stored experiences and all learned knowledge. For example, a student's memory of what occurred in class the previous day is stored in permanent memory, sometimes referred to as episodic memory (Buckner & Barch, 1999). Students' understanding of a topic like the cell membrane or the Civil War is also stored in permanent memory, sometimes referred to as a declarative memory (Anderson, 1995). Finally, permanent memory is where skills and processes such as balancing an algebraic equation, editing a composition for overall logic, or hitting a baseball are stored. This is sometimes referred to as production memory or procedural memory (Anderson, 1995).

The relationships between the three types of memory help explain triggered situational interest and maintained situational interest. If information does not get into working memory, it has no chance of being processed. Because working memory cannot hold very much information for a single situation, there is a constant battle, so to speak, between the outside world and the inside world (permanent memory) as to what working memory will store. The information from the outside world must trigger interest to get into working memory. However, simply triggering interest does not suffice. Information must be kept in working memory throughout a class period or at least part of a class period if it is to be encoded. Sustained occupation of working memory is called maintained situational interest.

The preceding description highlights the challenges a teacher faces on a day-to-day basis. While in class, a teacher is always vying for students' attention. If what is occurring in class does not capture and hold students' attention (enter and then occupy their working memories), then students will turn their attention to information from their permanent memories that has nothing to do with the classroom, such as last night's basketball game or seeing a boyfriend or girlfriend during the previous class. Here we discuss four ways to trigger and maintain situational interest: (1) using game-like activities, (2) initiating friendly controversy, (3) using unusual information, and (4) using effective questioning strategies.

Game-Like Activities

A number of classroom activities have the potential to capture and hold students' attention. Game-like activities help trigger situational interest and provide a foundation for maintained situational interest because they tap into the psychological principle of *clozentropy* (see Broadhurst & Darnell, 1965; Darnell, 1970, 1972; Taylor, 1953; Weiner, 1967). Basically, the theory of clozentropy states that the human mind will naturally attend to situations that have missing details. Hermann Ebbinghaus (1987) addressed this point, noting that human beings tend to fill in the blanks when presented with incomplete information. Based on this theory, Wilson Taylor (1953) developed a method of testing English proficiency that systematically leaves out words from text. To illustrate, consider the following: Mary went to the _____ to swim but she found that she forgot her _____. As you read this incomplete sentence, your mind naturally fills in words such as *pool* and *bathing suit*.

Incongruity Theories

Incongruity theories also support the utility of game-like activities to generate situational interest. As George Loewenstein (1994) explained, incongruity theories postulate that human beings have a natural tendency "to make sense of the world" (p. 82). Fundamentally, any activity with a rich contextual background that presents students with missing information will trigger situational interest. Games certainly fit into this category (Mitchell, 1992). A number of meta-analyses have been conducted on the effects of games and game-like activities on student achievement (see table 1.1).

Table 1.1: Meta-Analyses of the Effects of Games and Game-Like Activities on Student Achievement

Synthesis Study	Number of ESs	Average ES	Percentile Gain
Szczurek, 1982[a]	58	0.33	13
VanSickle, 1986[a]	42	0.43	17
Haystead & Marzano, 2009	62	0.46	18

[a]Reported in Hattie (2009)

Table 1.1 reports the results of three meta-analyses. Critical to understanding table 1.1 are the concepts of meta-analysis and effect size (ES), which appendix B (page 183) explains in some depth. Briefly though, a *meta-analysis* is a research technique for synthesizing a series of studies on the same topic. Typically, meta-analytic studies report their findings in terms of average ESs (see the average ES column in table 1.1). An *effect size* tells you how many standard deviations larger (or smaller) the average score for a group of students who were exposed to a given strategy (in this case, games and game-like activities) is than the average score for a group of students who were not exposed to a given strategy (in this case, no games). In short, an ES tells you how powerful a strategy is; the larger the ES, the more the strategy increases student learning.

ESs are typically small numbers. However, small ESs can translate into big percentile gains. For example, the average ES of 0.43 calculated by Ronald VanSickle (1986) translates to a 17 percentile point gain. (See appendix B, page 183, for a detailed description of ESs and a chart that translates ES numbers into percentile gains.) Another way of saying this is that researchers would predict a student at the fiftieth percentile in a class where games and game-like activities were not provided (an average student in that class) to rise to the sixty-seventh percentile if he or she were provided with games or game-like activities.

The third report in table 1.1 (Haystead & Marzano, 2009) was conducted at Marzano Research Laboratory with classroom teachers. It is particularly relevant to the perspective of this book because it informed many of the strategies presented in chapter 3.

Inconsequential Competition

Inconsequential competition is an aspect of games that can help trigger and maintain situational interest. Good and Brophy (2003) explained:

> The opportunity to compete can add excitement to classroom activities, whether the competition is for prizes or merely for the satisfaction of winning. Competition may be either individual (students compete against everyone else) or group (students are divided into teams that compete with one another). (p. 227)

As its name implies, inconsequential competition has no consequence regarding students' grades or status, it is simply done for fun (Marzano, 2007). However, this type of competition can stimulate a mild form of pressure that naturally comes with a competitive situation. It is important to note that pressure can be deleterious to well-being in general (Ito, Larsen, Smith, & Cacioppo, 2002; Roozendaal, 2003). However, it is also true that mild pressure can help focus attention (Cahill, Gorski, & Lee, 2003; Shors, Weiss, & Thompson, 1992; Van Honk et al., 2003).

Consequently, when playing games, pressure should remain at the right level of intensity and duration to provide positive benefits for engagement. Specifically, teachers should organize competitive games in such a way that students enjoy the challenge but do not feel compelled to win. Competition might have a negative consequence in that it could embarrass some students on losing teams (Epstein & Harackiewicz, 1992; Moriarity, Douglas, Punch, & Hattie, 1995; Reeve & Deci, 1996). In response to losing, team members may scapegoat individuals they believe are responsible for the team loss (Ames, 1984; Grant & Dweck, 2001; Johnson & Johnson, 1985). This caution noted, if teams are constantly reorganized so all students have a chance to experience winning and losing, teachers can avoid this potentially negative consequence.

Friendly Controversy

Another way to trigger and maintain situational interest is through controversy. David Johnson and Roger Johnson (1979) explained that within any learning situation, academic conflicts will naturally arise: "They will occur no matter what the teacher does" (p. 51). However, they noted that "the current evidence indicates that in most classrooms conflicts are avoided and suppressed" (p. 51). In their review of the research, they built a strong case for the fact that conflict can be used in the classroom to enhance student achievement, noting that "controversies among students can promote transitions to higher stages of cognitive and moral reasoning" (p. 55).

Good and Brophy (2003) described controversy strategies in the following way: "Controversy strategies include eliciting divergent opinions on an issue and then inviting students to resolve their discrepancies through sustained discussion" (p. 240). Johnson and Johnson (1985) explained that "*controversy* exists when one person's ideas, information, conclusions, theories, or opinions are incompatible with those of another person and the two seek to reach an agreement" (p. 238). They distinguished this from *debate*: "*Debate* exists when two or more students argue positions that are incompatible and a winner is declared on the basis of who presented their position best" (pp. 238–239).

Nancy Lowry and David Johnson (1981, as cited in Loewenstein, 1994) conducted one of the most frequently cited studies on the positive effects of controversy in the classroom. Fifth and sixth graders were randomly assigned to groups that foster either consensus or controversy. The hypothesis under investigation was that the controversy groups would stimulate more curiosity in students. In fact, students in the controversy group expressed more interest in the topic, reported more study time on the topic, and used more special sources such as those found in the school library. Perhaps the most interesting finding in the study was that, when presented with opportunities to view an optional film about the topic during recess, 45 percent of the controversy group attended, whereas only 18 percent of the consensus group attended.

In a later study, Johnson and Johnson (1985) examined the effects of three treatments of a specific topic. One group of fifth- and sixth-grade students studied the topic individually, though they were involved in group discussion about the topic. Another group engaged in a cooperative debate, the purpose of which was to logically debate the two sides of the issue. The third group engaged in cooperative controversy. Where the cooperative debate group focused on winning an argument, the cooperative controversy group focused on exploring differences in perspective and opinion. Relative to the other groups, the cooperative controversy group excelled in actively searching for information about the topic, re-evaluating its own position, and developing accepting and supportive relationships among students with and without physical challenges. Members of the group also demonstrated the most attitudinal change, the most interest in the subject matter, and the highest self-esteem. The students in the cooperative debate group were superior to those in the individual learning group but not superior to the cooperative controversy group on these measures. Johnson and Johnson (1985) concluded that both cooperative debate and cooperative controversy are useful instructional tools, but cooperative controversy is the more powerful relative to a variety of outcomes.

Unusual Information

A third activity that triggers and helps maintain situational interest is the use of unusual information. Brophy (2004) explained this in the context of curiosity, noting that "student curiosity is the driving force that underlies many theorists' suggestions for motivating students" (p. 227). Apparently, the behavioral effects of interest cross species. Loewenstein (1994) reported that "animals and humans seek out environmental variability. For example, a large number of studies showed that rats would explore the less familiar of two arms of a maze" (p. 77). Martin Covington and Karen Teel (1996) cited the use of oddities to help capture students' attention. Brophy (2004), however, warned that overuse and superficial use of unusual information and oddities "may focus [students'] curiosity on seductive but trivial details" (p. 227). Additionally, he noted that when they are used superficially, students "may lose interest in the topic once their initial curiosity is satisfied" (p. 227).

Effective Questioning Strategies

Finally, effective questioning strategies can trigger situational interest and help foster maintained situational interest. Specifically, it makes intuitive sense that when a student is answering a question, his or her working memory is fully attentive to the task at hand. Students' attention to questions is most likely due to the fact that a question, by definition, presents missing information. To this extent, questions are like games. Indeed, many games rely on questions. In the context of the classroom, questions can generate mild pressure that helps stimulate attention.

The research on the effects of questioning strategies supports their potential utility. Table 1.2 reports some of the findings on the effects of questioning.

Table 1.2: Studies on the Effects of Questioning Strategies on Student Achievement

Synthesis Study	Number of ESs	Average ES	Percentile Gain
Redfield & Rousseau, 1981[a]	14	0.73	27
Samson, Strykowski, Weinstein, & Walberg, 1987[a]	14	0.26	10
Gliessman, Pugh, Dowden, & Hutchins, 1988[a]	26	0.82	29
Gayle, Preiss, & Allen, 2006[a]	13	0.31	12
Randolph, 2007[a]	18	0.38	15
Wise & Okey, 1983[b]	11	0.56	21
Walberg, 1999[b]	14	0.26	10

[a]Reported in Hattie (2009)
[b]Reported in Marzano (2007)

As reported in table 1.2, the expected gains associated with questioning range from 10 to 29 percentile points. One of the problems with questioning as an engagement strategy is that once an individual student answers a question, the others in class may disengage. Consequently, increasing the number of students who respond to any given question helps capture the working memories of more students. Indeed, increasing the rate at which students respond is a commonly mentioned technique to increase the effectiveness of instruction (Good & Brophy, 2003).

Perceived Importance: Is This Important?

"Is this important?" is the third emblematic question that affects engagement. If the answer to this question is yes, students are more likely to stay involved in the tasks at hand. What then, makes something important or unimportant to a student? The answer to this question is found in the research and theory on goals.

Robert Marzano and Jana Marzano (2009) explained that the human mind is comprised of a hierarchy of goals. At the lower levels are goals that address basic subsistence needs such as food, comfort, and shelter. Above these are short-term goals such as scheduling a date or getting a good grade on a quiz. Above short-term goals are long-term goals such as making a varsity sports team and playing first-string all season or completing a semester-long thesis for an honors class. Even higher on the hierarchy are longer-term goals—those at the very top being lifelong goals. When a student is operating on higher levels of the hierarchy, he or she is more engaged. Therefore, the more a teacher can tap into students' higher-level goals, the more engaged the class as a whole will be. Here we discuss where all goals are stored, the self-system, as well as how personal goals motivate student engagement. We also address the role of cognitively challenging tasks in helping students perceive classroom activities as important.

The Self-System

Some cognitive psychologists postulate that human goals are housed in the *self-system* (Harter, 1982; Markus & Ruvolo, 1989). By definition, the self-system is part of permanent memory. Rather than memories of past events (episodic memories), information (declarative memory), or skills and processes (procedural memory), the self-system contains goals that individuals bring to every situation. Whether an individual engages in a particular activity or not is dependent on whether he or she perceives that activity as relevant to one or more goals in the self-system. From this perspective, the self-system can be viewed as the architect of human motivation. Barbara McCombs and her colleagues (McCombs, 1984, 1986, 1989; McCombs & Marzano, 1990) described the self-system in the following way:

> The self as agent, as the basis of will and volition, can be thought of, in part as a generative structure that is goal directed. . . . It . . . consciously or unconsciously defines who we are, what we think, and what we do. (McCombs & Marzano, 1990, p. 66)

Mihaly Csikszentmihalyi (1990) described the self-system as follows:

> The self is no ordinary piece of information. . . . In fact, it contains [almost] everything . . . that passes through consciousness: all the memories, actions, desires, pleasures, and pains are included in it. And more than anything else, the self represents the hierarchy of goals that we have built up, bit by bit over the years. . . . At any given time, we are usually aware of only a tiny part of it. (p. 34)

Monique Boekaerts (2009) echoed Csikszentmihalyi's comments about the hierarchic nature of goals:

> It is generally accepted that a small set of higher order goals, or principles, should be placed at the apex of a hierarchical goal network. This set of basic principles contributes most to a person's sense of Self, because the principles represent the person's basic values and the traits that he or she considers ideal. As such, higher order goals provide general organization and orientation to a person's life and optimize personal meaning and making processes. (p. 110)

Goals then, are endemic to the human condition. In some manner, people view every situation in their lives through the filter of their goals. As Boekaerts (2009) explained, every student enters class every day with goals that drive his or her behavior:

> I am convinced that all students live in a multigoal environment, and that much of their daily activities concern decision making about how much of their limited resources they will invest in the many goals that they consider salient at that point in time. (p. 106)

Unfortunately, the error that some educators make is to assume that the academic goals offered by the district, school, or individual teacher overlap with students' personal goals.

Personal Goals

One clear message from the research and theory on the goal-directed nature of human behavior is that students are more likely to engage in school goals that are linked to their personal goals. As we shall see in chapter 4, this generalization provides guidance for a number of classroom strategies that increase the probability that students will perceive the activities in a classroom as important. Of course, the challenge comes when students do not initially perceive school goals as related to any of their personal goals. Research points to *choice* as a possible remedy for this situation.

Choice appears to be a viable way to help students attach importance to classroom tasks. Richard Ryan and Edward Deci (2009) explained that "research has shown that providing students of all ages with choice typically increases intrinsic motivation" (p. 174). Erika Patall, Harris Cooper, and Jorgianne Robinson (2008) conducted a major meta-analysis of the research on choice. Selected findings from their study are reported in table 1.3.

Table 1.3: Selected Findings From Meta-Analysis of Research on Choice

Outcome Affected by Choice	Number of ESs	Average ES	Percentile Gain
Intrinsic motivation	46	0.30	12
Effort	13	0.22	9
Task performance	13	0.32	13
Subsequent learning	14	0.10	4

Source: Patall, Cooper, & Robinson, 2008

Table 1.3 indicates that choice has an effect on a variety of outcomes. Specifically, choice seems to increase intrinsic motivation, effort, task performance, and subsequent learning. To produce these impressive findings, classroom tasks that offer choice must be robust enough to allow students to make direct connections to their personal goals.

Cognitively Complex Tasks

Another way to facilitate connections between students' short and long term goals is to use cognitively complex tasks with real-world applications. When students are asked merely to regurgitate information in a repetitive fashion, they will not see the relevance of the information they have learned. In contrast, when students are challenged to use the information they have learned to solve problems, make decisions, conduct investigations, and create hypotheses regarding real-world issues, they are much more likely to see what they are learning as important.

Csikszentmihalyi's theory of *flow* dissects exactly what is happening when people are completely engaged in a task. Brophy (2004) offered this description:

> We remain aware of the goals of the task and of the feedback generated by our responses to it, but we concentrate on the task itself without thinking about success or failure, reward or punishment, or other personal or social agendas. At least for a little while, we focus completely on meeting the challenges the task offers, refining our response strategies, developing our skills, and enjoying a sense of control and accomplishment. (p. 11)

Csikszentmihalyi (1993) examined the kinds of activities people were engaged in when they found themselves completely absorbed in the task at hand—which he refers to as flow. While he expected those activities to be ones that, as described by Brophy (2004), "occur during relaxing moments of leisure and entertainment" he found quite the opposite. In fact, flow experiences "occur when we are actively involved in challenging tasks that stretch our physical or mental abilities" (pp. 10–11). Brophy (2004) notes that Fred Newmann also found that students are more engaged in tasks that are challenging. Newmann defined classes that challenged students with cognitively complex tasks as ones that used *thoughtfulness*. Thoughtful tasks:

- Focus on sustained examination of a few topics rather than superficial coverage of many.

- Encourage discourse that is characterized by substantive coherence and continuity.

- Challenge students to clarify or justify their assertions.

- Generate original and innovative ideas.

Newmann found that students reported thoughtful classes as being more difficult than those that were not, but they also reported being more engaged by these classes (Brophy, 2004).

Clearly cognitively challenging tasks are engaging in their own right, and this helps students answer affirmatively to the question "Is this important?" Brophy (2004), though, noted that there is yet another effect of cognitively challenging tasks. He said "*cognitive modeling is powerful not just as an instructional device but as a way to show students what it means to approach a task with motivation to learn*" (p. 295). Stated differently, when students are challenged they are more likely to see what they are learning as being important, and they are more likely to see *learning itself* as important and influential in their lives.

Cognitively challenging classrooms are important for a bigger picture reason as well. It is clear that the 21st century has brought many changes worldwide. Ken Kay (2010) noted that "More than three-quarters of all jobs in the United States are now in the service sector. Manual labor and routine tasks have given way to interactive, nonroutine tasks—even in many traditional blue-collar occupations" (p. xvii). Students today will hold more cognitively demanding jobs than ever before. They will hold a greater number of jobs as well, and many of those jobs are in fields that have yet to be invented (ASCD, 2009). As an Apple supervisor said, "any employee who needs to be managed is no longer employable" (Kay, 2010, p. xxi). Tasks that require use of cognitively challenging skills are not simply engaging then, they are essential. To ensure long-term success, students will need to see importance in the content being addressed as well as in education as a whole.

In some cases, classroom activities and tasks can transcend the confines of the actual classroom and require students to apply their knowledge and skills in the natural setting of the real world. Brophy (2004) noted the importance of the setting in which learning takes place: "if we want students to learn knowledge in a form that makes it useable for application, we need to make it possible for them to develop that knowledge in a natural setting, using methods and tasks suited to that setting" (p. 200). He suggested that teachers provide "activities of special significance such as service learning projects, student-led assessment conferences . . . or science or social studies projects that culminate in some service to the community or lobbying of local authorities to adopt some policy or take some action" (p. 201). We discuss incorporating the natural setting of the local community into instruction in chapter 5.

Perceptions of Efficacy: Can I Do This?

The answer to the final emblematic question, "Can I do this?," also affects engagement. Again, if the answer is yes, students are more likely to engage. If the answer is no, students might lessen or abort their involvement—even if they have positive feelings about the task (How do I feel?), are interested in the topic (Am I interested?), and perceive it as related to their personal goals (Is this important?). This issue has been addressed in great detail within cognitive psychology under the nomenclature of *self-efficacy*. Indeed, self-efficacy theory is a recognized branch of cognitive psychology. Dale Schunk and Frank Pajares (2009) explained that "self-efficacy refers to the perceived capabilities for learning or performing actions at designated levels" (p. 35).

In a meta-analysis of thirty-eight studies, Karen Multon, Stephen Brown, and Robert Lent (1991) found that self-efficacy has an effect size of 0.82 relative to students' academic performance. As shown in appendix B (page 183), this effect size translates to an expected 29 percentile point gain. In a meta-analysis of 114 studies regarding the relationship between self-efficacy and work-related performance, Alexander Stajkovic and Fred Luthans (1998) found exactly the same effect size of 0.82, indicating that self-efficacy is associated with a 29 percentile point gain in work-related performance. From these findings and the Multon et al. (1991) meta-analysis, it appears that perceptions of self-efficacy are substantially related to how both adults and children perform. Here we discuss two ways students foster their self-efficacy: (1) possible selves and (2) self-theories.

Possible Selves

The work of Hazel Markus and her colleagues (Cross & Markus, 1994; Markus & Nurius, 1986; Markus & Ruvulo, 1989) adds an interesting perspective to the concept of self-efficacy. They noted that efficacy is determined in part by students' sense of their *possible selves*. Possible selves are cognitive representations of an individual's future. The extent to which students have developed clear conceptions of who they might become in the future enables them to develop skills and gather resources that add up to a sense of self-efficacy.

Tamara Murdock (2009) added a powerful caution regarding how minority students grow to perceive themselves. She explained that for members of minority groups in the United States, their "identities are constructed within a larger social context where stereotypes and discrimination still pervade. Moreover, race, like gender, is a strong filter through which we view ourselves" (p. 447). Consequently, some identities or future possible selves that minority students generate may differ from what is typically considered successful in the greater culture. For example, some students may develop distinctly anti-academic identities or future possible selves because, among their peers, academic success is perceived as a "white behavior or evidence that the person has sold out or bought into an unjust system" (Murdock, 2009, p. 447).

Self-Theories

Carol Dweck expressed perhaps one of the most popular and powerful theories of self-efficacy. In a series of works, Dweck and her colleagues (Dweck, 2000, 2006; Dweck & Master, 2009) articulated a perspective that has challenged some long-held, even cherished, beliefs. Specifically, Dweck challenged the belief that the best way to motivate students is to boost their confidence by frequently praising them and assuring them of their intelligence:

> In elementary school, parents and teachers may constantly praise these children for how well they do, how smart they are, how quickly they learn. It might seem that these early successes would lay the foundation for a life of self-confidence and high academic achievement. Yet, many of these students struggle when they reach junior high school, and their grades begin to show a downward trajectory. Suddenly classes are challenging,

and hard work is necessary for success. How do students respond when the going gets tough? Do they remind themselves that they are intelligent and capable, roll up their sleeves and get down to work? Unfortunately, many of them do not. Instead many choose to give up, to take the easy way out, and try to get by with the minimum amount of effort. Why does this happen and what can educators do? (Dweck & Master, 2009, p. 123)

Dweck and her colleagues reached their conclusions by noticing two rather distinct patterns of responses to challenging situations (Diener & Dweck, 1978). One group of students demonstrated a helpless pattern of responses when asked to solve challenging problems. The students blamed their lack of success on their abilities and even expressed negative emotions through statements such as "I don't like this anymore. This isn't fun." Additionally, their performance decreased over time. The other group established a different orientation, characterized as a "mastery-oriented pattern" (Dweck & Master, 2009, p. 123). These students remained optimistic even when tasks were challenging, making statements such as "I've almost got this." They expressed positive emotions with statements such as "I like it when I can figure out something hard like this." Additionally, their performances were better, and they used more effective strategies than their counterparts to solve the problems.

Over time, Dweck and Master concluded that a big part of the discrepancies between these two types of students could be tied to the differences in their beliefs or their theories about intelligence. Stated differently, they hypothesized that students develop *self-theories* that make a major difference regarding the way they approach challenging situations. Carol Dweck and Allison Master (2009) explained:

> Some students believe that intelligence is a fixed attribute. They believe they have only a certain amount and that's that. We call this an "entity theory." Students with an entity theory believe that intelligence is something fixed and unchanging. They believe that if individuals have a lot of it, then they are in good shape, but if they don't, there is not really anything they can do about it. Moreover, students with an entity theory may constantly worry about whether they have it or not. Other students see intelligence as a changeable attribute, something that can be grown and strengthened over time. We call this an "incremental theory." These students think that the more effort they put in, the more they will learn and the better their ability will be. These beliefs about intelligence have important implications for students. (p. 124)

For Dweck, then, self-theories are at the core of student motivation, particularly in the face of challenging tasks. If a student has developed a "fixed theory" regarding human competence, he or she will tend to shrink from challenging tasks and experience negative effect. If a student has developed a "growth theory" regarding human competence, he or she will tend to embrace challenging situations and experience positive effect.

The intricacies of Dweck's model and the nuances of the relationship between self-theories and human behavior are many, and we cannot address them in the space provided here. This noted, following are some important aspects of self-theories.

- Self-theories are relatively stable. Once a student has developed a self-theory, he or she tends to stay with this theory.

- Self-theories can be specific to a domain. For example, a student might hold a fixed theory regarding mathematics but a growth theory regarding music.

- Different self-theories lead to different goals. When students have a fixed theory regarding competence, they tend to pick tasks that will show off or highlight their perceived innate abilities. Getting good grades and demonstrating that they are smart comes first for these students. Those with a growth theory will seek goals that help them learn since learning new skills will enhance their performance.

- Different self-theories lead to different beliefs about the value of effort. Students who hold a fixed theory of human competence will tend to devalue effort. Ability is paramount. If a student has ability, he or she will perform well. If he or she doesn't, effort will not help much. In fact, fixed-theory students tend to see effort as a negative characteristic. If you have to work hard to achieve, then you're not smart. Dweck and Master (2009) noted that:

  > this may be precisely why many high-achieving students stop working when junior high school becomes difficult. They have coasted along on low effort, showing how smart they are. Now effort is required and they are not willing to take the risk. They would prefer to do poorly and be regarded as smart but lazy than to exert effort and feel inept. (p. 127)

- Growth theorists tend to believe that effort is not only useful but a vital component of success. Growth theorists tend to support statements like "The harder you work at something, the better you will be at it."

- Different theories foster different reactions to failure. Students who have fixed theories desire success in school, and as long as they are successful, their theories may have little impact on their performance. However, once these students begin to experience setbacks or begin to worry about their performance, the theories they hold start to work against them. To those who hold a fixed theory, failure at a particular task is an indication of low ability, and when faced with failure, fixed theorists will ascribe their failure to things outside of their control ("I really don't like this subject"). Given that failure is connected with things out of their control, fixed theorists have little chance of getting better. By contrast, when the growth theorist fails, it's an indication he or she didn't try hard enough. Where failure promotes little or no action for the fixed theorists, it stimulates new and more focused action in the growth theorist.

From the perspective of this book, one of the most exciting aspects of self-theories is that they can shift. To illustrate, Dweck and Master (2009) reported on a study by Joshua Aronson, Carrie Fried, and Catherine Good (2002) in which African American college students were taught that intelligence is malleable. In spite of their stereotypical beliefs about African Americans in academic settings, these students produced higher grades than in previous semesters. In another study, college students taught seventh graders that they could increase their intelligence. The college students had one ninety-minute mentoring session each semester with the seventh graders and then communicated through email during the rest of the semester. During the semester, the college mentors simply talked about the fact that intelligence can expand at any time because neurons and dendrites form new neural connections. The seventh-grade students also learned from a Web-based computer program how to increase intelligence. This rather modest intervention provided relatively large and statistically significant gains in both reading and mathematics (Good, Aronson, & Inzlicht, 2003). Blackwell, Trzesniewski, and Dweck (2007) have reported similar results.

A Model of Attention and Engagement

The discussion thus far regarding the four emblematic questions allows for a rather straightforward model classroom teachers can use to make instructional decisions that help foster student engagement. Again, motivation, engagement, and their related processes are very complex constructs that are difficult to fully understand. However, for the purpose of busy classroom teachers, our goal is simply to develop an internally consistent model for planning and carrying out instruction.

Our model focuses on the related constructs of attention and engagement, for which we provide operational definitions. However, we do not attempt to explain the overlap and interaction between attention and engagement and related concepts such as motivation and involvement.

At the core of our model are the four emblematic questions that were used to organize the research and theory:

1. How do I feel?

2. Am I interested?

3. Is this important?

4. Can I do this?

We define *attention* as positive responses to both questions one and two ("How do I feel?" and "Am I interested?"). These questions deal with whether information from the outside world gets into working memory (see figure 1.1, page 7). Recall that if information does not make it into working memory, an individual has no conscious experience of it. If students have negative emotions or low energy, they are not very likely to entertain new information in working memory. Similarly, if the information is not considered interesting, working memory will not process it.

We define *engagement* as positive responses to questions three and four ("Is this important?" and "Can I do this?"). The answers to both of these questions affect how long information is kept in working memory. If information is not deemed important, working memory will not maintain it for long. If students do not believe they can perform voluntary or required tasks relative to the information, the brain will eventually reject it.

From this perspective, one might say that a teacher is always asking and answering two questions about students:

1. Do I have their attention?

2. Are they engaged?

If the answer to the first question is no, the teacher looks for ways to raise the emotional tone of the classroom and pique students' interests. If the answer to the second question is no, the teacher looks for ways to help students recognize the importance of the content and raise their senses of efficacy regarding the content.

In the next four chapters we consider specific instructional strategies. Each chapter deals with one of the four emblematic questions, the answers to which affect attention and engagement.

Translating Research and Theory Into Classroom Practice

In subsequent chapters, we draw from the research and theory in this chapter and from sources such as *The Art and Science of Teaching* (Marzano, 2007) and *Classroom Management That Works* (Marzano, 2003) to translate our model of attention and engagement into both short-term and long-term strategies. The use of these strategies in a coherent and connected fashion can create a classroom in which students are highly engaged.

As mentioned in the introduction, as you progress through the remaining chapters, you will encounter exercises that ask you to examine the content presented. Some of these exercises ask you to answer specific questions or identify specific strategies. After completing each exercise, you can check your answers with those in the back of the book. Other exercises are more open-ended and ask you to generate applications for what you have read.

Chapter 2

HOW DO I FEEL?

As we saw in chapter 1, a student's answer to the emblematic question "How do I feel?" is a composite function of at least three factors: the student's level of energy, the demeanor of the teacher, and the student's perception of acceptance by the teacher and peers. If a student has little energy, he or she most likely will not attend to what is occurring in class. If a teacher's general demeanor establishes a negative or overly serious affective tone, the student most likely will not attend to what is occurring in class. Finally, if a student does not feel accepted by the teacher or by peers, he or she will most likely not pay attention in class.

How students feel at any moment in time is a function of many factors, most of which are outside of a teacher's sphere of influence. For example, a student's home environment may not be emotionally supportive, or the student may not receive proper nutrition or proper rest. Similarly, a student could have rather severe psychological problems that lead to a clinical diagnosis. Unfortunately, teachers have little chance to address these issues in any systematic way. However, every teacher's classroom can become a place that all students experience as lively, positive, and accepting. In this chapter, we consider five strategies teachers can use to increase the chance that students will have a positive response to the question "How do I feel?": (1) using effective pacing, (2) incorporating physical movement, (3) demonstrating intensity and enthusiasm, (4) using humor, and (5) building positive teacher-student and peer relationships.

Using Effective Pacing

Pacing is a basic but often overlooked aspect of keeping students' energy levels high. It is usually thought of as an aspect of classroom management (see the book *Classroom Management That Works*, Marzano, 2003), but its direct tie to students' energy levels makes it a critical determinant of attention. If pacing is too slow, energy drops and attention wanes. If it is too fast, students can become confused and frustrated. A proper balance keeps energy high but allows students adequate time to process information. To help achieve that balance, focus on pacing when handling administrative tasks, making transitions, assigning seatwork, and presenting new content.

Administrative Tasks

Administrative tasks typically come into play when beginning or ending a class period or school day or when using class materials and equipment. In general, procedures for administrative tasks like the following should be in place: handing in assignments, distributing materials, storing materials after an activity, and getting organized into groups. If students have clear and well-practiced routines for these tasks, pacing is not slowed down; however, lack of routines or unpracticed routines can adversely affect pacing. The following vignette demonstrates how teachers can utilize efficient routines for administrative tasks in class.

> *Mr. Polumbus is an elementary physical education teacher. Many of his lessons involve the use of equipment such as balls, bats, and racquets. In order to make the most of each class, he assigns two students to be equipment marshals. Each month, Mr. Polumbus trains two new students to perform the equipment marshal job. By training the marshals to the point of routine, Mr. Polumbus knows he can begin class with a presentation or demonstration and then seamlessly transition into an activity that requires the use of equipment. Further, at the end of class he knows that the marshals will properly gather and store all equipment the students used.*

Transitions

Within a given lesson, there are numerous activities, each of which has its own purpose and structure. A lack of clear transitions from one activity to the next can negatively affect pacing. When well paced, each activity has a clear beginning and conclusion. Students should know when an activity starts, how long it will last, and when it will end. The following vignette depicts the use of transitions.

> *Mr. Fiore is masterful at using the cooperative learning structure called* jigsaw. *In this structure, students are part of a home group, and each member of this group is responsible for learning a specific piece of the content and then teaching it to the rest of the group. During a typical class period, students work in three phases: (1) an independent phase, during which they learn about their piece; (2) a collaborative phase, during which they work with an "expert group" that consists of members of other home groups who are learning the same piece of information; and (3) a final phase, during which they gather with their home group to take turns teaching each piece of content. When Mr. Fiore uses this structure, transitions are seamless. The required materials are sitting on the desks when students walk into class. The directions for each phase—directions which have been taught and used in previous lessons—are projected from his computer as is a small timer with a gentle, audible chime. Students are given a specific amount of time to work in each phase, and they have one minute to move from one phase to the next.*

Seatwork

Another important component of effective pacing is ensuring that students have activities they can engage in once they complete their seatwork. No matter how well organized the seatwork activity is, some students will finish sooner than others. This can cause problems in that students who finish early may become distracted or bored and, at worst, distract other students and disrupt the flow of the class. Teachers should plan activities, such as the following, for those students who do finish early:

- Helping other students

- Beginning to work on more advanced content

- Beginning to work on an activity that addresses the content of the seatwork from another perspective

- Studying a topic of their own choice

The following vignette depicts effective seatwork in the classroom.

> *For seatwork, Ms. Littleton has assigned her science class a practice quiz on carbon dating. Students are to complete the quiz and raise their hands when they finish. She will then hand the student an answer sheet so that the student can check his or her answers. It reads, "If you finish checking your answers before class ends, write a few sentences about the items you missed. Do you understand why your answer was incorrect? Do you have questions about it?" She knows that even with this multistep assignment, some students will finish before class ends. In order to prevent those students from becoming bored or disruptive, she provides a few challenge questions that require students to use what they know about carbon dating to solve a real-world problem such as determining the age of an archeological object.*

Presentation of New Content

When presenting new content, it is important to consistently monitor the pace at which information is being presented. Detailed attention to content students already know may bore them, creating a slow or dragging pace. However, moving too quickly through new content may frustrate students because they will not feel they have had adequate time to process what they have learned. In general, teachers should present information in small pieces or chunks of knowledge. After each chunk, students in small groups interact by summarizing or answering a question about what was presented. Some teachers refer to this sequence as "chunk and chew."

Additionally, while information is being presented, teachers should continually monitor students' levels of attention. If energy is waning, the teacher might shorten the length of the chunk so that students can begin processing the information in small groups. The following vignette depicts this type of interaction.

Mr. LaCroix is presenting his art history class with new content on postimpressionism. He is using the work and life of Paul Gauguin to demonstrate how society and art were changing from impressionism to postimpressionism. In order to keep the pace of the class lively, he splits up his initial lesson into four chunks: how the art and artists of impressionism and postimpressionism were alike, how the art and artists of impressionism and postimpressionism were different, Gauguin's societal and political influences, and Gauguin's artistic influences and ambitions.

Mr. LaCroix begins by presenting his class with some basic information about postimpressionism, emphasizing that many of the artists who created influential impressionist art also created influential postimpressionist art. He presents his class with a Gauguin painting and asks the students to get into prearranged small groups and compare what they know of impressionist paintings to what they see.

Next, he presents the class with information on the key elements that define postimpressionism as being its own distinct movement. Students gather in small groups again and discuss a different painting, this time focusing on what makes it different from what they know about impressionism. "What are the key differences you see? What were these artists trying to achieve by changing their work in these specific ways?"

Then, he gathers the class to present information on the social and political changes during Gauguin's time. However, he notices that many students have questions regarding what they have already seen and discussed. He knows that moving on before these questions have been answered will cause confusion and frustration, so he adjusts his instruction and allows for a large group discussion for the remainder of class.

Exercise 2.1 provides an opportunity to test your understanding of pacing and its role in attention. Answering these questions will require making connections and inferences that may not be obvious. In other words, the answers to these questions are not found explicitly in the text. (See page 48 for a reproducible of this exercise and page 160 for a reproducible answer sheet. Visit **marzanoresearch .com/classroomstrategies** to download all the exercises and answers in this book.)

Exercise 2.1
Using Effective Pacing

1. What is the relationship between pacing, working memory, and attention?
2. What are some limitations of pacing strategies in terms of keeping students' attention?
3. Which aspects of pacing are you effective at, and which aspects are you ineffective at?

Incorporating Physical Movement

Like pacing, physical movement can have an impact on energy, which in turn affects students' ability or disposition to attend. In essence, any classroom activity that employs movement increases the probability that students will have a positive response to the question "How do I feel?" A number of sources provide a variety of ways teachers can integrate physical movement into classroom activity, such as the following:

- *Brain Gym: Simple Activities for Whole Brain Learning* by Paul Dennison and Gail Dennison (1986). This book provides simple physical exercises anyone can do to increase energy and cognitive function.

- *Hands On: How to Use Brain Gym in the Classroom* by Isabel Cohen and Marcelle Goldsmith (2003). This book takes the ideas and exercises in *Brain Gym* one step further by providing teachers with age-conscious strategies for applying the exercises to specific skills and content addressed in the classroom.

- *Making the Brain/Body Connection: A Playful Guide to Releasing Mental, Physical and Emotional Blocks to Success* by Sharon Promislow (2005). This book uses simple language to discuss the connections between the mind and the body and offers a ten-step process for using those connections to release the mental and physical blocks that hinder success.

- *Smart Moves: Why Learning Is Not All in Your Head* by Carla Hannaford (1995). This book provides a more in-depth discussion of the body's role in emotional development and speech development as well as academic achievement.

Movement can be incorporated into class to lift energy, deepen or further understanding of content, or galvanize an entire class or school.

Movement to Lift Energy

Sometimes physical movement used in class is not intrinsically related to the content of a lesson. Rather, it is used to infuse energy into a lethargic classroom atmosphere. One such activity is referred to as a *stretch break*. With a stretch break, a teacher asks students to physically move in order to get more blood and oxygen flowing to the brain. Though these activities may be completely unrelated to content, they can have a legitimate place in promoting attention. For example, a teacher who notices his students becoming lethargic while taking a state-mandated test might ask them to stand during an allotted five-minute break and perform some basic exercises such as stretching their arms up over their heads while standing on their toes and then touching their fingers to their toes. Next, they might touch their right elbow to their left knee and then their left elbow to their right knee.

Another way movement can be used to lift energy is to associate it with *rehearsal*. Rehearsal refers to repeating important information in a way that helps students remember it. Teachers can use movement to punctuate certain aspects of content or to create a pattern to help remember it. Even though this type of movement is not inherently related to the content, it can help students remember what they are learning and increase their energy levels. For example, a teacher who has noticed her students are having difficulty recalling units of measurement might ask them to represent the largest of the units by standing straight up, the smaller measurements by bending over, and the smallest measurements by kneeling down. So, when she says *gallon*, they stand straight up; *quart*, they bend; and, *pint*, they kneel. The same is done with *yard*, *foot*, and *inch* and *ton*, *pound*, and *ounce*. She might then mix all of the measures and call them one after another (*ton*, *pint*, *inch*, and so on) so students move quickly from position to position.

The following vignette depicts a teacher incorporating movement into a class for the purpose of lifting energy.

> *Ms. Earnshaw notices students in her morning class appear to be tired and struggling with remembering the names of the planets in the Milky Way solar system. She asks them to stand and do a few simple stretches to get oxygen flowing to their brains and then asks for a volunteer to create a silly movement for the planet closest to the sun—Mercury. A silly movement is created for each of the planets, and then, when Ms. Earnshaw calls the names of the planets in their respective order from the sun, the students string each movement into a silly dance.*

Movement That Furthers Understanding of Content

Sometimes tasks are designed that use movement as a tool to deepen students' understanding of content. Often, these activities involve gathering or organizing information about a topic. In such situations, students must leave their seats to perform an activity that is necessary to further understand the content. One strategy to this end is *give one, get one*. Give one, get one is a process in which pairs of students compare their understanding of specific information. This is most effectively done when students are keeping notes or notebooks. As a review activity, the teacher has students stand and find a partner. The teacher then directs students to review their notes on a specific topic that has been the subject of a number of lessons. The partners compare notes on the topic in an effort to both give new information (give one) as well as get new information (get one). Pairs may also generate questions that the teacher answers in a whole-class setting. For example, a language arts teacher addressing a unit on how mythology affects language might ask students to pair up and employ the give one, get one strategy. One student might share how he discovered that the word *panic* came from the god *Pan*. The second student might share that the ancient race of giants called Titans, who fought Zeus, influenced the name of the famous ship *Titanic*. While sharing and gathering new information, students might write down any questions they have to address with the entire class during a group discussion.

Another strategy that uses physical movement to further students' understanding of the content is referred to as *voting with your feet* or the *human graph*. Voting with your feet is an activity in which students move to different parts of a room to signify which answer they believe is correct. This is best done with multiple-choice questions. For example, for a lesson on WWII, a teacher might design a few multiple-choice items that address the idea that different people have different perspectives related to historical events. Each item would have four possible answers: A, B, C, and D. On the day of the activity, the teacher places a poster with one letter (*A* through *D*) on each wall of the classroom. When the teacher presents students with one of the multiple-choice items, students are asked to line up under the letter that represents what they believe to be the correct answer. For example, a teacher might pose the following question: "Based on what you have heard and read, decide if you believe the attack on Pearl Harbor was (A) an unprovoked attack by Japan, (B) consciously and strategically provoked by Truman, (C) not intentionally provoked but motivated by America's actions, or (D) other." Students would then move to the wall with the letter representing what they believe to be the correct response. Before discussing the correct answer, the teacher asks one student under each alternative to explain why he or she believes that answer is correct. With questions such as these, it is important to consider the validity of answers not initially thought of as "correct."

Corners activities also help students move physically while furthering their understanding of the content. During corners activities, students assemble in corners to discuss different aspects of a topic being addressed in class. For example, a social studies teacher might have a unit that focuses on the topic of civil disobedience. The teacher would design four questions about civil disobedience such as:

1. What are the defining characteristics of civil disobedience?

2. How can civil disobedience advance democracy?

3. How can civil disobedience impede democracy?

4. What is an example in your life when you used civil disobedience to a good end?

Each question is posted in a specific corner of the room. Each corner has chart paper and one student who is assigned to use the chart paper to record what group members say. After splitting the class into four roughly equally sized groups, the teacher provides directions for the activity; students begin by going to one of the four corners. Each group stays in a corner for about five minutes. The recorder for each corner briefly summarizes students' comments on the chart paper. Students then move to another corner, but the recorders stay in their assigned spot. When students have been to all four corners, the recorders read what each group has discussed.

Teachers can also incorporate physical movement to help students understand content in a different way or from a different perspective. Drama is a very versatile way to do this. With drama-related activities, students act out an event that is being studied, taking the roles of various participants in that event. Events can stem from a variety of sources such as historic situations, current events, and literature. For example, a teacher with English learners might ask students to re-enact stories they have been reading. The students might work in groups to plan, rehearse, and then perform short scenes, borrowing dialogue from the story and adding their own words as well.

Finally, physical representations can deepen students' understanding of content because they require students to use their bodies to represent abstract or concrete content. With these activities, the physical movement is intended to depict critical aspects of a topic. For example, a math teacher might ask students to stand and physically represent terms such as *radius*, *diameter*, and *circumference*.

The following vignette illustrates a teacher incorporating physical movement into a lesson for the purpose of furthering understanding of the content being addressed.

> *Ms. Valdez's class has been reading* Winesburg, Ohio *by Sherwood Anderson. As a review of the book, Ms. Valdez sets up the classroom for a corners activity. Four students are assigned the job of recorder, and they each sit at a desk at one of the four stations set up around the room. As students move in assigned groups through the four stations, the recorders ask the following questions prepared by Ms. Valdez:*
>
> • *Corner A: Authors such as Ernest Hemingway and William Faulkner often cited* Winesburg, Ohio *as having been an important influence on their own work. In the context of the themes in and structure of* Winesburg, Ohio, *why do you think this book would have been so important to Hemingway and Faulkner? What would they have seen as original, inventive, or important about the work?*

- *Corner B: How do you think the setting of a small town in Ohio was important to the story?*

- *Corner C: How would you interpret the connections made or missed between the characters in each story, and how would those connections compare to those made or missed by the characters between stories? What kind of message emerges from these connections?*

- *Corner D: How important do you think the prologue is; how would your understanding of the book differ had you not read it?*

Movement for the Whole Class or School

As we saw in chapter 1, classwide or schoolwide programs that promote physical exercise and physical movement can have a positive effect on students' abilities to attend. While an individual teacher cannot implement a schoolwide program immediately, small groups of teachers can collaborate to initiate change. The following are real-world examples of schoolwide programs.

Oakwood Intermediate School in Allendale, Michigan, created an "exer-learning lab" that is equipped with minitrampolines, treadmills, and stationary bikes connected to video-game consoles. Three times a week, selected students come to the lab about a half-hour before school starts, spending a few minutes at each station. Their heart rates are periodically monitored, and they complete surveys about how they feel before they leave, so that teachers know participating students are not becoming exhausted. For now, the program is aimed at students with potential obesity issues or academic concerns, but teachers and community leaders are working to expand the program and include a study on the value of movement prior to reading (Ogg, 2009).

San Rafael High School in San Rafael, California, has created an exercise course for freshmen in the school's "adventure room." The adventure room was once an outdated wrestling venue, but now contains rock-climbing walls and elements of a ropes course. After students complete safety training, they set personalized goals to achieve at the completion of the course based on individual interests and skill levels. The school's principal says that the course is designed not only to improve physical fitness, but also to teach cooperation and problem-solving skills and to build self-esteem. Teachers have noticed a difference in students, saying that their freshmen now are more grounded and mature than the freshmen they taught before the adventure curriculum (Rapaport, 2008).

> *Many elementary schools in New Hampshire are participating in CircusFit, an exercise program created by Ringling Bros. and Barnum and Bailey. Clowns, acrobats, and trapeze artists in the company visit schools to have some fun and show off physical skills. Kids learn that these skills require fitness and practice. Teachers can visit the website, www.circusfit.com, to learn how to create a safe and fun classroom circus program that meets the President's Challenge criteria (www.presidentschallenge.org); classes that stick with it are rewarded with circus tickets or in-school visits from performers (Snyder, 2008).*

Exercise 2.2 provides some practice at identifying how physical movement can be used to increase students' energy levels. (See page 49 for a reproducible of this exercise and page 161 for a reproducible answer sheet. Visit **marzanoresearch.com/classroomstrategies** to download all the exercises and answers in this book.)

Exercise 2.2
Incorporating Physical Movement

After reading each of the following classroom scenarios, determine which of the following strategies for physical movement is being employed:

  A. Stretch break

  B. Movement related to rehearsal

  C. Give one, get one

  D. Vote with your feet

  E. Corners activities

  F. Drama

  G. Physical representation

1. Mr. Rush's language arts class has been reading some poetry. In order to help the students begin to think about the abstract concepts in the poems and to lift the energy level in the room, he asks his students to stand. "I'm going to call out a word and I want you to do something with your body that you think represents its meaning." When he begins by calling out the word *beauty*, his students are a bit hesitant, but as the exercise continues they begin to have more fun with it and create many different poses.

2. The students in Mr. Ulrick's first class of the day are often still tired and lethargic. In order to energize them a bit, he often asks them to stand in the beginning of class and do some simple exercises that are designed to wake up both sides of the brain.

3. Ms. Rollin's choir class has been looking at potential songs for an end-of-year performance. She has put together four possible programs students can choose from. She gives them the song list for each of the four programs at the end of class one day, giving each program a number 1–4. She asks them to think overnight about which program they like best and why. Before class the next day, she places four posters, each with a number (1–4) in different places around the room. When class begins, she asks them to stand under the number that represents the program they have chosen. She then asks students under each number to explain why they like that program the best. However, simply liking or disliking the songs in each program is not sufficient. She asks each of them to provide technical justifications, using vocabulary and concepts they have learned throughout the year to articulate their opinions. She finds that while they have not had many in-depth discussions about music in the past, many of her students are able to speak technically and articulately and even have strong opinions. Finally, she gives them a chance to change their votes after having heard the opinions of some classmates.

4. Mr. Holmes is having a review session for an upcoming social studies test on different governmental systems in place throughout the world. He tells his students to gather the notes they have on each of the different systems and the countries in which they are employed. He calls out two names randomly and those students pair up. When everyone is paired, he says, "You have five minutes to share your notes with one another. You can glean new information that might be on the test this way, and you can clear up any mistakes you may have in your notes." After the five minutes are up, he calls out names in random pairs again and students repeat the process with a new partner.

Demonstrating Intensity and Enthusiasm

A teacher's intensity and enthusiasm are contagious and can have a positive effect on students' levels of attention. When teachers demonstrate intensity and enthusiasm for content being addressed in class, they are indirectly communicating the messages "This is exciting" and "This is fun," which helps create an atmosphere that invites attention. Teachers can use a number of strategies to demonstrate personal intensity and enthusiasm for the content being addressed. Among these are sharing personal stories, being conscious of verbal and nonverbal signals, and reviving the zest for teaching.

Personal Stories

In some situations, a teacher might have a personal story that relates to the content being addressed. Personal stories communicate that the teacher is excited about and interested in the content. For example, a specific piece of content may have provided an insight for the teacher, or it may have been very difficult at first for the teacher to understand. A teacher's stories invite students to look for their own personal connections to content. The following vignette illustrates the use of personal stories.

> Mr. Thompson is a performing arts teacher, and he often has students who are nervous about performing in front of an audience of any kind. When they are nervous or self-conscious, they have a difficult time getting into character, and they do not enjoy the experience on stage. He often tells his students that he once felt the same way. "When I was young, I was really shy," he says. "I hated to be called on in class! So at first, the idea of being on stage in front of an entire audience did not sound like my idea of a good time. But I did read a lot, and I wound up reading a play adaptation of Beowulf. I really loved the hero and how strong and smart he was. I think I identified more with him because the story had been adapted into a play, so he had actual lines, and when I read them aloud it was easy to pretend I really was him. I noticed that I could be really different when I read a character like that; I could carry him around with me and feel braver even when I wasn't reading the play. I read more plays after that, and when my school was doing a production of Brave New World, I decided to try out. I was so nervous on the day of the audition that I threw up and almost chickened out completely. But then, I just kept reading the script, reading aloud the lines of the character I was auditioning for, and once I started to feel like I really was that character, I wasn't scared anymore."

Verbal and Nonverbal Signals

Teachers can communicate intensity and enthusiasm in a variety of verbal and nonverbal ways that include the following:

- Speaking with a loud voice

- Smiling while presenting content

- Using hand gestures indicating excitement

While it is best that these behaviors occur spontaneously, it is certainly legitimate for a teacher to remind himself or herself to show intensity and enthusiasm in appropriate ways and at appropriate times. The following vignette demonstrates the use of verbal and nonverbal signals.

> *Ms. Olson is a physical education teacher who played basketball in college. She no longer plays because she hurt her knee, but she still stays active through yoga and swimming. Her enthusiasm for the game is contagious. Her tone of voice, the frequent thumbs-up signs she uses, and a permanent smile all communicate her love for the game. Even the students who are not particularly fond of basketball give extra effort.*

Zest for Teaching

Over the years, it is very easy and natural for teachers to forget the original intensity and enthusiasm they had when they first began teaching. When this occurs, it is helpful for teachers to remind themselves why they got into teaching in the first place. To this end, teachers should take a few moments each day to remind themselves of their original feelings for the teaching profession. The following vignette illustrates reviving the zest for teaching.

> *Ms. Alvarez became a teacher just out of graduate school because she really loved children and wanted to change lives. Fifteen years into her career, though, she sometimes loses sight of her original enthusiasm. She has seen that factors such as family and community heavily influence early learning as well, and sometimes she does not feel she can make the difference she once thought possible. She has also married and had her own children since her career began, and she sometimes feels torn. At the advice of a colleague, she watches the movie* Stand and Deliver, *which chronicles the story of Jaime Escalante. She is well aware that movies based on true stories are sometimes overdramatized, but the story of the commitment to students moves her and reminds her why she chose teaching. Feeling revitalized, she makes a commitment to herself to watch the movie, and others with similar themes, at least once a year.*

Using Humor

Humor is another aspect of a teacher's demeanor that can positively affect attention. When teachers use humor, students feel better about the content, the teacher, and perhaps even themselves. Humor can be employed in many ways. For the most part, teachers who consistently use humor in the classroom have a keen eye for occurrences that they could turn into humorous episodes. For example, the power could go out right as the teacher begins showing a video clip. To turn a potentially awkward situation into an opportunity for humor, the teacher might say, "Well, how did you like it so far?" Capitalizing on opportunities to inject humor comes with attention and practice. Over time, a teacher learns which incidents generate humor in appropriate ways. Using self-directed humor, funny headlines or quotes, movie clips or other media entertainment, and creating a class symbol for humor are all time-tested and dependable sources for humor.

Self-Directed Humor

It is usually risky to use students as the subject of humor, since it might embarrass them. This noted, occasionally there are students who invite humor and friendly taunting about which they are not offended but actually enjoy. In such cases, friendly banter with students may be appropriate, but teachers should always approach it with great caution. In contrast, a teacher using himself or herself as the subject of humor is appropriate and useful in almost all environments. The following vignette depicts how a teacher might use self-directed humor.

> *Ms. Patrick is teaching a social studies unit on cultural norms and mores. She is using fashion and music trends to show how what is desirable and fashionable in one culture may be offensive or laughable in another. To demonstrate her point, she brings in photos of herself as a teenager, when the style was very different. She assures her students that she was very cool back then, and when they laugh, she shows them some clips of music videos that were popular during that time. "Do you see how big her hair was?" Ms. Patrick asks. "Now look at my hair in those pictures. See? Very cool." Her students laugh both at the outdated fashions and at the photos of their teacher, but her point about changing social trends and mores is well illustrated.*

Funny Headlines or Quotes

Teachers can also use funny headlines or quotes to keep humor in the classroom. Ideally, these quotes or headlines are directly related to the content. For example, a teacher who is focusing on revision and editing in the writing process might display funny mistakes in headlines such as "Honors for Academic Excellense" or "Give Blood This Month and Help Feed the Needy." The headlines make the students laugh, but the teacher's point about the importance of being attentive to their own writing is also stressed. Additionally, students might bring in funny headlines they found independently in sources such as national and local newspapers, magazines, papers distributed by local universities, or neighborhood or school newsletters.

Another good source for funny headlines is the *Tonight Show*. The comedian Jay Leno has made humorous headlines famous in his talk show. Following are some headlines featured on the show (Vickers, 2010):

- "Nearly $1 Available to Encourage Organic Farming"

- "Stimulus Funds Help Pay for Jobs That Handle Stimulus Funds"

- "Large Selection of Fresh Caught Canadians"

- "Cash is the Key to Ending Financial Woes"

- "Open Government Seminar Will be Closed to the Public"

- "Live Main Lobster $24.95/lb"

- "Total Lunar Eclipse Will Be Broadcast on Norwoods Public Radio"

- "Lawyers Back Despite the Use of Bug Spray"

- "Americans Watch Television 27 Hours a Day"

Teachers can also incorporate humor in the classroom through quotations from famous people. Websites such as www.brainyquote.com, www.quotationspage.com, and www.quotegarden.com have a good collection of humorous quotations. Quotations found on www.brainyquote.com include the following:

- "Electricity is really just organized lightning."—George Carlin

- "Drawing on my fine command of the English language, I said nothing."—Robert Benchley

- "Get your facts first, then you can distort them as you please."—Mark Twain

- "I always wanted to be somebody, but now I realize I should have been more specific."—Lily Tomlin

- "Originality is the fine art of remembering what you hear but forgetting where you heard it."—Laurence J. Peter

- "Television is a medium because anything well done is rare."—Fred Allen

- "If at first you don't succeed, failure may be your style."—Quentin Crisp

- "I don't like books, they're all fact, no heart."—Stephen Colbert

- "I had a stick of Carefree gum, but it didn't work. I felt pretty good while I was blowing that bubble, but as soon as the gum lost its flavor, I was back to pondering my mortality."—Mitch Hedberg

- "Two things are infinite: the universe and human stupidity; and I'm not sure about the former."—Albert Einstein

Even though humorous headlines or quotations may not directly relate to classroom content, teachers can still use them to create a humorous tone in the classroom. The following vignette depicts a teacher using funny quotes or headlines.

> *Ms. Downyweather is a middle school language arts teacher who uses humor with homophones. When writing sentences on the board or in classroom activity directions, she will occasionally make an intentional homophone error to see if anyone catches it. Sentences such as "If you could meat any person in the world, who would it be?" often make students laugh and keep them on their toes when reading her directions.*

Movie Clips and Media Entertainment

Movies and other forms of media entertainment provide a rich source of humor for the classroom. Of course, it is usually not appropriate to watch a full-length movie, but teachers can find short clips that are appropriate for different subject areas and grade levels. The following vignette shows the use of movie clips in class.

> *Mr. Singer's science class is working in pairs to complete a series of experiments he has assigned. To keep the tone in the class light but emphasize the importance of the scientific method, he frequently shows a brief movie clip about a successful or unsuccessful science experiment. He shows clips from movies such as* Honey, I Shrunk the Kids; Weird Science; Innerspace; *and* The Nutty Professor. *He says with each clip, "Science is funny, because Hollywood wouldn't make so many movies about science if it wasn't funny."*

A Class Symbol for Humor

One safe way to generate humor is to create a fictitious class character or symbol that becomes the subject of jokes and quips. It is safe because neither the teacher nor the students are directly or indirectly the subject of jokes. The following vignette depicts the use of a class symbol.

> *Ms. Lancaster is an art teacher. She stresses to her students the importance of creative self-expression and the importance of staying true to their own artistic visions and personal hopes and dreams. To stress this, she has created a humorous character she calls "the Critic." She has a life-sized drawing of the Critic in her classroom, a menacing, somewhat ridiculous-looking cartoon villain. She begins the school year by asking her students about their favorite artists, be it through mediums of music, writing, film, or visual arts. When students volunteer their favorite artists, she reads a critique of that artist. Over the years she has collected critiques on as many popular artists as possible, so she finds herself almost always prepared. When she reads the quote, she asks the student what he or she thinks. "Tell the Critic what you think of him!" she says. She even brings in some of her own art and reads what local newspaper critics said about her. The Critic becomes the symbol of criticism that no artist likes but all artists need to improve their craft.*

Use Exercise 2.3 to practice identifying how teachers can use intensity, enthusiasm, and humor to create a positive demeanor. (See page 51 for a reproducible of this exercise and page 163 for a reproducible answer sheet. Visit **marzanoresearch.com/classroomstrategies** to download all the exercises and answers in this book.)

Exercise 2.3
Demonstrating Intensity and Enthusiasm and Using Humor

After reading each of the following classroom scenarios, determine which of the following strategies for exhibiting intensity and enthusiasm or using humor is being employed:

Intensity and Enthusiasm

    A. Personal stories

    B. Verbal and nonverbal signals

    C. Zest for teaching

Humor

    D. Self-directed humor

    E. Funny headlines or quotes

    F. Movie clips and media entertainment

    G. A class symbol for humor

1. Ms. Amnell is a language arts teacher, and when she is teaching creative writing to her students, she finds they sometimes have a hard time thinking of original ideas. To help them along, she brings in short clips from films the students have probably never seen. Sometimes the clip is of a brief conversation between two people, sometimes it is an explosion or an alien ship landing on earth. All clips are humorous in some way. They must use the clip as the beginning of a narrative piece. She finds that when they are given a beginning, especially a funny beginning they wouldn't have thought of on their own, students show a lot of imagination.

2. Mr. Dermot tells his students that he has an imaginary brother named Leon Swankis. He tells his class a few stories about some of his adventures with Leon. It seems Leon is always getting Mr. Dermot in trouble. Sometimes he means well, but it is usually better when Mr. Dermot follows his own plan instead of listening to Leon's ideas. Every day when class lets out, he reminds his students: "If you meet Leon, don't listen to him! He'll get you into trouble!" Throughout the year, he finds that students adopt Leon as their symbol for trouble, and their stories of him can be quite outlandish and funny. Some of them meet Leon, and though Leon tried to get them in trouble, they didn't listen to him. Occasionally, a student does find himself in trouble, whether it be in class or in school or even at home. If the student talks to Mr. Dermot about it, he will ask, "Was Leon there?" The student usually smiles and nods, affirming Leon was there. "I've told you, you can't listen to Leon, you have to listen to yourself."

3. Ms. Mason is an art teacher who happens to enjoy magic shows. When she demonstrates a technique in class, she uses the exaggerated and theatrical hand movements magicians use. She has the serious demeanor of a magician, and when the demonstration is complete, she holds out her arms and says, "Ta-da! Magic!" When students execute a technique particularly well or produce something they are really proud of, she does the same thing, telling them in a dramatic voice that what they have done is nothing short of magic!

4. Mr. Starr has been teaching science for over fifteen years. Sometimes teaching the same or similar content can get old and feel stale. When he feels uninspired about teaching, he takes the time to read science-based magazines and articles about new advancements and breakthroughs. Thinking about how many discoveries are being made in science today—and the ramifications of those discoveries—re-energizes him about teaching science.

Building Positive Teacher-Student and Peer Relationships

Teacher-student relationships are key to ensuring that students feel good about being in class. Without a strong relationship with the teacher, it is hard for students to respond positively to the question "How do I feel?" If students perceive that the teacher respects and likes them, they are more likely to attend to classroom content. One of the most interesting aspects of powerful teacher-student relationships is that they are forged by behavior and words as opposed to thoughts and feelings. Stated differently, it is not what a teacher thinks and feels about a particular student that forges a positive relationship with the student. Rather, it is how the teacher speaks to and behaves with the student that communicates respect and acceptance. This fact is very liberating because no matter what a teacher thinks about a student or how he or she feels about a student, the teacher can behave in a way that communicates respect and acceptance. By ensuring fair and equitable treatment of all students, showing interest in and affection for students, and identifying and using positive information about them, teachers can forge positive relationships with each student as well as encourage strong peer relationships.

Ensure Fair and Equitable Treatment of All Students

As we saw in chapter 1, if students feel rejected by their peers, they will likely disengage from classroom activities. If they experience a pattern of rejection for an extended period of time, students can develop negative attitudes about school that are difficult to reverse. While teachers cannot follow students around to ensure they are both giving and receiving fair and equitable treatment throughout the day, they do have a basic legal and ethical obligation to ensure that their classrooms are places where all students feel safe. Often this means curbing disruptive or hurtful behavior and letting students know that teachers will provide help to any student in need. Teachers also have an obligation to stop bullying or hurtful behavior schoolwide. For example, if a teacher hears that his student's friend in another class is being bullied, that teacher has a responsibility to inform the teacher of the bullied student and to do whatever else within his power to stop his student's friend from being hurt. Resources that provide strategies to prevent classroom bullying include the following:

- Stop Bullying Now! (www.stopbullyingnow.hrsa.gov)

- Striving to Reduce Youth Violence Everywhere (www.safeyouth.gov)

- *Bullying Prevention and Intervention: Realistic Strategies for Schools* by Susan M. Swearer, Dorothy L. Espelage, and Scott A. Napolitano (2009)

- *The Bully, the Bullied, and the Bystander: From Preschool to High School—How Parents and Teachers Can Help Break the Cycle of Violence* by Barbara Coloroso (2003)

Common strategies for stopping bullying include the following:

- Identifying specific positive and negative aspects of the social environment of the school

- Getting the support of staff and parents and training the staff in bullying prevention

- Creating and consistently enforcing rules and policies regarding bullying

- Encouraging students to become witnesses instead of merely bystanders

- Providing support for victims (See National Youth Violence Prevention Resource Center, 2010, and Coloroso, 2003, for more information.)

Beyond ensuring students' basic safety, teachers can help students have positive feelings about class by actively encouraging behavior that demonstrates respect. From the first day of class, the teacher can establish the expectation that all students will not only be safe but valued and respected as well. *A Handbook for Classroom Management That Works* (Marzano, Gaddy, Foseid, Foseid, & Marzano, 2005) identifies a number of ways to accomplish this. One technique is to establish a set of basic rights, such as the following, that applies to all students:

- All students have the right to be treated with respect.

- All teachers have the right to be treated with respect.

If time permits, the class can establish a more extensive list of rights. Figure 2.1 presents a list of rights that builds on the work of Manuel Smith (1975) and Robert Alberti and Michael Emmons (1982).

- I have the right to evaluate my actions and the right to be accountable for them, but I do not have the right to criticize the behavior of my peers.

- Unless someone is in danger, I have the right to choose whether or not I want to help solve a peer's problems. If a peer is in danger, he or she can count on me to help or to find an adult who can help.

- Unless my actions hurt another, I have the right to change my mind and make mistakes. If my actions do hurt someone, I can be counted on to make amends.

- I have the right to decide who I view as a close friend; I do not have to try to make everyone like me.

- I have the right to feel safe; I don't have the right to make others feel unsafe.

- I have the right to a private life, free of gossip; I don't have the right to gossip about or invade anyone else's privacy.

- I can be counted on to be respectful to others, and I have the right to be treated with respect.

- I have the right to talk about my feelings as long as I don't hurt or embarrass others in the process.

- I have the right to be listened to. My opinions count, as do the opinions of my peers.

- I have the right to say no without feeling guilty. No one can force me to do something I am uncomfortable with, just as I cannot force my peers to do something they don't want to do.

Figure 2.1: Extended list of students' rights.

Typically, statements of students' rights are generated at the beginning of the school year. Once rights are established, the teacher and students make sure basic rights are being enforced throughout the year. The following vignette depicts a teacher enforcing agreed-upon students' rights in the classroom.

> *Mr. Carter began the school year by discussing with his class the importance of equality in his classroom. In order to make sure all students would be treated equally and with respect, the class created a list of rights and responsibilities that is now displayed in the front of the classroom. He knows from discussions with his students that Yanko and James do not get along. They have had problems outside of the classroom, and while Mr. Carter knows he cannot control what his students do at all times, he can do his best to make sure that they are in control and respectful during his time with them. When Yanko is out sick one day, he hears James telling Grace that she shouldn't be friends with Yanko. He starts to talk about why he thinks so, but Mr. Carter stops him.*
>
> *"Look at our list. See the part that says you don't have the right to hurt or embarrass another student?"*
>
> *James says it doesn't count, because Yanko isn't in the room.*
>
> *"It still counts, James," he says. "And look at this part that says you do not have the right to gossip about others. That counts too."*
>
> *After class, Mr. Carter speaks with Grace, making sure she knows she has the right to choose her friends—no matter what anyone else thinks.*

Show Interest in and Affection for Students

Teachers can display interest and affection in many ways and in a variety of situations. Again, it is important to remember that demonstrating interest and affection has nothing to do with how a teacher feels about a particular student. Rather, it has everything to do with how the teacher behaves toward the student. A teacher can show interest in and affection toward all students, regardless of how he or she feels about them.

Simple Courtesies

Simple courtesies include greeting students at the door, calling them by their names, saying "good morning," and the like. The simple act of acknowledging a student can be a powerful message that the teacher likes and accepts him or her.

Making eye contact is another simple courtesy. It is a subtle behavior but an effective one. For example, when making an announcement about an upcoming dance club meeting, a teacher might make eye contact with a student he knows enjoys dancing. The simple act of making eye contact lets the student know that the teacher likes and accepts him or her. This noted, for some students, returning eye contact may be uncomfortable or even contrary to how they were taught to show respect to elders. As with all strategies, teachers must adapt their approaches in the classroom to ensure the desired effect. The following vignette depicts a teacher displaying simple courtesies.

> *Ms. Darnay has noticed that while Cassandra pays attention in class and completes her assignments on time, she does not seem very confident. In order to encourage her, Ms. Darnay calls on her during class even though Cassandra didn't raise her hand. She doesn't seem to know the answer at first, but when Ms. Darnay maintains eye contact and waits for a few moments instead of moving on to another student, Cassandra comes up with something very close to the correct answer. Ms. Darnay gives her positive feedback, maintains eye contact, and uses facial expressions to give Cassandra subtle hints and encourage her when she gets closer to the correct answer.*

Physical Contact and Physical Gestures

At times, subtle physical contact can be used to demonstrate interest and affection. For example, a teacher might give a student a pat on the back when he or she understands something that has been a struggle in the past. Of course, physical contact should be used with attention to each student's age level, gender, and culture. What may seem appropriate with one student could be inappropriate with another. For example, while an elementary school teacher might acknowledge a student by touching him or her on the head, a high school teacher might use a handshake or a high five.

Teachers can also use physical gestures to communicate affection for students. These too are a subtle but effective form of communication because they can make students feel good about themselves and about the atmosphere of the classroom. Physical gestures that communicate affection include the OK gesture, thumbs up, the touchdown sign, a wink, nod, or smile. For example, a teacher who knows a student has a difficult time interacting with others and making friends might catch his eye and give him a wink or a thumbs up to encourage him and let him know he is accepted.

Physical proximity is perhaps the most subtle and nuanced behavior that teachers can use to communicate affection for students. In general, physical proximity communicates caring and familiarity. For example, a teacher who sees a student struggling with a problem or an activity might kneel next to her to encourage a discussion that could help the student be successful. Of course, this generalization does not hold for all cultures or all students. Teachers should take care to ensure that their use of physical proximity is appropriate. The following vignette depicts use of physical contact and physical gestures for the purpose of demonstrating interest in and affection for students.

> *Mr. Forrester works in a small alternative school in a large city. He knows his students have had a difficult time in other schools. Often because of lack of confidence, learning disabilities, or low expectations, his students have been previously overlooked or ignored in classrooms. He wants them to know that they are valued and will be held accountable for their own learning in his classroom. One of the things he does is maintain close physical proximity to the students when he is teaching. Instead of standing at the front of the class during lectures, he walks*

around the room, between aisles and rows so that students know sitting in the back doesn't mean they are invisible.

When students are answering questions, he stands closer to them instead of at the front of the room. He uses encouraging gestures as well so students know they have his full attention and that he believes they can answer the question correctly. When a student has success, he always offers a high five.

Students' Needs and Concerns

Teachers can display affection simply by attending to special needs students might have. Again, many accommodations are not just good practice but required by law. Teachers will certainly need to support students with poor vision or learning disabilities, for example, but students might also have more personal needs that teachers can take note of and make accommodations for. A student who has missed school because of a serious illness or a death in the family might need a little more support catching up than normal, or a student whose family has moved and has joined the class in the middle of the school year might need a bit more tutoring or emotional support than other students. Making accommodations for students with these kinds of needs sends a message to all students that the teacher is concerned about their well-being.

In addition to unique needs, students often have personal concerns. One very straightforward way to communicate affection for students is to listen carefully to those concerns and then respond to them. For example, a student might have an upcoming sporting event that he or she is very nervous about competing in. Acknowledging these personal concerns lets students know they are personally important to the teacher. The following vignette depicts the strategy of attending to students' needs and concerns.

Ms. Alvarez notices on the first day of class that one student, Frank, is the younger brother of a recent graduate who was a very accomplished athlete. She usually takes some time to get to know her class on the first day by asking about their personal interests and accomplishments, and she takes note when Frank says, "Everyone thinks I play basketball like my brother, but I don't. I like to paint and take pictures. I'm not an athlete." His comment makes it clear to Ms. Alvarez that Frank feels overshadowed in school by his brother, so she makes an effort in the following weeks to use art and artists in her classroom examples. She is also careful not to compare Frank to his brother in class or in private conversations.

Identify and Use Positive Information About Students

One simple way to communicate respect and acceptance is to find something positive about students and then use that information to both plan instruction that addresses students' interests and communicate concern for specific students. This is particularly true for students who may have discipline issues or who appear alienated from the rest of the class or the teacher. Structured opportunities in class for students to share interests and accomplishments, conversations with parents and guardians, and conversations with fellow teachers are all excellent ways to learn and use positive information about students.

Structured Opportunities to Highlight Interests and Accomplishments

A class inventory is one of the numerous structured ways to highlight positive information about students. A technique teachers have used for decades, it can provide a rich source of information. Typically, inventories include questions such as the following:

- What is your favorite movie?

- What do you like to read?

- What are some of your hobbies?

- What are your favorite subjects in school?

- If you could have any career when you grow up, what would it be?

Teachers can use a number of sources to obtain or develop inventories. Some sites that can help create inventories include the following:

- Scholastic Printables (http://printables.scholastic.com/printables/detail/?id=35571)

- Education World (www.educationworld.com/tools_templates)

- Scribd (www.scribd.com/doc/17020655/Student-Interest-Survey)

- SurveyMonkey (www.surveymonkey.com)

In addition to questions that deal with students' hobbies, favorite movies, and the like, students can complete indirect sentence stems such as the following:

- Three words that describe me are . . .

- Learning is fun when . . .

- I like classes that . . .

- I wonder a lot about . . .

- Sometimes I worry about . . .

- I like people who . . .

- Something that really challenges me is . . .

For example, on the first day of class a teacher might hand each of her students a 3 × 5 index card as they enter the room. When class begins, she asks them to write their full name and three favorite books or movies. Additionally, she asks them to write a sentence or two about what they are looking forward to experiencing in the coming school year.

In general, the more students know about each other, the more they tend to get along. Anything a teacher can do to help students become familiar with one another will help create a positive classroom atmosphere. Class discussions can be a rich source of information about students' interests. As students engage in dialogue, they provide information that can help forge positive peer relationships as well as information that the teacher can use to direct instruction toward topics that interest them. For example, a teacher who discovers a student's family is from Sri Lanka might include information and updates about a presidential election happening in the country when he is teaching a unit on government.

Structured opportunities to learn about students and allow them to highlight their interests and accomplishments can be more extensive as well, going beyond a single class period. Marzano et al. (2005) recommend activities similar to the following:

- Establish a "show off" schedule in which a different student each week talks a little about himself or herself, showing pictures or trophies—anything that lets the class know more about who he or she is. During this time, any student should have the opportunity to announce important events or accomplishments.

- Let students get to know you better by telling personal stories, displaying photos or certificates, and announcing important events in your life.

- Create recognition displays, such as an "aced it" display. Students can decorate a card shaped like an ace with whatever represents their strengths—maybe a picture of an award-winning science-fair project or a blue ribbon. A student on the swim team who beat a previous time might write his new time on his ace. The class should display all the student aces and update them whenever students have accomplished something new. Using stickers or Post-it notes, students can also congratulate or compliment their peers. They might also communicate other messages such as thanking a classmate for help on an assignment.

The following vignette depicts a teacher using a structured activity to learn more about students.

> *Mrs. Hurst begins the school week by making an announcement: "This weekend I finished my first triathlon!" She has told her students about her training all along, and on Friday they wished her good luck. She has a photo her husband took of her crossing the finish line, and she adds it to the personal display board over her desk. Before class begins, she asks if anyone else had an exciting weekend. Bea says her family's dog had puppies, and she too brought a photo to put on the board. "It's hard work taking care of all of those puppies, but I really love them!" she says. Finally, Seth raises his hand and says he went to Kenneth's baseball game over the weekend and saw him hit his first home run. Kenneth is in Mrs. Hurst's class as well, but he is one of the shyer students, so she appreciates that Seth makes sure his friend is acknowledged.*

Parents and Guardians

Parents and guardians can be a source of important information about students. Typically, parents and guardians will volunteer information about their children to help teachers better understand their students. Teachers can use this information to interact with students in a way that indicates they are supported and accepted. The following vignette depicts the use of information gathered from parents and guardians.

During a phone conversation with Lana's father, Mr. Johnson learns that Lana is diabetic, and that her blood sugar levels can sometimes affect her energy and level of engagement. Not knowing anything about diabetes, Mr. Johnson asks Lana's dad to give him a basic understanding of the disease, and what he can say or do for Lana if he notices her becoming inattentive or lethargic in class. The next week, he privately lets Lana know that he is aware of her condition and that she can always come to him if she needs help or someone to talk to about any difficulties that may arise.

Fellow Teachers

Teachers should try to communicate the message that they are proud of students and interested in their accomplishments. Fellow teachers often provide such information. For example, a high school teacher who coaches a speech and debate team might email the other teachers in the school to inform them that the team recently won a statewide tournament and is scheduled to compete nationally in Washington DC. She might include the names of each student on the team so that teachers can individually congratulate them on the accomplishment.

Just as teachers can provide positive information about students, they can also spread negative information about students. This occurs most frequently when teachers complain about students to their colleagues. While it is certainly a natural behavior to be disappointed in certain students and even angry at times, it does no good to complain about students to colleagues at school. In the extreme, complaining about students can generate a negative halo effect for students labeled as "troublemakers" or worse. When a teacher or teachers complain about a specific student, the appropriate response is to counter the negative comments with positive comments. For example, a teacher might counter with, "That's not my experience with that student. I find her quite interesting," or, "I think we need to give her the benefit of the doubt. I know she's had some tough things happen to her." This takes courage as it may elicit negative reactions from the complaining teachers, but it is the right thing to do. Negative comments that foster a bad reputation for students have no place in a professional community.

The following vignette depicts a teacher learning about a student from fellow teachers.

Ms. Chao and Mr. Thompson teach at the same school and have been friends for quite some time. During a break in the school day, they are discussing their classes.

"Most of my students are fine, but Billy is driving me crazy," Mr. Thompson says. "He is so lazy and he has the worst attitude. Janet had him last year, and she said the same thing, the kid was nothing but a problem all year long."

"Jared is Billy's older brother, right?" Ms. Chao asks.

Mr. Thompson nods.

"I had Jared two years ago. He was tough at first, I admit. But did you know their dad was killed in a car accident?"

Mr. Thompson says he had not been aware of that.

"Both of them have had a hard time. I spoke to their mother several times, and I think she is pretty rough on them. I don't think they get much support at home. Billy's probably not trying to make trouble."

Mr. Thompson doesn't respond, and the moment is a bit awkward between the two teachers. However, Mr. Thompson begins to rethink his position about Billy. He even speaks to the school's basketball coach, who tells him Billy is actually a very hard worker for something he is passionate about.

Exercise 2.4 provides practice identifying strategies teachers use to create relationships with students. (See page 53 for a reproducible of this exercise and page 165 for a reproducible answer sheet. Visit **marzanoresearch.com/classroomstrategies** to download all the exercises and answers in this book.)

Exercise 2.4
Building Positive Teacher-Student and Peer Relationships

After reading each of the following classroom scenarios, determine which of the following strategies for creating positive relationships with students are being employed. Note that in each scenario the teachers are using more than one strategy.

Ensure Fair and Equitable Treatment

    A. The class constitution

Show Interest in and Affection for Students

    B. Simple courtesies

    C. Physical contact and physical gestures

    D. Students' needs and concerns

Identify and Use Positive Information About Students

    E. Structured opportunities to highlight students' interests and accomplishments

    F. Parents or guardians

    G. Fellow teachers

1. Mr. Briggs usually gets the chance to talk with his students' families at the school's Back to School Night. However, Rodney's mother did not attend Back to School Night, so Mr. Briggs calls her at home on an evening Rodney said she would be home. She tells him that Rodney has recently been diagnosed with Asperger's syndrome, and that while they are doing what they can to get him all the help he needs, he still has a bit of a hard time socially at school. "He loves math," she says. "He loves chess, too. Puzzles of any kind fascinate him." After learning this information, Mr. Briggs watches out for Rodney. Sometimes he makes eye contact with Rodney so he knows he is as important as the other students; sometimes they have lunch together and do puzzles. When a fellow teacher decides to form a chess club, Mr. Briggs talks to Rodney and encourages him to join. He also talks to Rodney's mother once a week to get updates and see if there is anything else he can do to help.

2. After greeting her students by name as they come into class, Ms. Landis asks her students, as she does every Monday, if there is anything they would like to change about their personal profiles. The personal profiles are placed around the room and feature photos of each student as well as pictures or illustrations of hobbies, pets, friends, or anything else the student finds important. After taking a few minutes to allow students to add to or change their profiles, the class gets into small groups to continue work on a class project. Ms. Landis circulates the room to monitor progress, and when a student has questions or comments, she kneels beside his or her chair to talk. She finds that some of her more soft-spoken students will open up a little more if she is closer and at eye level with them.

3. While in search of information about his new students, Mr. Heim asks another teacher about a student named Li. The teacher says Li is a bully and will likely try to hurt other students. During a private meeting with Li, Mr. Heim asks him to share a little bit about himself. Li tells him that last school year was his first at this school, and it was tough for him. Mr. Heim asks why, and Li tells him that he didn't know anyone when he moved here and that where he comes from, kids have to prove they are tough to make friends and be respected. "I don't think it's like that here," Li says, "but it took me a while to figure it out. Now most of the kids are afraid of me." Mr. Heim tells Li he will do what he can to help him make some friends, and later shares his conversation with the teacher he originally spoke with. "He is not a bully," Mr. Heim says. "He just didn't know how to fit in. The rules at his old school don't apply here. I think we should give him a chance before making assumptions; negative presumptions will only make life harder for him."

4. Ms. Ballard is a physical education teacher. In the beginning of the year, she likes to initiate a class discussion in which she asks students what their favorite sports are and what kinds of games and sports they would like to learn. Over the course of the year, she tries to fit in as many requests as possible, asking the students who made the requests to assist during that unit. She uses high and low fives to encourage her assistants as well as all of her other students and sometimes uses elaborate handshakes she and the students make up.

5. Mr. Fuentes learns from Gage's mother that he recently lost a grandfather to whom he was very close. Mr. Fuentes knows Gage won't want to talk much about it at school, but he wants to show that he recognizes his student is going through a hard time. When he sees Gage in the hallway or as he is coming or going from class, Mr. Fuentes simply puts his hand on Gage's shoulder and gives him a smile.

Analyzing Your Strengths and Weaknesses

In this chapter, we have provided a variety of suggestions across five general categories of strategies, all of which increase the chances that students will have a positive response to the question "How do I feel?" One step to becoming more skilled in these strategies is to identify your strengths and weaknesses regarding these methods. In table 2.1 (page 46) we have provided a scale for self-analysis along with a list of all the strategies within each category. (See page 55 for a reproducible of this scale. Visit **marzanoresearch.com/classroomstrategies** to download all self-assessment scales in this book.)

The scale has five values—0 through 4. A score of 0 (not using) indicates that you never use this strategy or are not even aware of it. A score of 1 (beginning) means that you have used this strategy, but are aware of the fact that you are not using it correctly. A score of 2 (developing) indicates that you use the strategy without significant error, but do so in a rote mechanical way. You have to think about how to execute the strategy before you use it. A score of 3 (applying) indicates that you use the strategy without having to think much about it and always make sure to monitor how well it is working, making adaptations as needed. Finally, a score of 4 (innovating) means that you know the strategy so well that you have developed your own version of it. Score yourself on each of the strategies to identify specific areas you may wish to work on.

Table 2.1: Self-Assessment Scale for Chapter 2

	0 **Not Using** I never use this strategy.	1 **Beginning** I sometimes use this strategy, but I don't think I use it correctly.	2 **Developing** I use this strategy, but I do so mechanically.	3 **Applying** I use this strategy and monitor how well it works.	4 **Innovating** I know this strategy well enough that I have created my own version of it.
Using Effective Pacing					
Administrative tasks	0	1	2	3	4
Transitions	0	1	2	3	4
Seatwork	0	1	2	3	4
Presentation of new content	0	1	2	3	4
Incorporating Physical Movement					
Movement to lift energy	0	1	2	3	4
Movement that furthers understanding of content	0	1	2	3	4
Movement for the whole class or school	0	1	2	3	4
Demonstrating Intensity and Enthusiasm					
Personal stories	0	1	2	3	4
Verbal and nonverbal signals	0	1	2	3	4
Zest for teaching	0	1	2	3	4
Using Humor					
Self-directed humor	0	1	2	3	4
Funny headlines or quotes	0	1	2	3	4
Movie clips and media entertainment	0	1	2	3	4
A class symbol for humor	0	1	2	3	4
Building Positive Teacher-Student and Peer Relationships					
Ensure fair and equitable treatment of all students	0	1	2	3	4

Show interest in and affection for students	0	1	2	3	4
Identify and use positive information about students	0	1	2	3	4

Summary

This chapter began with a brief discussion about the first question in the model of attention and engagement, "How do I feel?" If students are low on energy or feeling bored, frustrated, or rejected by the teacher or their peers, it is likely that they are not attending to classroom activities. If a teacher does not have a student's attention, there is little hope that the content being addressed will enter his or her working or permanent memory. Teachers can use effective pacing and incorporate physical movement into lessons to help students feel energized; they can also demonstrate intensity and enthusiasm and use humor to help students feel stimulated. Finally, to help students feel accepted and valued, they can establish personal relationships and foster positive peer relationships in a fair and supportive classroom atmosphere.

Exercise 2.1

Using Effective Pacing

1. What is the relationship between pacing, working memory, and attention?

2. What are some limitations of pacing strategies in terms of keeping students' attention?

3. Which aspects of pacing are you effective at, and which aspects are you ineffective at?

Exercise 2.2

Incorporating Physical Movement

After reading each of the following classroom scenarios, determine which of the following strategies for physical movement is being employed:

A. Stretch break

B. Movement related to rehearsal

C. Give one, get one

D. Vote with your feet

E. Corners activities

F. Drama

G. Physical representation

1. Mr. Rush's language arts class has been reading some poetry. In order to help the students begin to think about the abstract concepts in the poems and to lift the energy level in the room, he asks his students to stand. "I'm going to call out a word and I want you to do something with your body that you think represents its meaning." When he begins by calling out the word *beauty*, his students are a bit hesitant, but as the exercise continues they begin to have more fun with it and create many different poses.

2. The students in Mr. Ulrick's first class of the day are often still tired and lethargic. In order to energize them a bit, he often asks them to stand in the beginning of class and do some simple exercises that are designed to wake up both sides of the brain.

3. Ms. Rollin's choir class has been looking at potential songs for an end-of-year performance. She has put together four possible programs students can choose from. She gives them the song list for each of the four programs at the end of class one day, giving each program a number 1–4. She asks them to think overnight about which program they like best and why. Before class the next day, she places four posters, each with a number (1–4) in different places around the room. When class begins, she asks them to stand under the number that represents the program they have chosen. She then asks students under each number to explain why they like that program the best. However, simply liking or disliking the songs in each program is not sufficient. She asks each of them to provide technical justifications, using vocabulary and concepts they have learned throughout the year to articulate their opinions. She finds that while they have not had many in-depth discussions about music in the past, many of her students are able to speak technically and articulately and even have strong opinions. Finally, she gives them a chance to change their votes after having heard the opinions of some classmates.

4. Mr. Holmes is having a review session for an upcoming social studies test on different governmental systems in place throughout the world. He tells his students to gather the notes they have on each of the different systems and the countries in which they are employed. He calls out two names randomly and those students pair up. When everyone is paired he says, "You have five minutes to share your notes with one another. You can glean new information that might be on the test this way, and you can clear up any mistakes you may have in your notes." After the five minutes are up, he calls out names in random pairs again and students repeat the process with a new partner.

Exercise 2.3

Demonstrating Intensity and Enthusiasm and Using Humor

After reading each of the following classroom scenarios, determine which of the following strategies for exhibiting intensity and enthusiasm or using humor is being employed:

Intensity and Enthusiasm

    A. Personal stories

    B. Verbal and nonverbal signals

    C. Zest for teaching

Humor

    D. Self-directed humor

    E. Funny headlines or quotes

    F. Movie clips and media entertainment

    G. A class symbol for humor

1. Ms. Amnell is a language arts teacher, and when she is teaching creative writing to her students, she finds they sometimes have a hard time thinking of original ideas. To help them along, she brings in short clips from films the students have probably never seen. Sometimes the clip is of a brief conversation between two people, sometimes it is an explosion or an alien ship landing on earth. All clips are humorous in some way. They must use the clip as the beginning of a narrative piece. She finds that when they are given a beginning, especially a funny beginning they wouldn't have thought of on their own, students show a lot of imagination.

2. Mr. Dermot tells his students that he has an imaginary brother named Leon Swankis. He tells his class a few stories about some of his adventures with Leon. It seems Leon is always getting Mr. Dermot in trouble. Sometimes he means well, but it is usually better when Mr. Dermot follows his own plan instead of listening to Leon's ideas. Every day when class lets out he reminds his students: "If you meet Leon, don't listen to him! He'll get you into trouble!" Throughout the year, he finds that students adopt Leon as their symbol for trouble, and their stories of him can be quite outlandish and funny. Some of them meet Leon, and though Leon tried to get them in trouble, they didn't listen to him. Occasionally, a student does find himself in trouble, whether it be in class or in school or even at home. If the student talks to Mr. Dermot about it, he will ask, "Was Leon there?" The student usually smiles and nods, affirming Leon was there. "I've told you, you can't listen to Leon, you have to listen to yourself."

3. Ms. Mason is an art teacher who happens to enjoy magic shows. When she demonstrates a technique in class, she uses the exaggerated and theatrical hand movements magicians use. She has the serious demeanor of a magician, and when the demonstration is complete, she holds out her arms and says, "Ta-da! Magic!" When students execute a technique particularly well or produce something they are really proud of, she does the same thing, telling them in a dramatic voice that what they have done is nothing short of magic!

4. Mr. Starr has been teaching science for over fifteen years. Sometimes teaching the same or similar content can get old and feel stale. When he feels uninspired about teaching, he takes the time to read science-based magazines and articles about new advancements and breakthroughs. Thinking about how many discoveries are being made in science today—and the ramifications of those discoveries—re-energizes him about teaching science.

Exercise 2.4

Building Positive Teacher-Student and Peer Relationships

After reading each of the following classroom scenarios, determine which of the following strategies for creating positive relationships with students are being employed. Note that in each scenario the teachers are using more than one strategy.

Ensure Fair and Equitable Treatment

    A. The class constitution

Show Interest in and Affection for Students

    B. Simple courtesies

    C. Physical contact and physical gestures

    D. Students' needs and concerns

Identify and Use Positive Information About Students

    E. Structured opportunities to highlight students' interests and accomplishments

    F. Parents or guardians

    G. Fellow teachers

1. Mr. Briggs usually gets the chance to talk with his students' families at the school's Back to School Night. However, Rodney's mother did not attend Back to School Night, so Mr. Briggs calls her at home on an evening Rodney said she would be home. She tells him that Rodney has recently been diagnosed with Asperger's syndrome, and that while they are doing what they can to get him all the help he needs, he still has a bit of a hard time socially at school. "He loves math," she says. "He loves chess, too. Puzzles of any kind fascinate him." After learning this information, Mr. Briggs watches out for Rodney. Sometimes he makes eye contact with Rodney so he knows he is as important as the other students; sometimes they have lunch together and do puzzles. When a fellow teacher decides to form a chess club, Mr. Briggs talks to Rodney and encourages him to join. He also talks to Rodney's mother once a week to get updates and see if there is anything else he can do to help.

2. After greeting her students by name as they come into class, Ms. Landis asks her students, as she does every Monday, if there is anything they would like to change about their personal profiles. The personal profiles are placed around the room and feature photos of each student as well as pictures or illustrations of

The Highly Engaged Classroom © 2011 Marzano Research Laboratory • marzanoresearch.com
Visit **marzanoresearch.com/classroomstrategies** to download this page.

hobbies, pets, friends, or anything else the student finds important. After taking a few minutes to allow students to add to or change their profiles, the class gets into small groups to continue work on a class project. Ms. Landis circulates the room to monitor progress, and when a student has questions or comments, she kneels beside his or her chair to talk. She finds that some of her more soft-spoken students will open up a little more if she is closer and at eye level with them.

3. While in search of information about his new students, Mr. Heim asks another teacher about a student named Li. The teacher says Li is a bully and will likely try to hurt other students. During a private meeting with Li, Mr. Heim asks him to share a little bit about himself. Li tells him that last school year was his first at this school, and it was tough for him. Mr. Heim asks why, and Li tells him that he didn't know anyone when he moved here and that where he comes from, kids have to prove they are tough to make friends and be respected. "I don't think it's like that here," Li says, "but it took me a while to figure it out. Now most of the kids are afraid of me." Mr. Heim tells Li he will do what he can to help him make some friends, and later shares his conversation with the teacher he originally spoke with. "He is not a bully," Mr. Heim says. "He just didn't know how to fit in. The rules at his old school don't apply here. I think we should give him a chance before making assumptions; negative presumptions will only make life harder for him."

4. Ms. Ballard is a physical education teacher. In the beginning of the year, she likes to initiate a class discussion in which she asks students what their favorite sports are and what kinds of games and sports they would like to learn. Over the course of the year, she tries to fit in as many requests as possible, asking the students who made the requests to assist during that unit. She uses high and low fives to encourage her assistants as well as all of her other students and sometimes uses elaborate handshakes she and the students make up.

5. Mr. Fuentes learns from Gage's mother that he recently lost a grandfather to whom he was very close. Mr. Fuentes knows Gage won't want to talk much about it at school, but he wants to show that he recognizes his student is going through a hard time. When he sees Gage in the hallway or as he is coming or going from class, Mr. Fuentes simply puts his hand on Gage's shoulder and gives him a smile.

Self-Assessment Scale for Chapter 2

	0 Not Using I never use this strategy.	1 Beginning I sometimes use this strategy, but I don't think I use it correctly.	2 Developing I use this strategy, but I do so mechanically.	3 Applying I use this strategy and monitor how well it works.	4 Innovating I know this strategy well enough that I have created my own version of it.
Using Effective Pacing					
Administrative tasks	0	1	2	3	4
Transitions	0	1	2	3	4
Seatwork	0	1	2	3	4
Presentation of new content	0	1	2	3	4
Incorporating Physical Movement					
Movement to lift energy	0	1	2	3	4
Movement that furthers understanding of content	0	1	2	3	4
Movement for the whole class or school	0	1	2	3	4
Demonstrating Intensity and Enthusiasm					
Personal stories	0	1	2	3	4
Verbal and nonverbal signals	0	1	2	3	4
Zest for teaching	0	1	2	3	4
Using Humor					
Self-directed humor	0	1	2	3	4
Funny headlines or quotes	0	1	2	3	4
Movie clips and media entertainment	0	1	2	3	4
A class symbol for humor	0	1	2	3	4

1 of 2

The Highly Engaged Classroom © 2011 Marzano Research Laboratory • marzanoresearch.com
Visit **marzanoresearch.com/classroomstrategies** to download this page.

Building Positive Teacher-Student and Peer Relationships					
Ensure fair and equitable treatment of all students	0	1	2	3	4
Show interest in and affection for students	0	1	2	3	4
Identify and use positive information about students	0	1	2	3	4

Chapter 3

AM I INTERESTED?

As described in chapter 1, the extent to which students pay attention in class is a function not only of how they feel but also of their level of interest. In other words, students will attend to activities in the classroom if they can affirmatively answer the question "Am I interested?" In this chapter, we consider four categories of strategies that stimulate student interest: (1) using games and inconsequential competition, (2) initiating friendly controversy, (3) presenting unusual information, and (4) questioning to increase response rates.

Using Games and Inconsequential Competition

Games and inconsequential competition help trigger and maintain situational interest. Games should always have an academic focus. One way to maintain such a focus is to organize games around relevant vocabulary terms. After each game, the teacher leads students in a brief review of the terms that students found most challenging. *Inconsequential competition* can accompany games. As its name implies, this type of competition is just for fun. Students are organized into ad hoc groups or groups that last for a single lesson or unit. Throughout the year, students are continually regrouped so that all students experience winning and losing. Points are tallied to identify winning teams, but points are not used to increase or decrease students' scores or grades. Here we consider two general categories of games and inconsequential competition: (1) vocabulary games and (2) turning questions into games.

Vocabulary Games

In the book *Vocabulary Games for the Classroom*, Carleton and Marzano (2010) identify thirteen different types of games that teachers can adapt to almost any subject or grade level. Two games— *Which One Doesn't Belong?* and *What Is the Question?*—are briefly described here. For a more detailed description of the games, along with game items and sample vocabulary terms for the games, see Carleton and Marzano (2010).

Which One Doesn't Belong? can be used with students of all ages. It allows students to use their knowledge of vocabulary terms and phrases to find similarities and differences among a group of terms. The teacher prepares by creating word groups containing three terms that are similar in some way and one term that is different. On game day, students can work independently or in groups. The teacher displays one word group at a time, and students have a set amount of time to pick out the term that does not belong and write down why. This game can be played formally with points or informally without strict rules or points. It can be played spontaneously as well, at times when a lesson lends itself to such an activity.

What Is the Question? is best for older elementary through high school students. It is modeled after *Jeopardy!* and allows students to team up and test knowledge of terms and facts. The teacher prepares a game board with relevant categories and creates game items to test students' knowledge within those categories. Each item is in the form of an answer, and the students must frame their responses in the form of a question. Students can work independently, or the class can be split into small groups. Just like *Jeopardy!*, a student or team is chosen to select a category and begin the game, and whoever responds correctly is given the opportunity to select the next category.

Turn Questions Into Games

In addition to vocabulary games, any set of questions on a specific topic can be turned into an ad hoc game. For example, a teacher might design four multiple-choice questions as part of a mathematics lesson on estimation. Before asking the questions, the teacher organizes students into equally sized groups. Each group is given one minute to name itself. Once the teacher asks the question, group members caucus for one minute to discuss the correct answer and record it on a piece of paper or whiteboard. When the teacher gives the signal, each group holds up its answer. On the board, the teacher keeps a record of the groups that select the correct answer. After all four questions have been asked, points are totaled, and the group with the highest point total is acknowledged.

The following vignette illustrates a teacher using games and inconsequential competition to stimulate attention.

> Ms. Derringer is teaching a unit on El Niño. She has prepared four multiple-choice questions to ask the class throughout the lesson. At the beginning of class, she divides the class into four equally sized groups. After an allotted minute, each group comes up with a name, and Ms. Derringer writes the four names on the board. They are: the Animators, the Smashing Pumpkins, the Football Team, and Weathering Heights.
>
> Once the teams have been named, she begins the lesson. After a brief overview of what El Niño is, she pauses to ask the first question: "How does El Niño affect the fishing industry in Peru? Is it (a) El Niño helps the fishing industry because it brings warmer water that fish like for mating, (b) El Niño hurts the fishing industry because it brings warmer water that does not have the nutrients fish need to survive, (c) El Niño does not affect the fishing industry, but it does affect the tourist industry, or (d) El Niño hurts the fishing industry because it brings warmer water that attracts larger predators who, in turn, eat the fish the industry depends on?"
>
> The groups take a minute to decide which answer they think is correct, and when Ms. Derringer signals, one member of each group holds up a piece of paper with the agreed-upon answer. The Animators and Weathering Heights both have chosen

d as the answer, while both the Smashing Pumpkins and the Football Team have chosen b. After each group explains the logic behind their answer, Ms. Derringer reveals that the correct answer is b and awards the two correct teams one point each. "Everyone seemed to understand that El Niño hurts the fishing industry by bringing warmer water, so that's great," she says.

She continues the lesson, stopping three more times to ask questions and award points. At the end of class, the Animators have two points, the Smashing Pumpkins have one point, the Football Team has four points, and Weathering Heights has three points. "Congratulations to the Football Team, you guys did a great job!" Ms. Derringer says. As the students walk out of class, she notices they are talking about the lesson and challenging each other to a rematch.

Exercise 3.1 provides an opportunity to test your understanding of how using academic games and inconsequential competition creates student interest. Answering these questions will require making connections and inferences that may not be obvious. In other words, the answers to these questions are not found explicitly in the text. (See page 80 for a reproducible of this exercise and page 168 for a reproducible answer sheet. Visit **marzanoresearch.com/classroomstrategies** to download all the exercises and answers in this book.)

Exercise 3.1
Using Games and Inconsequential Competition

> 1. Why do academic games stimulate attention?
> 2. What would be appropriate teacher behavior if many students did poorly on the questions in an academic game?
> 3. What are some ways you have used games in the past?

Initiating Friendly Controversy

Controversy can both trigger situational interest and maintain situational interest. In general, when people express opposing views, they are engaged. As we saw in chapter 1, when structured well, controversy can stimulate students to delve deeply into content even outside of class time.

Teachers should take care when structuring controversy activities for the classroom to ensure that discussion does not become too heated. They can accomplish this by establishing rules for interaction such as the following:

- Even if you are anxious to say something, listen when others are talking and wait your turn.

- You may criticize ideas but not people.

- As others speak, try to listen to what they are saying and understand why they think their opinion is accurate.

- When you state your opinion, try to provide evidence or reasons for it.

These cautions noted, controversy should not be avoided. In fact, the goal of friendly controversy activities should be to leave students with some unanswered questions so that they seek more information. Here we consider five strategies for implementing friendly controversy: (1) class vote, (2) debate model, (3) town hall meeting, (4) legal model, and (5) perspective analysis.

Class Vote

Perhaps the simplest strategy to help stimulate friendly controversy is to initiate a class vote. Here the teacher simply asks students to vote on a particular issue. Both before and after the vote, though, students discuss the merits of various positions. This discussion encourages students to carefully consider their positions and change their minds (and votes) as more information is disclosed. In this way, the vote is not used to decide the winning position. For example, a secondary economics teacher might ask the class to vote on whether or not the United States should switch from an income tax to a flat tax. After the initial vote, the class would discuss the merits and drawbacks of each position, and then the teacher might initiate another vote. The following vignette depicts the use of a class vote.

> After finishing the story "Jack and the Beanstalk," Mr. Donaldson asks the class to vote on whether or not it was okay for Jack to steal the harp and the goose given that the giant was mean and threatening. When students have voted, he asks for volunteers to explain their reasoning. After a class discussion about whether or not an act that is normally considered to be morally wrong can, in certain situations, be seen as justified, the class votes again. Students are then invited to explain why they changed or did not change their votes.

Debate Model

To stimulate friendly controversy, teachers can also focus on debate. Formal debates take several forms, but a common one is the Lincoln-Douglas debate format. It has the following four characteristics:

1. The Lincoln-Douglas debate model seeks to encourage students to use evidence, logic, and persuasive techniques to effectively argue a controversial viewpoint.

2. The teacher chooses two teams to debate opposing sides of a specific policy or issue. Usually one side argues in favor of a policy (affirmative team) while the other side argues against it (negative team).

3. Each side gets a chance to make an opening argument, cross-examine the negative team, and present a rebuttal.

4. Each team evaluates the group performance after the debate, and each student evaluates his or her performance as a member of the team.

The debate model can be used in a wide variety of circumstances. For example, a science teacher might invite debate regarding the merits versus drawbacks of zoos, or an art teacher might invite debate regarding the benefits versus harm of spending tax money to support art and artists. The following vignette depicts the use of the debate model in the classroom.

Ms. Lucas is a middle school social studies teacher who is finishing a unit on the rights and responsibilities of U.S. citizenship. She wants her students to understand those rights and responsibilities, but she also wants them to understand how such things are relevant in their own lives. She wants them to feel a sense of responsibility regarding issues involving their government. She knows from previous class discussions that they are particularly interested in minimum age requirements for laws like voting and military service. She decides to put together a class debate based on the Lincoln-Douglas model.

To begin, she splits the class into two groups—one group that will debate the minimum voting age, and the other that will debate the minimum age for military service. Next, she assigns students to the affirmative and negative sides of each issue, making sure that each team is made of some of the more vocal students in the class and some of the more reserved students. Once students are in their teams (there are four teams in all), she explains the Lincoln-Douglas debate model. Ms. Lucas also provides all teams with a list of resources to use and a few tips, such as being prepared for a cross-examination from the opposing team and speaking clearly and slowly enough for the audience. She also outlines explicitly what they will be graded on during the debate.

On debate day, Ms. Lucas acts as a moderator as the students debate both issues. At the conclusion of each debate, students who were not involved in that particular debate vote on which team was the most persuasive.

The next day, the students are given the opportunity to reflect on their own performances and that of their team. They list things they thought were successful and things they would do differently in another debate.

Town Hall Meeting

Another model is based on a town hall meeting (Hess, 2009). It has the following four characteristics:

1. The purpose of a town hall meeting is not to win a debate. Instead, it seeks to encourage students to see a complex issue from multiple perspectives.

2. The teacher and the class create roles for the meeting. The teacher designates each student or group of students to a role. Roles are based on those people most likely to have strong opinions about an issue or most likely to be affected by a new policy or change in existing policy.

3. Students participate in an open discussion that the teacher mediates. Students stay in their roles, arguing from that point of view for the duration of the discussion.

4. Students participate in a *debriefing*. The debriefing is designed to allow students to evaluate their own performances as well as evaluate the discussion as a whole.

The following vignette depicts the use of the town hall–meeting model. For more information, see *Controversy in the Classroom* (Hess, 2009).

Ms. Twain is a high school teacher who wants her students to see complex, controversial issues from multiple viewpoints and to communicate effectively with people whose opinions are different from their own. To this end, she creates a town hall–meeting activity on the topic of eminent domain.

To begin, she discusses the specific learning goals that the students will be graded on during the town hall meeting, and she shows videos of effective and ineffective town hall meetings as models. Next, Ms. Twain provides a packet of background material on eminent domain and specific circumstances in which it has been used and dedicates a class period to familiarizing students with the issue. Once students have had time to digest the information in the packets, the class works together to craft specific roles for the participants in the town hall meeting—that is, they imagine the broadest possible range of arguments about the initiative. The roles include a government agent tasked with enforcing eminent domain, a private citizen who is being forced to sell property, a citizen who supports the sale because it would benefit him, and a citizen who disagrees with the decision even though he would benefit from it. Over the next few days, students research their roles and craft their positions and arguments.

On the day of the town hall meeting, Ms. Twain acts as a mediator, calling on students who play the assigned roles. Students present their arguments for or against the use of eminent domain. The town hall meeting lasts ninety minutes, after which (in class the next day) the students participate in a debriefing of the meeting. In the debriefing, students discuss what went well and what didn't, focusing on the original learning goals presented. They also discuss how they felt arguing from a perspective different than their own.

Legal Model

The legal model is still another approach (Hess, 2009). The structure of controversy here is in scrutinizing the decisions of the U.S. Supreme Court. The legal model has the following four characteristics:

1. The legal approach seeks to encourage students to critically examine how court decisions affect policy. It also seeks to encourage students to form opinions or make arguments based on textual evidence.

2. Each student completes a "ticket" before the discussion to ensure students are aware of the arguments made by each of the Supreme Court justices in the case. A ticket outlines the essential arguments each Supreme Court justice made in relation to the case being studied. Students keep their tickets with them during the seminar to serve as a reference guide.

3. The teacher holds a class seminar using probing questions. Questions can focus on fact, opinion, or idea, but all questions require students to refer to their tickets and the court-case text.

4. After the seminar, students debrief and evaluate their own performances as well as the performance of the class.

The following vignette demonstrates the use of the legal model in the classroom. For more information, see *Controversy in the Classroom* (Hess, 2009).

> *Mr. Park is a middle school social studies teacher who wants his students to have a contextual understanding of the nuances of the U.S. Supreme Court and the impact of the justices' decisions. He presents his students with the Supreme Court case of* Feiner v. New York, *in which the Supreme Court looked at whether or not freedom of speech protected someone making inflammatory political statements on a street corner. After becoming familiar with the case, students are given a ticket assignment that requires them to identify the basic arguments made by each of the nine Supreme Court justices. Additionally, Mr. Park splits them into groups to discuss the basic facts of the case and its movement to the Supreme Court.*
>
> *When their tickets are completed, students then sit in a circle and participate in a seminar—a group discussion guided by specific rules and regulations the students have previously become familiar with. The main discussion consists of using the text of the court case as well as their tickets to answer specific, probing questions such as: "The First Amendment is frequently challenged in court. Why do you think this is? Use the court-case text in your answer." Mr. Park also asks about the ultimate decision in the case and how that decision influenced our current interpretation of the First Amendment. Some of the questions require information on the case and some require opinions, thoughts, or ideas, but each question asks students to refer directly to the court text. After the seminar, students participate in a debriefing, in which they evaluate their own performances as well as the performance of the group according to the learning goals Mr. Park presented at the beginning of the unit. At the end of class, students turn in their tickets to Mr. Park for later assessment.*

Perspective Analysis

In perspective analysis, students scrutinize their opinions on a given issue and the logic behind those opinions. In addition, students consider a contrasting position and the logic behind it. Marzano (1992) identifies a formal process that teachers could introduce students to:

1. Identify your position on a controversial topic.

2. Determine the reasoning behind your position.

3. Identify an opposing position.

4. Describe the reasoning behind the opposing position.

5. When you are finished, summarize what you have learned.

They can also present this process to students as a series of questions, such as the following:

- What do I believe about this?

- Why do I believe it?

- What is another way of looking at this?

- Why might someone else hold a different opinion?

- What have I learned?

The following vignette depicts the use of the perspective analysis in the classroom.

Ms. Ippoliti's language arts class has been studying the use of research in persuasive compositions. She notices that some students have cited Wikipedia in a past essay. She decides to put together a perspective analysis to address the issue of whether or not Wikipedia is a valid research source. "What do you think?" she asks. "What criteria make a valid research source? Do all articles on Wikipedia meet those criteria?"

After students have had time to discuss the issue and form an opinion, Ms. Ippoliti leads the class through the questions in the perspective analysis model. Students first go through the questions independently, articulating their opinions and answering the questions in writing. They also discuss what they have learned about the complexities of the Supreme Court and the impact its rulings have on society. Next, she invites a class discussion during which students verbalize their opinions and the justifications for those opinions. Many of her students feel that Wikipedia is a valid resource because all entries contain reference lists. Others feel that because anyone can change an entry and the site is not closely monitored, Wikipedia is not a valid source.

Next, students on opposing sides of the issue pair up in order to summarize what they have heard on both sides of the issue. Finally, students consider the discussion

> *and come back to class the next day ready to discuss what they have learned and any possible change in their opinions. Specifically, they are asked to examine the impact of sitting down with someone on an opposing side of an issue to discuss and summarize both positions.*

Exercise 3.2 provides an opportunity to test your understanding of how initiating friendly controversy creates interest in students. Answering these questions will require making connections and inferences that may not be obvious. In other words, the answers to these questions are not found explicitly in the text. (See page 81 for a reproducible of this exercise and page 169 for a reproducible answer sheet. Visit **marzanoresearch.com/classroomstrategies** to download all the exercises and answers in this book.)

Exercise 3.2
Initiating Friendly Controversy

1. Compare the defining features of the debate model, the town hall–meeting model, and the legal model.
2. What is unique about perspective analysis as compared to other approaches described in this section?

Presenting Unusual Information

Unusual information almost always piques the interest of students. Given that human beings are naturally curious, information that is not typical within a given content area can help capture students' attention. For example, what student in a geometry class would not be interested to learn that a Möbius strip is a one-sided surface (Pappas, 1989)? What student in a science class studying the human body would not be interested to learn why knuckles pop?

Teachers can use many sources to find intriguing information. The following are some useful online sources:

- The *New York Times* (www.nytimes.com)—This site is useful for finding interesting and current information for science (John Tierney's column is especially fun), social studies, and language arts. You can also search the *New York Times* archives and find historical articles on almost any topic.

- Federal Resources for Educational Excellence (http://free.ed.gov)—This site is a federal resource geared specifically toward education. It provides information and educational links in the subjects of language arts, math, science, and social studies. Pictures and videos are available as well.

- Edutopia (www.edutopia.org)—This site is geared toward educators and provides information on hot topics in education, current events in education, and new or inventive instructional strategies and ideas.

- PBS (www.pbs.org)—This site provides access to PBS and NOVA videos as well as webinars on various topics from *PBS Teachers LIVE!* You can also find unusual information or innovative ideas for instruction on the PBS link to the Idea Lab blog.

- National Geographic (www.nationalgeographic.com)—This site is especially useful for finding information on new species as well as intriguing photos. Feature stories relevant to science and social studies are available as well.

- LiveScience (www.livescience.com)—This site provides videos and information in the subjects of space, animals, health, environment, technology, culture, and history. A section of the site is even dedicated to strange news.

- Discover (http://discovermagazine.com)—This site provides information on health and medicine, mind and brain, technology, space, human origins, the living world, environment, and physics and math. It also features interesting articles and blog links.

- Science Daily (www.sciencedaily.com)—This site provides interesting information on the results of recent studies or discoveries in scientific arenas such as health and medicine, ancient species, and technology and mathematics.

- Scientific American (www.scientificamerican.com)—This site provides information on space, evolution, energy and sustainability, mind and brain, health and medicine, and technology. It also features articles and images from *Scientific American Mind* magazine as well as various blog links.

- The History Channel (www.history.com)—This site provides videos of television shows featured on the History Channel. Many of these shows, such as *Life After People*, take unique perspectives on the past, present, and future of Earth and mankind. The site also includes "This Day in History" facts and curriculum guides to help teachers link information found on the site to their own lesson plans.

- Listverse (http://listverse.com)—This site provides lists ranking a variety of interesting topics such as "Top 15 Fascinating Planets Outside Our Solar System," "Top 10 Extraordinary People With Disabilities," and "Top 10 Individual Protests."

- Trivia-Library (www.trivia-library.com)—This site provides trivia on a wide range of topics that teachers could creatively apply to almost any content area.

- The *New Yorker* (www.newyorker.com)—This site provides articles and essays on a variety of topics and interviews with a variety of relevant artists and politicians.

- Arts & Letters Daily (www.aldaily.com)—This site provides many articles on art and current events. It is also useful for its variety of links. It provides links to many newspapers, magazines, columnists, blogs, and even radio stations.

- Kids' Planet (www.kidsplanet.org)—This site provides kid-friendly information about animals as well as some teacher lesson plans. It also provides a list and basic fact sheet about all endangered species worldwide.

- Kids Know It Network (www.kidsknowit.com)—This site is a "children's learning network," geared specifically for student users. It provides content and links to social studies and science information as well.

- Smithsonian Education (www.smithsonianeducation.org)—This site provides lesson plans, information, and resources for virtually any content area. It also allows teachers to access state standards and provides resource links for almost all of those standards.

- NASA (www.nasa.gov)—This site provides all kinds of space-related information, including information on the history of NASA; information on past and present shuttles, space stations, and missions; information on technology and aeronautics; and information on the Earth, our solar system, and the universe.

- Mudd Math Fun Facts (www.math.hmc.edu/funfacts)—Mudd Math Fun Facts provides puzzles and math tricks in areas such as algebra, geometry, number theory, probability, and calculus.

- Coolmath (http://coolmath4kids.com)—This site provides instructional tips for younger math students. It also has math lessons and a few math games, and it provides fun math "brain benders."

In addition, teachers can adapt the following books containing unusual and intriguing information for classroom use:

- *Legends, Lies, and Cherished Myths of American History* by Richard Shenkman (1988). This book debunks popular notions of American history that we often mistake for being fact. For example, many of the artistic likenesses of famous figures in history such as Christopher Columbus and John Harvard are fictitious inventions. No portraits were painted of Columbus during his time, and the famous statue of John Harvard was created after his death and depicts only a scholarly looking gentleman, not John Harvard himself.

- *Legends, Lies, and Cherished Myths of World History* by Richard Shenkman (1993). This book debunks popular notions of world history that we often mistake for being fact. For example, Winston Churchill was not a popular candidate for prime minister. In fact, the only reason he got the job was because the most popular candidate (Lord Halifax) turned it down.

- *Don't Know Much About Geography: Everything You Need to Know About the World but Never Learned* by Kenneth Davis (1992). This book connects interesting historical facts with geography, and it answers many off-the-wall geography questions. For example, it explains the reasons behind the names and nicknames for all fifty states. Nevada comes from the Spanish word for *snow capped*, which is interesting because Nevada ranks as the driest state in the country.

- *Dr. Joe & What You Didn't Know: 177 Fascinating Questions & Answers About the Chemistry of Everyday Life* by Joe Schwarcz (2003). This book answers all kinds of questions about everyday science, such as "What are smelling salts?" (p. 28). Smelling salts are technically ammonium carbonate. They actually have no medicinal value and are no longer used in medical contexts; however, bakers still use smelling salts as a leavening agent in cookies and crackers because ammonium carbonate releases gas as it is heated.

- *They All Laughed . . . From Light Bulbs to Lasers: The Fascinating Stories Behind the Great Inventions That Have Changed Our Lives* by Ira Flatow (1992). This book discusses in detail the efforts and accidents behind great inventions. For example, a scientist named Roy J. Plunkett was trying to invent a nontoxic refrigerant in 1938, but accidentally invented Teflon instead.

- *Napoleon's Buttons: 17 Molecules That Changed History* by Penny Le Couteur and Jay Burreson (2004). This book blends science and history in a humorous way. For example, the buttons for all soldiers in Napoleon's army were made of tin. When the tin met the extremely cold temperatures of a Russian winter, the buttons crumbled into powder. The soldiers needed their hands to keep their clothes on, which made fighting very difficult and could have been a major contributing factor to the downfall of the French army.

As indicated, there are many resources for a teacher seeking unusual information in class. Appendix C (page 187) lists some unusual information drawn from these sources in the areas of mathematics, science, language arts, and social studies.

Teachers can use unusual information to stimulate attention in the classroom in a variety of ways. Here we consider introducing a lesson, allowing students to research and collect interesting facts, and inviting guest speakers.

Introduce a Lesson

Teachers can introduce a lesson with unusual information. This is particularly effective when the unusual information provides a reason for examining the upcoming content. The following vignette depicts this use of unusual information.

> *Mr. Reyes is an elementary science teacher. He introduces a unit on the solar system by telling his students that the solar system is pretty strange: "When you heat up a burner on the stove, the burner gets a lot hotter than the heat it gives off, right? After all, if you held your hand a few inches above a burner it wouldn't hurt, but if you touched it, it would burn you badly. Did you know the sun doesn't work like that? The sun's surface is only about six thousand degrees Celsius, but the atmosphere surrounding the sun is millions of degrees hotter. Does anyone know why? Believe it or not, scientists don't know either! In this lesson, we are going to consider how heat is conducted. Maybe that will provide some clues."*

Allow Students to Research and Collect Interesting Facts

A class-generated collection of facts is one way to use unusual information. A teacher can ask students to compile an electronic database of unusual or little-known information about content being studied. This database can become a kind of in-class wiki, with students adding to the list and (where appropriate) correcting misperceptions or inaccuracies. Each class can transmit a legacy of arcane but interesting information about the content for other classes and future students to reflect upon. For example, students in an art class might collect information about the unusual or surprising materials many artists have used for sculptures. Students in the same class the next school year might be interested in the information their predecessors discovered and be inspired to look for facts about the painters' use of unusual materials or photographers' or writers' unusual inspirations.

Creating history files is another approach to using unusual information. As the name implies, this strategy is used with historical information and involves researching differences among perceptions of facts related to specific content being studied. For example, science students might research and document how the prevalent models of our solar system have changed over time, or students in a health class might collect information about how definitions of "healthy eating" have changed over time.

The following vignette depicts students gathering unusual information.

> *Ms. Olivier began to collect a compendium of information about her favorite authors and the ideas and inspirations behind their books as a personal project several years ago. When her class was reading* The Divine Comedy *by Dante Alighieri, one of her students asked if Beatrice was based on a real person. "No one knows for certain, but evidence suggests that there really was a Beatrice," she said. "Dante met her when he was nine and loved her all his life, even though she married another man. She died when she was only twenty-four, and after that Dante began composing poems about her." She found that her students were even more engaged in the book after hearing about Dante's real unrequited love. As an experiment, she decides to have her students collect knowledge about Kurt Vonnegut before reading* Cat's Cradle, *their next book. One student finds that Vonnegut and Dr. Seuss were fraternity brothers in college. Another finds that he coauthored a children's book titled* Sun Moon Star *that was about the birth of Jesus. The students collect the information on an online wiki so that each of them can add unusual facts, correct grammar mistakes or misunderstandings, and even comment on facts other students have found. Ms. Olivier's class enjoys the challenge so much that she decides to keep the database and use it to challenge students she will have the next school year.*

Invite Guest Speakers

Guest speakers and firsthand consultants are another way to provide unusual information. Teachers can invite individuals to the classroom who can share direct experience regarding the content being addressed in class. The following vignette depicts this approach.

> *Mr. Driver knows his high school economics students will be more interested in subjects relevant to their everyday lives. He asks a journalist with the* Economist *to join his class via video conference to discuss the recent economic recession. Students prepare questions about the causes and effects (both long and short term) of the recession and are encouraged to ask the journalist advice about what might happen in the future. Some students ask what is safe to invest in, and some ask what fields of study will ensure safe and successful careers. One student is an aspiring painter and wants to know what might happen to grants and scholarships in the near future. After the conference, students have a roundtable discussion about what they learned and why the state of the economy is relevant to politics, history, scientific and artistic movements, and their own daily lives.*

Exercise 3.3 (page 70) provides an opportunity to test your understanding of how teachers can use unusual information to create interest in students. Answering these questions will require making connections and inferences that may not be obvious. In other words, the answers to these questions are not found explicitly in the text. (See page 82 for a reproducible of this exercise and page 170 for a reproducible answer sheet. Visit **marzanoresearch.com/classroomstrategies** to download all the exercises and answers in this book.)

Exercise 3.3
Presenting Unusual Information

1. What is the underlying dynamic behind using unusual information to capture students' attention?
2. How might the use of unusual information facilitate class participation and cooperation?
3. How have you utilized unusual information in the past? Are there specific topics you teach that could use unusual information?

Questioning to Increase Response Rates

Answering a question occupies a student's working memory. Thus, asking questions elicits a student's attention. The only problem with this generalization is that once a student is called on to answer a question, the other students in class may disengage and focus on something else. Consequently, if questioning activities are used to capture students' attention, they must increase the number of students who answer each question. A teacher can use a number of activities to increase response rates, some of which are addressed in the book *The Art and Science of Teaching* (Marzano, 2007). Here we take a more in-depth look at effective questioning strategies.

Call on Students Randomly

Calling only on students who raise their hands is an ineffective practice because typically only a small number of students volunteer to answer teacher-posed questions. This creates an environment in which students know that once a question is asked, they can simply relax because only those who raise their hands are responsible for the answer. Another pattern that decreases response rates is for the teacher to typically call on only a select group of students. Again, this pattern signals to the students who are not typically called on that they do not have to attend when a question is asked.

In contrast, calling on students in an obviously random manner can increase response rates in that all students have to at least think about the answer even though they might not actually be called on. Some strategies for calling on students randomly are drawing names out of a hat, writing students' names on tongue depressors that are kept stored in a glass or jar, and using technology available with an interactive system. Regardless of which method a teacher uses, if students know that a teacher will call on any student at random after asking a question, they are more likely to attend to classroom lessons. For example, a student in a class where the teacher typically calls only on volunteers might skip a homework assignment that is not graded because he knows he is not likely to be called on if he remains quiet during the class period. By contrast, a student who understands that he is just as likely to be called on as any of his peers might be sure to complete his homework so he can be prepared. The following vignette depicts a teacher calling on students randomly.

> *Julia is taking French, which is not her favorite subject. She has trouble with pronunciation and avoids speaking in French aloud because she finds it awkward. She is proficient with pencil-and-paper tests, though, because they involve memorization,*

which isn't hard for Julia. In past classes, the best way to get a good grade in the class was to rely on her test scores and stay as quiet and invisible in class as possible. If the teacher saw her scores on paper, she got good grades, but if he heard her speaking in class, his opinion of her ability was likely to go down. Unfortunately, staying quiet in her current French class is not easy because her new teacher draws names out of a hat when he asks questions, so Julia is as likely as any other student to be called on. She decides that for this class she will have to get some after-school help to work on her pronunciation.

Paired Response

One easy way to increase the response rate among students is to use *paired response*. With this strategy, the teacher organizes students into pairs. When a question is asked, the pairs are first given time to confer, which allows all students to be engaged in answering the question. The group time to collaborate and prepare an answer is critical, as it can set students up for success. When a pair is randomly called on, the teacher can ask one of the students to verbalize the answer, the students can decide who will act as the speaker, or each student can contribute part of the answer. The following vignette illustrates the use of paired response.

Vanessa and Colin have been partnered in math class for the day. Ms. Jones writes an equation on the board and asks each pair to work together to solve it. They were given a few minutes to discuss the problem and come up with a solution. Vanessa doesn't have much confidence in her math skills, so usually when the teacher asks for a solution to an equation she pretends to work and then lets someone else answer. But if she has a partner, she has to at least try to complete the problem. When the allotted time is up, Ms. Jones calls on Vanessa and Colin. Vanessa verbalizes the answer they came up with and, because Colin is more confident in the answer, he verbalizes how they arrived at that answer. After a few equations, Vanessa finds she is catching on, and she is even able to verbalize how she and Colin arrived at their answer when Ms. Jones calls on her.

Wait Time

Wait time refers to pausing at strategic points during questioning. Waiting before calling on students allows them to process the question and encourages them to think through their answers instead of impulsively responding. To serve this purpose, the teacher explains ahead of time to the students that once a question is asked there will be time allotted for thinking through their answers—no one will be called on during that time. The amount of time a teacher waits is a function of the complexity and type of question. Stated differently, a teacher can use less wait time after asking a straightforward question with one correct response and more wait time when asking a complex or open-ended question that requires interpretation. Other types of wait time are addressed in *The Art and Science of Teaching* (Marzano, 2007).

By encouraging all students to think through their answers to a question, a teacher is more likely to increase the rate of response. In other words, a student who is given some time to thoughtfully tailor a response is more likely to offer it than a student who has not been given that time and therefore does not have an answer he or she can offer with confidence.

The following vignette depicts wait time in the classroom.

> *A mathematics teacher draws a set of parallel lines and a transversal line and labels each of the angles. He asks the class, "Who can name a pair of corresponding interior angles?" A fair number of students raise their hands, but Desiree is not one of them. She thinks she doesn't know the answer, but then her teacher waits before calling on someone. This gives her an opportunity to consider the definition of corresponding angles. After thinking about it, she realizes she knows the definition and then applies what she knows to the question. By the time the teacher is ready to call on someone for the answer, Desiree is prepared and confident enough to raise her hand.*

Response Chaining

Response chaining involves linking or "chaining" students' responses. The teacher begins by asking a question, to which one student responds. Other students are then asked to respond to that student's response. This pattern can continue with one response being linked to another like links in a chain. This approach can be adapted to both questions that are straightforward (questions with one correct answer) and questions that are open ended.

If chaining is used with questions that require short answers, students respond to another student's answer in one of three ways: the answer was correct, partially correct, or incorrect. When a student contends that a previous student's response was correct, the teacher asks him or her to explain why it is correct or add information to the first student's answer. When a student contends that a previous student's response was partially correct, he or she is asked to explain which part of the answer was correct and which part was incorrect. When a student contends that a previous student's response was incorrect, he or she is asked to provide the correct answer. For example, a language arts teacher might ask a question about a cause-and-effect relationship in a narrative text. After one student offers an answer, the teacher would call on another student at random. This student might say that the previous answer was partially correct because the cause and effect were identified, but the previous student did not note that the effect had more than one cause. After identifying one or more other causes, the teacher would call on a third student.

If chaining is used with open-ended questions that require extended responses, the pattern is a bit different. Instead of first stating whether the answer was correct, partially correct, or incorrect, a student would paraphrase the previous response to link his or her answer with a peer's. Next, the student states whether he or she agrees or disagrees with the last response and explains why. In this way, students are listening to their peers and processing their answers as well as generating their own. For example, a social studies teacher might pose a question about the morality of a first-world country abstaining from getting involved in a brutal civil war in a third-world country. After an initial response, the teacher might call on a second student. The student summarizes his peer's answer by noting that she felt a first-world country has a responsibility to help put a stop to bloodshed, because human lives are worth more than the money it would cost to intervene. He would then continue by saying he disagrees with the previous answer because a first-world intervention might actually cause more bloodshed. He argues further that the financial security of a first-world nation does not entitle its citizens to police the rest of the world. The teacher would then call on a third student to continue the pattern. The following vignette depicts a teacher using response chaining.

> Charlotte has answered the question "How do crystals grow?" Mr. Limon asks Omar if he thinks Charlotte's answer was correct. He says he thinks it was partially correct, and Mr. Limon asks him to explain why. "Crystals do grow from water that has a lot of dissolved minerals, so she was right about that," he says. "But they can also grow from melted rock and from vapor." Mr. Limon asks Vance what he thinks about Omar's statement. He thinks it was partially correct because "crystals can grow from melted rock and vapor, but only under the right conditions." After the three responses, Mr. Limon makes sure to clear up anything he feels was inaccurate or incomplete.

Choral Response

Choral response increases the rate of response simply because all students are answering a question in unison. Teachers should reserve this strategy for situations in which it is clear that the students are having trouble with specific information. For example, if students have trouble explaining a certain principle, the teacher would provide a brief explanation of the principle and then ask them to repeat the explanation in a choral response. The intent of choral responses is not that all students are to learn content in a verbatim fashion; rather, the intent is to provide an "imprint" of the correct information. The following vignette depicts the use of choral response in the classroom.

> After Ms. Ashcroft completes a demonstration, she asks students which principle was in play. No one seems to know the answer, so she asks them all to recite the principle, "The angle of incidence is equal to the angle of reflection." Although it is difficult to determine if all students are participating equally in the choral response, Ms. Ashcroft can get a rough sense of participation, and all students at least hear the correct information.

Simultaneous Individual Response

While choral response invites participation from the entire class, it does not guarantee participation from each student, nor does it require any student to provide a response to a question; and while paired and chained response increase response rates, they do not ensure the participation of the entire class. Simultaneous individual response employs a voting format, asking each student to select from a number of possible responses. By tracking both individual student responses and the overall responses of the entire class, a teacher receives valuable feedback. This feedback is both student specific (the teacher can gauge what each student does and does not understand) and class specific (the teacher is able to get an idea of how the entire class is progressing).

One simple way to invite simultaneous individual response is to use *hand signals*. It is important to note that when hand signals are used, questions must employ a selected-response format. For example, a multiple-choice item is a selected-response format. If four responses are provided in a multiple-choice item, students can signal the correct answer by holding up one finger for the first option, two fingers for the second option, and so on. To use this technique, the teacher first presents students with the question and the numbered options. The teacher then gives students some time to consider the four answers to the question and then, when prompted, each student holds up the number of fingers he or she believes indicates the correct answer. This technique is also common with true/false questions. For example, a math teacher might ask students whether or not it is true that the Pythagorean theorem is $a^2 + b^2 = c^2$. After a few moments, students who believe the statement to be true are prompted to give a thumbs up, and students who believe the statement to be false are prompted to give a thumbs down. After each student has responded, the teacher might ask one student who believed the statement false and one student who believed it to be true to explain their answers. Then he would reveal and explain the correct answer.

Response cards also elicit responses from all students simultaneously. To utilize response cards, the teacher must provide students with a reusable material such as a 12 × 12–inch whiteboard. Students use these boards to record their responses to teacher-posed questions. Typically, teachers compose short constructed-response items for response cards (although they can also use selected-response items). For example, a Spanish teacher might say, "Please write the Spanish word for *elephant*." Each student would write the word on the whiteboard and show it to the teacher when prompted.

One of the easiest and most comprehensive ways to use simultaneous individual response is to employ *response technologies*. These are devices that allow students to cast their votes to answer a teacher-posed question. All versions of these electronic devices have some sort of keypad that students use to choose the correct or preferred answer from multiple choices and then send their answers to a hub attached to a computer. Answers are then projected on a screen. Although everyone can see the pattern of answers, individual students are not identified. For example, assume that a teacher asks the following multiple-choice item with four responses: "How much of the coral in the Gulf of Eilat is dead? Is it (A) none, (B) less than half, (C) roughly three-quarters, or (D) the entire coral reef is now dead?" The teacher would then ask students to respond using the voting device. When all students had responded, the teacher would display the results in a graph similar to that in figure 3.1.

Notice that the bar graph in figure 3.1 shows what percentage of students chose each item. In this case, 50 percent of the students selected *D*, 20 percent selected *C*, and so on. What it does not show is the individual response of each student, thus allowing students to participate without the risk of embarrassment. This anonymity gives students a sense of safety and makes participation more likely.

Although the devices are used mainly for responding to selected-response items; open-ended questions (such as questions that elicit an opinion) and questions that gauge confidence levels and attitudes can be used as well. This is particularly valuable because in addition to the general voting display, most interactive technologies are capable of allowing a teacher to see how each student responded to any given question. This does not mean that students are being singled out, as only the teacher would have access to this type of detailed information. Table 3.1 (page 76) depicts what this type of display might look like if a teacher gave students a six-question quiz.

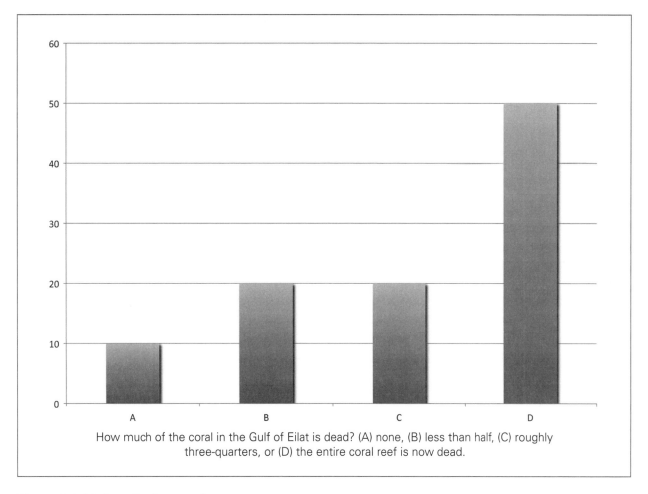

How much of the coral in the Gulf of Eilat is dead? (A) none, (B) less than half, (C) roughly three-quarters, or (D) the entire coral reef is now dead.

Figure 3.1: Voting display results.

The first column in table 3.1 lists students' names. The second column lists the device each student was using during the class. The remaining six columns represent each student's response to each of the six items. A blank cell indicates the student answered the question incorrectly. A checked cell indicates that the student answered the question correctly. As shown in table 3.1 (page 76), Angela Barber answered questions two and five correctly, Brian Benoti answered all of the items correctly, and so on. Of course, this type of display provides the teacher with a great deal of information about the status of each student.

In addition to the features shown in figure 3.1 and table 3.1, many technologies now enable students to select more than one answer or even use a keyboard to generate and then send a short answer. With this type of class-specific and student-specific information, teachers can make any necessary instructional adjustments and can also create individualized plans for each student. The following vignette depicts a teacher using simultaneous individual response questioning.

> *Mr. Walsh's elementary class has been working on identifying and extending patterns. He uses a whiteboard to display a relatively simple pattern and gives his students a minute to study it. He then asks them how the pattern should be extended, and he displays four different possible answers—labeled A, B, C, and D respectively. "Using your voting device, enter the answer you believe is correct." He gives the class a bit more time and then displays the anonymous results of the*

Table 3.1: Record of Correct and Incorrect Student Answers

Name	Voting Device	Question 1	Question 2	Question 3	Question 4	Question 5	Question 6
Angela Barber	A1		✓			✓	
Brian Benoti	A2	✓	✓	✓	✓	✓	✓
Grace Carlson	A3			✓		✓	✓
Kaleb Castle	A4	✓		✓		✓	✓
Nick Easton	A5		✓		✓		✓
Redmond Frontier	A6		✓	✓	✓		✓
Samuel Heinrick	A7		✓	✓			
Dale Hoffer	A8		✓	✓	✓	✓	✓
Justine Johnson	A9	✓	✓	✓	✓	✓	✓
Linus Kirkpatrick	A10	✓		✓			✓
Harrison Lewis	A11	✓	✓	✓	✓	✓	✓
Terence Made	A12	✓	✓		✓		✓
Juan Marquez	A13	✓		✓	✓	✓	
Amelia Mercer	A14	✓	✓	✓	✓	✓	✓
Luis Olano	A15	✓		✓	✓		
Finn Olson	A16			✓	✓		✓
Indira Petrova	A17	✓	✓	✓	✓	✓	
Patrick Regan	A18	✓	✓	✓	✓	✓	✓
Iona Remmington	A19	✓		✓	✓		
Carmen Vargas	A20	✓	✓		✓	✓	✓
Carolina Vargas	A21		✓	✓	✓		✓

vote. "Great job!" he says. "Most of you thought B was the correct answer, but some of you gave other responses. Before I tell you the correct answer, let's look carefully at each option." After explaining the pattern and its correct extension, he moves on, giving the class a more difficult pattern to evaluate. He continues the process of displaying more difficult patterns until he can see that only a few students got the right answer. "You guys did really well," he tells them at the end of class. "Some of these were tough patterns." After class he looks at the teacher display results that tell him how each student answered. This display gives him valuable data about how each student is progressing in the unit. He plans his next lesson based on what he learns, and he is able to offer personal assistance to the individual students he knows need it.

Exercise 3.4 provides practice identifying questioning strategies used to increase response rates. (See page 83 for a reproducible of this exercise and page 171 for a reproducible answer sheet. Visit **marzanoresearch.com/classroomstrategies** to download all the exercises and answers in this book.)

Exercise 3.4
Questioning to Increase Response Rates

After reading each of the following classroom scenarios, determine which of the following questioning strategies is being employed:

    A. Call on students randomly

    B. Paired response

    C. Wait time

    D. Response chaining

    E. Choral response

    F. Simultaneous individual response

1. Mr. Severs is beginning a social studies unit about current events, and he would like to get an idea of what his students already know about the national and global stages. He prepares a number of questions about recent political happenings. At the start of class, he hands out voting devices in alphabetical order. When each student has one, Mr. Severs asks his first question. "Which of these people is not a member of President Obama's cabinet? Is it (A) Hillary Clinton, (B) William Reilly, (C) Janet Napolitano, or (D) Rahm Emanuel?" He gives his students a few moments to think about the question and vote for the answer they think is correct. When all of the votes are in, he shows everyone a bar graph depicting how the class voted. He asks more questions as class goes on, each time showing the class the results and explaining the correct answer. When class is over, he takes a deeper look at the individual responses of each student. Now he knows that, in general, his class doesn't know much about current events, but he has three or four students who do appear to keep up.

2. Ms. Palmer has drawn names in order to pair up students in the beginning of her language arts class. During the lesson she asks a few questions about the book they have been reading and gives the students a set amount of time to construct a reply. After her first question, "How did Jacob respond when he didn't make the Olympic team the first time?" she waits a few minutes and then calls on Jared and Kendra. "He was really depressed about it, and he stopped training and went to work for his dad's restaurant," Jared says. Ms. Palmer asks Kendra how she might respond in the same situation. "I would be really upset too. Gymnastics is a sport that traditionally really young athletes compete in.

I might have stopped training too, but I would have gone to college instead of working for my dad. I probably would have moved on from athletics." Ms. Palmer then asks another pair to discuss the outcome of Jacob's next Olympic quest. After one student responds, she asks the other student how he feels about Jacob's decision to continue his quest given that he did eventually make the team but did not win a medal.

3. Mr. Vinci has four students who are quite interested in various aspects of photography and will consistently volunteer to answer his questions or show the class the photos they took for the previous assignment. Although he appreciates their enthusiasm, he has noticed that many of his other students will refrain from volunteering because they know these four students will. He institutes a new policy in response. At the beginning of every class, he gathers the photos from the last assignment, and when he asks a question, he selects a photo at random. The student who took the photo is called on to answer the question. He finds that doing this also means that more photos taken by his students are shown in class.

4. Ms. Montrose likes to get an idea of how confident students feel in what they are learning in the days and weeks before an exam. If they are confident, they are more likely to do well, and if they are not, Ms. Montrose can offer some personal one-on-one time prior to the exam. As the last activity in class one day, she asks the students how well they feel they understand the topic: "Give me a thumbs up if you think you understand this well enough to get an A on the test; hold your thumb out to the side if you think you are getting better but are not quite ready for a test yet, and give me a thumbs down if you don't feel you understand this material very well at all." Once they have signaled their feelings, she reminds them before the bell rings that she is available for extra help before and after school by appointment.

Analyzing Your Strengths and Weaknesses

In this chapter, we have presented a variety of suggestions across four general categories of strategies, all of which increase the chances that students will have a positive response to the question "Am I interested?" Table 3.2 provides the self-assessment scale introduced in chapter 2. Using the scale in table 3.2, rate yourself on each strategy listed. (See page 85 for a reproducible of this scale. Visit **marzanoresearch.com/classroomstrategies** to download all self-assessment scales in this book.)

Summary

This chapter began with a brief discussion of the second question in the attention and engagement model: "Am I interested?" It makes logical sense that if a student finds the material presented in class boring or irrelevant, he or she will most likely not attend to classroom activities. The content of instruction, however, is not always obviously interesting to students. Teachers can help trigger and maintain situational interest in students by utilizing academically based games and turning questions directed at the class into spontaneous chances for inconsequential competition. By using structured models, teachers can also create friendly controversy among the students, which can extend student interest in a topic beyond the confines of the classroom. Unusual information also interests students because it creates a sense of curiosity and invites them to fill in pieces that may be missing. Similarly, switching up questioning techniques elicits many student responses (as opposed to just a few), which keeps all students engaged.

Table 3.2: Self-Assessment Scale for Chapter 3

	0 **Not Using** I never use this strategy.	1 **Beginning** I sometimes use this strategy, but I don't think I use it correctly.	2 **Developing** I use this strategy, but I do so mechanically.	3 **Applying** I use this strategy and monitor how well it works.	4 **Innovating** I know this strategy well enough that I have created my own version of it.
Using Games and Inconsequential Competition					
Vocabulary games	0	1	2	3	4
Turn questions into games	0	1	2	3	4
Initiating Friendly Controversy					
Class vote	0	1	2	3	4
Debate model	0	1	2	3	4
Town hall meeting	0	1	2	3	4
Legal model	0	1	2	3	4
Perspective analysis	0	1	2	3	4
Presenting Unusual Information					
Introduce a lesson	0	1	2	3	4
Allow students to research and collect interesting facts	0	1	2	3	4
Invite guest speakers	0	1	2	3	4
Questioning to Increase Response Rates					
Call on students randomly	0	1	2	3	4
Paired response	0	1	2	3	4
Wait time	0	1	2	3	4
Response chaining	0	1	2	3	4
Choral response	0	1	2	3	4
Simultaneous individual response	0	1	2	3	4

Exercise 3.1

Using Games and Inconsequential Competition

1. Why do academic games stimulate attention?

2. What would be appropriate teacher behavior if many students did poorly on the questions in an academic game?

3. What are some ways you have used games in the past?

Exercise 3.2

Initiating Friendly Controversy

1. Compare the defining features of the debate model, the town hall–meeting model, and the legal model.

2. What is unique about perspective analysis as compared to other approaches described in this section?

Exercise 3.3

Presenting Unusual Information

1. What is the underlying dynamic behind using unusual information to capture students' attention?

2. How might the use of unusual information facilitate class participation and cooperation?

3. How have you utilized unusual information in the past? Are there specific topics you teach that could use unusual information?

Exercise 3.4

Questioning to Increase Response Rates

After reading each of the following classroom scenarios, determine which of the following questioning strategies is being employed:

    A. Call on students randomly

    B. Paired response

    C. Wait time

    D. Response chaining

    E. Choral response

    F. Simultaneous individual response

1. Mr. Severs is beginning a social studies unit about current events, and he would like to get an idea of what his students already know about the national and global stages. He prepares a number of questions about recent political happenings. At the start of class, he hands out voting devices in alphabetical order. When each student has one, Mr. Severs asks his first question. "Which of these people is not a member of President Obama's cabinet? Is it (A) Hillary Clinton, (B) William Reilly, (C) Janet Napolitano, or (D) Rahm Emanuel?" He gives his students a few moments to think about the question and vote for the answer they think is correct. When all of the votes are in, he shows everyone a bar graph depicting how the class voted. He asks more questions as class goes on, each time showing the class the results and explaining the correct answer. When class is over, he takes a deeper look at the individual responses of each student. Now he knows that, in general, his class doesn't know much about current events, but he has three or four students who do appear to keep up.

2. Ms. Palmer has drawn names in order to pair students up in the beginning of her language arts class. During the lesson she asks a few questions about the book they have been reading and gives the students a set amount of time to construct a reply. After her first question, "How did Jacob respond when he didn't make the Olympic team the first time?" she waits a few minutes and then calls on Jared and Kendra. "He was really depressed about it, and he stopped training and went to work for his dad's restaurant," Jared says. Ms. Palmer asks Kendra how she might respond in the same situation. "I would be really upset too. Gymnastics is a sport that traditionally really young athletes compete in. I might have stopped training too, but I would have gone to college instead of working for my dad. I probably would have moved on from athletics." Ms. Palmer then asks another pair to discuss the outcome of Jacob's next Olympic quest. After one student responds, she asks the other student how he feels about Jacob's decision to continue his quest given that he did eventually make the team but did not win a medal.

3. Mr. Vinci has four students who are quite interested in various aspects of photography and will consistently volunteer to answer his questions or show the class the photos they took for the previous assignment. Although he appreciates their enthusiasm, he has noticed that many of his other students will refrain from volunteering because they know these four students will. He institutes a new policy in response. At the beginning of every class, he gathers the photos from the last assignment, and when he asks a question, he selects a photo at random. The student who took the photo is called on to answer the question. He finds that doing this also means that more photos taken by his students are shown in class.

4. Ms. Montrose likes to get an idea of how confident students feel in what they are learning in the days and weeks before an exam. If they are confident, they are more likely to do well, and if they are not, Ms. Montrose can offer some personal one-on-one time prior to the exam. As the last activity in class one day, she asks the students how well they feel they understand the topic: "Give me a thumbs up if you think you understand this well enough to get an A on the test; hold your thumb out to the side if you think you are getting better but are not quite ready for a test yet, and give me a thumbs down if you don't feel you understand this material very well at all." Once they have signaled their feelings, she reminds them before the bell rings that she is available for extra help before and after school by appointment.

The Highly Engaged Classroom © 2011 Marzano Research Laboratory • marzanoresearch.com
Visit **marzanoresearch.com/classroomstrategies** to download this page.

Self-Assessment Scale for Chapter 3

	0 **Not Using** I never use this strategy.	1 **Beginning** I sometimes use this strategy, but I don't think I use it correctly.	2 **Developing** I use this strategy, but I do so mechanically.	3 **Applying** I use this strategy and monitor how well it works.	4 **Innovating** I know this strategy well enough that I have created my own version of it.
Using Games and Inconsequential Competition					
Vocabulary games	0	1	2	3	4
Turn questions into games	0	1	2	3	4
Initiating Friendly Controversy					
Class vote	0	1	2	3	4
Debate model	0	1	2	3	4
Town hall meeting	0	1	2	3	4
Legal model	0	1	2	3	4
Perspective analysis	0	1	2	3	4
Presenting Unusual Information					
Introduce a lesson	0	1	2	3	4
Allow students to collect interesting facts	0	1	2	3	4
Invite guest speakers	0	1	2	3	4
Questioning to Increase Response Rates					
Call on students randomly	0	1	2	3	4
Paired response	0	1	2	3	4
Wait time	0	1	2	3	4
Response chaining	0	1	2	3	4
Choral response	0	1	2	3	4
Simultaneous individual response	0	1	2	3	4

Chapter 4

IS THIS IMPORTANT?

Chapters 2 and 3 addressed attention—teaching strategies that encourage students to occupy their working memories with what is occurring in class. This chapter and the next deal with *engagement*. Engagement is a much deeper and more long-term phenomenon than attention. Where attention applies to a specific event in class, engagement goes well beyond a single activity and even beyond a single class period. When students are engaged, they tend to think about the topic frequently and in-depth. Although the strategies addressed in this chapter and the next all have the goal of stimulating engagement, they do so in varying degrees and in different ways. To produce high engagement, teachers should use many of the strategies in this chapter and the next in concert.

This chapter focuses on fostering engagement using strategies that help students affirmatively answer the question "Is this important?" Obviously, if students do not perceive classroom tasks as important, engagement will be muted or nonexistent. As we have seen in chapter 1, something is considered important when it relates to the self-system—to that hierarchy of goals that can be considered the architect of motivation. To one extent or another, students are always behaving in such a way as to accomplish one or more goals. For example, at a very basic level, students (as well as everyone else) are always working to ensure that basic subsistence goals are being met regarding safety, food, and shelter. Perhaps a level up from subsistence goals are those regarding acceptance by peers and adults. Above those goals are a wide array of goals that address increased knowledge or skill in specific areas. For example, an individual might have the goal of increasing her knowledge of famous artists—not because she wishes to become an artist herself, but simply because increased understanding of the topic provides her with satisfaction. Another individual might have the goal of becoming a better golfer—one who can play eighteen holes of golf with a score under one hundred. Again, this is not because the individual wishes to make a living playing golf or wishes to become a champion at golf. Increased skill at the sport simply provides satisfaction.

Perhaps at the highest level are goals that address life ambitions. These goals typically deal with accomplishments that people perceive as defining their future lives. For example, an individual might have the life ambition of being the good mother or father to a large family. Still another individual might have the life ambition of being a doctor who provides care in poverty-stricken or war-torn places.

Fundamentally, classroom activities that make connections to the real world help generate a positive response to the question "Is this important?" With this understanding in mind, we consider three main ways that a teacher can help students affirmatively answer the emblematic question "Is this important?":

(1) connecting to students' lives, (2) connecting to students' life ambitions, and (3) encouraging application of knowledge.

Connecting to Students' Lives

In their personal lives, students have many goals that relate to learning more about a specific topic or becoming more skilled at a particular activity. Teachers can help students make connections to these personal goals through well-structured comparison tasks and analogical reasoning tasks.

Comparison Tasks

Using comparison activities is certainly a strategy commonly used in K–12 classrooms. It is probably safe to say that teachers at every grade level and in every subject area use comparison activities—some quite routinely. While any comparison activity will probably stimulate students' interests (in other words, capture their attention), comparison activities can also stimulate engagement if students are allowed to relate new content to topics of personal interest. Briefly, the process of comparing can involve the following four steps. (Not all comparison tasks have to include all steps.)

1. Identify the items to be compared.

2. Select the characteristics on which the comparison will be based.

3. For each characteristic, identify the similarities and differences.

4. Explain what was learned from doing the comparison.

Crucial to the success of direct comparison activities is the selection of the characteristics on which the comparison will be based. The teacher should be clear about which aspects of the content are to be used in student comparisons. Some common aspects for comparison are based on physical characteristics, processes, a sequence of events, cause-and-effect relationships, psychological characteristics, and fame or notoriety.

A teacher might use *physical characteristics* as the criteria for a comparison activity. Physical characteristics are important to content that involves persons, places, animals, and things. For example, if a particular unit in science addresses alligators, the teacher might set up an activity that asks students to compare the physical characteristics of an alligator with anything of their choice. One student might compare the fast but brief land speed of an alligator to Usain Bolt's sprints. He might enjoy track and field and compare his own performances to the alligator as well.

A *process* can also be used as criteria for a comparison. For example, assume a science teacher was focusing on the functions and processes of the cell. He might ask the students to focus on the selectively permeable membrane when making their comparisons. A student who really enjoys the Star Trek series might compare a selectively permeable membrane to the transporter on the Starship Enterprise because, like the membrane allows nutrients to enter the cell, the transporter allows the good guys to enter the ship. Similarly, just as the membrane keeps toxins out of the cell, the transporter does not allow bad guys like the Romulans to board the ship.

A *sequence of events* can also be used as a basis for student comparisons. Historical content frequently involves important sequences of events. For example, within a unit on the era of the Kennedys, a social studies teacher might focus on the events leading up to and immediately after the blockade of Cuba for a comparison activity. A particular student might compare that sequence of events to her cheerleading team. Over the summer, the team was selecting new uniforms, but the coaches and the team captains did not agree on which uniforms to select. The disagreement went on all summer, and they came really close to not having uniforms at all for the first fall football game.

A *cause-and-effect relationship* can be the basis for student comparisons as well. Cause-and-effect relationships can be found in many subject areas. For example, an economics teacher addressing the relationship between inflation and the devaluing of goods could assign a comparison activity, and one student who is interested in theater might compare the cause-and-effect relationship at work in inflation to standing ovations in the theater. Standing ovations are supposed to be rare—a real honor, but he has noticed that it seems like standing ovations have become common, almost standard at the end of a performance. Just like the value of a dollar decreases when more dollars are in circulation, the value of standing ovations decreases when they happen so frequently.

Psychological characteristics are another possible comparison criteria. Psychological characteristics refer to habitual behaviors or tendencies an individual might exhibit. Such characteristics typically apply to real people or characters from fiction. For example, during a unit on Abraham Lincoln, the teacher might make note of the fact that Lincoln demonstrated tremendous perseverance. He had many failures in life before he became a successful politician and ultimately president of the United States. As a comparison activity, the teacher might have students liken this psychological trait of Lincoln's to other individuals they are interested in. One student might compare Lincoln's early failures to those of Kurt Warner, his favorite football player. Warner had a lot of early failures as well, even bagging groceries the year before he came to the NFL. Also, like Lincoln, Warner eventually saw great success.

The *fame* or *notoriety* of a person or an event can also be used. Fame or notoriety refers to how well known someone or something is for negative or positive reasons. This characteristic can apply to people, places, things, and events. For example, a teacher might have a unit in which Genghis Khan is a key figure. The point might be made that Genghis Khan was initially portrayed in history as a villain, but more modern accounts identify many positives associated with his reign. During a comparison activity, a student might compare Khan to a book he read during the summer. When he first read it, he didn't like it at all; he thought it was boring. When school started though, the class began discussing the book. The teacher and other students pointed out things about the book he had never seen before, and by the end of the unit, he had re-read the book and decided he actually liked it a lot.

One thing to remember when providing comparisons to students' lives is to allow them the opportunity to expand and expound on their interests. For example, after students have described how the Starship Enterprise is like the cell membrane, the teacher might ask the students to describe some of their favorite parts about Star Trek. This encourages a positive affective tone in the classroom and may provide opportunity for further comparison. For more information on direct comparisons, see *Building Background Knowledge for Academic Achievement* (Marzano, 2004). The following vignette depicts a teacher using direct comparison.

> *Ms. Zettle's class has been studying different climates. She asks students to pick their favorite climate and find some appealing images of it. Next, she asks them to compare the elements in those images to something that interests them. J. D. chooses Antelope Canyon in Arizona. He likes it because over time, the wind and water have eroded the rock to look like an abstract painting. He likes the work of Georgia O'Keeffe and brings in a print of one of her paintings to make the comparison. "Even though a lot of her imagery was floral, her lines look just like the contours in Antelope Canyon," he says. "Her shading looks the same, too. What she did with a brush is what nature did with the canyon!"*

Analogical Reasoning Tasks

Most students are, at some point, challenged with solving analogy problems by filling in missing elements. The process involves matching the relationship between the first two elements to the same relationship between the last two elements. For example, with traditional analogy problems, students might be asked to complete the following:

carpenter : hammer :: painter : _____

When analogy problems are used to make connections to students' lives, a format like the following should be used:

heart : circulatory system :: _____ : _____

Only the first two elements are provided in this problem. One student might complete the analogy with "motor : car," while another student could apply the relationship to "drummer : band" or "mother : family." When students complete open-ended analogies and then explain how the relationships of the two pairs are similar, they are able to bring their own unique interests to academic content. The following vignette depicts the use of analogical reasoning to help students make connections to their personal lives.

> Mr. Uchida's language arts class has been reading Frankenstein. He presents his students with the following analogy:
>
> Victor Frankenstein : the monster :: _____ : _____
>
> He then asks them to complete the analogy using something of interest to them.
>
> Nick compares the relationship between Frankenstein and his monster with his own relationship with a car he has been rebuilding. He says, "My friends and I want to compete in the 24 Hours of LeMons competition this summer. You have to start with a car that is at least ten years old and is not in working condition, and then you can only spend one thousand dollars on getting it running. Then there is a twenty-four-hour race. We have it running now, and it has taken a lot of work to bring it back to life. Victor had to work hard on the monster, too. But just like the monster, our car is pretty ugly. It's not anything we'll be able to drive or sell after the race is over."
>
> Another student has been acting in the school's rendition of Macbeth, and she compares the relationship between Frankenstein and his monster to Macbeth and his father. She says, "Macbeth wound up betraying his father by killing him, just like the monster, Frankenstein's child, killed his father." Mr. Uchida finds students make many different comparisons, and the class discusses how those different comparisons speak to the complexity of the relationship between Frankenstein and his monster.

Exercise 4.1 provides some practice at identifying teachers in action connecting to students' lives. (See page 111 for a reproducible of this exercise and page 173 for a reproducible answer sheet. Visit **marzanoresearch.com/classroomstrategies** to download all the exercises and answers in this book.)

Exercise 4.1
Connecting to Students' Lives

Identify each of the following examples as one of the types of comparison activities:

   A. Physical characteristic comparison

   B. Process comparison

   C. Sequence of events comparison

   D. Cause-and-effect relationship comparison

   E. Psychological characteristic comparison

   F. Fame or notoriety comparison

   G. Analogical reasoning

1. Mr. Moyer's science class has been studying the Manhattan Project as an example of a scientific advancement that is remembered in both positive and negative ways. "What else is like this?" he asks. "Choose something you are interested in to make the comparison." Zane compares the Manhattan Project to spiders. "Some people think the atomic bomb saved a lot of lives in the long run and was a good thing, but some people think it was morally corrupt and made the world a more dangerous place. I think this is like spiders because a lot of people think spiders are gross or scary, but I really like them. I think they can spin really beautiful webs; and without spiders, entire ecosystems would be totally wiped out. They have a complex reputation, too, I guess."

2. Mr. Okpik's social studies class has been studying North and South Korea in a unit about current events. They have been looking specifically at the recent activities at the 38th parallel. "One of South Korea's responses to North Korea sinking one of their warships was to broadcast a South Korean pop song across the border at the 38th parallel. The song was chosen because of its sultry tone and its lyrics, which tout rebellion and independence. Acts like this are often referred to as psychological warfare. What do you think South Korea was trying to accomplish? What else can you think of that has a similar aim? Choose something you are interested in to make the comparison," he says. Torin compares South Korea's broadcast to some of the taunting that happens at his baseball games. He says, "I'm a catcher, and when a batter first comes to the box I sometimes make comments at him. They are harmless, but I'm trying to rattle him, break his concentration. I think South Korea's broadcast was similar in that it was harmless—no one was injured or killed because of it. I think they did it to rattle the North Koreans, to tease them a little and send a message that they aren't afraid of them." He also notes that while those mental games can seem kind of silly, they can also be quite effective. "I've been in the box as a batter before and been rattled by some of the comments the catcher has made to me," he says.

3. Ms. Kwon's science class has been studying migration. "Animals of various species have migration patterns they follow generation after generation. Can you think of something you know about and are interested in that has the same relationship?" she asks. Emma compares migration to her family's recent move to a new city. "We don't move around regularly like animals that migrate do, but animals basically migrate in order to get what they need, whether it's food or breeding grounds or a warmer climate. We moved because my mom got a job that she really wanted and because some of my cousins live here, too. So we came to a new place in order to get what we wanted," she says.

4. Ms. Philips wants the students in her mathematics class to understand the nature of inverse processes such as multiplication and division. She explains that multiplication and division use the same numerical concept but in opposite ways. She says, "What are some things you know of that have the same basic relationship? Choose something you are interested in, and fill in the following statement: Multiplication is to division as what is to what?" Brandy completes the statement with the words *toe loop* and *salchow*. She explains that she is an ice skater. Both the toe loop and the salchow are jumps where the skater spins a certain number of times in the air, but what makes them opposite is the takeoff. In the toe loop the skater takes off on the back foot, the foot the spin revolves around. In the salchow, though, the skater leads with the other foot, the foot that creates the revolution. So the two jumps are essentially opposites, just like multiplication and division.

Connecting to Students' Life Ambitions

Life ambitions probably represent the highest level of self-system goals. Students will not automatically connect classroom content and activities to their life ambitions, but teachers can still integrate content and life ambitions through the personal project. When engaged in a personal project, students identify a personal goal of their choice and work on it throughout the quarter, the semester, or even the entire year. The teacher facilitates the identification of the goal and the progress toward that goal.

One obvious drawback to personal projects is that they do not fit well into traditional subject areas of mathematics, science, social studies, and language arts. Indeed, students might select goals that deal with content outside the scope of traditional school curricula. However, personal projects can be the perfect venue for developing what some are referring to as 21st century skills. Specifically, Heidi Hayes Jacobs (2010) and others have pointed to cognitive processes like decision making, problem solving, and investigation as the basic skills of the 21st century. These skills are endemic to personal projects.

Personal Projects

The personal project is a seven-phase process that can be used to engage students by addressing their long-term goals. Each of the seven phases is associated with a question or set of questions students must address.

One nice feature of the seven phases in the personal-project process is that teachers do not have to address them every day. A teacher may devote a class or part of a class to the first phase, and then wait a few days to address the second phase, wait a few weeks to address the next phase, and so on. Thus, a class can participate in personal projects quite easily in a single quarter without taking an inordinate amount of instruction time.

Phase One: What Do I Want to Accomplish?

During the first phase, students are asked to identify a personal goal that interests them. Ideally, students select a topic they are greatly excited, even passionate about. In the beginning, students may be shy about sharing such goals, primarily because they do not want to be teased or ridiculed. To this end, it is highly useful if the teacher engages in the personal project along with the students and shares his or her reaction to each step of the process. If the teacher is willing to demonstrate vulnerability about personal goals, students will be encouraged to follow suit. Students may also be reticent to identify personal goals simply because they do not believe them to be possible. One powerful activity to help students think beyond their expectations is to have them address questions like, "What would I like to try if I knew I wouldn't fail?" Again, the teacher should also engage in this activity along with the students. The following vignette depicts the first phase of a personal project.

Damon is in Ms. Heatherwood's homeroom. Ms. Heatherwood and other teachers in the middle school use the class to teach goal-setting skills, problem-solving skills, and the like. Ms. Heatherwood elects to use personal projects as the vehicle for reinforcing these skills. She begins by asking all students to identify a personal goal they would like to work on during the quarter. It can be a goal that might require a year, a few years, or even decades to accomplish. At first, Damon identifies the goal of finishing high school. Other students have similarly modest goals.

Ms. Heatherwood challenges the whole class to think outside of the box. She says, "What would you like to try if you knew you wouldn't fail?" She shares with them that she has always wanted to write a novel. That will be her goal for her personal project. Spurred on by his teacher's example, Damon says, "I guess if I really didn't have to worry about anything, I would really love to become a fighter pilot in the navy or the air force." Ms. Heatherwood says she thinks that is a great goal and she would like to see him use that for the personal project. Damon is uncertain at first because just thinking about something that big makes him uncomfortable, but he agrees. Other students identify similarly challenging goals.

Phase Two: Who Else Has Accomplished the Same Goal? Who Will Support Me?

During the second phase, students look for heroes, role models, and mentors to establish a support system. Heroes and role models are people who have accomplished goals similar to the ones students have identified. Typically, students must gather information about their heroes and role models. This provides a wonderful opportunity for students to practice information-gathering techniques through Internet or library searches. It also provides an opportunity for students to practice synthesizing information. Unlike heroes and role models, mentors are people students actually interact with. Mentors may not have accomplished the same goals students are striving for, but they will encourage the students. The following vignette depicts the second phase of a personal project.

In his search for a hero or a role model, Damon finds out about Lee Archer. Archer was the only confirmed ace—an airman who shoots down several enemy aircrafts—of the Tuskegee Airmen, the United States' first African American military pilots. "He flew 169 missions in World War II and retired as a lieutenant colonel!" Damon thinks the accomplishment is really impressive because of how much racism was in the military at that time. "He really had to overcome a lot," Damon says. Looking to the people in his life who might help support him is more difficult. At first, he doesn't think his dad would be supportive, but when Ms. Heatherwood encourages Damon to speak with him, his dad thinks the goal is great. "He said he was surprised that I would want to do something like that," Damon says. "He said he thought I could do it if I really wanted to, and that was really cool! He even said he would be my mentor!"

Ms. Heatherwood also shares her progress in finding heroes, role models, and mentors. She explains to the class that she began reading some of her favorite books again, the ones that had inspired her to write in years past. One of the books was The Good Earth, *which reminded her about the life of its author, Pearl S. Buck. "She was such an interesting woman! She was a humanitarian as well as an author, and even though she didn't begin publishing books until her late thirties, she still won both the Nobel and Pulitzer prizes." Ms. Heatherwood has decided to read both of Buck's autobiographies, and that Buck will be her hero for her personal project. "I also discovered a place called Lighthouse Writers, Workshop" she says. "It's sort of a writers' community. They offer workshops and readings and even writers' retreats. I think being involved with them would really help support me in my project, and since all of the people who teach the workshops are published authors, I think they would be great mentors."*

Phase Three: What Skills and Resources Will I Need to Accomplish My Goal?

During this phase, students gather information about the requirements necessary to accomplish their personal goals. Whereas phase one is geared toward thinking without limits, the third phase focuses on the hard facts of accomplishing a specific goal. As with phase two, this phase provides opportunities for students to practice information-gathering skills and synthesis skills. The following vignette depicts the third phase of a personal project.

When researching his goal, Damon finds that he will need to be accepted at a good college or at the Air Force or Naval Academy. After college, he then needs acceptance into a pilot program. If he does exceptionally well he may be able to attend a prestigious program such as the U.S. Navy Strike Fighter Tactics Instructor program (SFTI program). He also finds out about health and vision requirements. "Only the best of the best become pilots," he says. "You really have to work hard for a long time. You have to be physically fit as well as smart."

Ms. Heatherwood also shares her progress on phase three: "I looked into the process for publishing a novel. I didn't realize that writing it is only part of the battle. You have to try to find an agent first, and that can take years. J. K. Rowling was turned down fifty times before she got an agent! Then, once you have an agent, your agent tries to find a publishing house that wants to publish your book. Even once you have a contract, your book probably won't hit the shelves for another two years!"

Phase Four: What Will I Have to Change in Order to Achieve My Goal?

This phase is usually the most challenging and confrontational of all the steps in the personal project. Students must identify what they need to change in their current behavior in order to accomplish their goals. The willingness to change current behavior that is not contributing to a goal is a centerpiece of all truly great accomplishments. Necessary changes may be behavioral or attitudinal. The following vignette depicts the fourth phase of a personal project.

When it is time for phase four of the process, Ms. Heatherwood takes some time to prepare students. She knows this will be the most challenging part of the whole process. She explains that accomplishing difficult goals entails being brutally honest with yourself because many times there are things about our own behavior that are obstacles to accomplishing our goals. To illustrate, she explains that she has never been disciplined about her writing. She writes only when she is in the mood. Often, she goes more than a month without writing. By the time she starts writing again, she has forgotten about her previous thinking regarding her novel. She has come to realize that she has to stop writing only when she feels like it and put herself on a schedule of writing for thirty minutes at least five times per week. She challenges students to address the question "What will I have to change in order to achieve my goal?"

Based on Ms. Heatherwood's example, Damon analyzes his own behavior relative to achieving his goal. He concludes that he will have to work much harder in school. "I will have to have excellent grades if I want to be accepted to the Air Force Academy for college," he says, "and my grades now are just OK. I will also have to dedicate more time to school clubs and sports, which means I will have to spend much less time playing video games and hanging out with friends who don't care about school." He decides to set a schedule for himself as well. "I will join the community service club at school, and in addition to attending meetings and service events, I will study for an hour and a half every day Sunday through Thursday."

Phase Five: What Is My Plan for Achieving My Goal, and How Hard Will I Have to Work?

During this phase, students generate a written plan to accomplish their goals. They should think of the plan as a general outline for the future, realizing that it will change as different circumstances and opportunities arise. This noted, students should attempt to make their plans as detailed as possible by listing milestones and significant events. This helps make the goal and the actions necessary to accomplish that goal more real in students' minds. The following vignette depicts the fifth phase of a personal project.

Ms. Heatherwood launches students into phase five. She explains that students have the next week to create a written plan for their goals. She tells them that plans change over time, but it is always a good idea to start with a written plan and then change it as needed. She tells them a story about how her plans during college changed every few years as her interests changed, and what she really wanted became clearer. Even though her original plan for college was altered many times, she's glad she was very concrete right from the very beginning.

Damon knows now that he will have to graduate high school with excellent grades and a clean record, attend and graduate from a good college or the Air Force or Naval Academy, and be accepted into a pilot program. High school graduation is clearly the closest of those landmarks, so he uses this as an initial point of reference. He creates the following plan:

1. *Join the community service club and follow the study schedule to pull my grades up by at least a full letter in each class (getting a B instead of a C in math, and so on).*

2. *Join the high school's track and basketball teams, and join the community service club.*

3. *Take the Preliminary SAT sophomore year in high school and the SAT and ACT junior year.*

4. *Complete applications to specific colleges and military academies by the fall of senior year in high school.*

5. *Graduate with no less than a 3.5 grade point average.*

6. *Participate in school activities all four years of high school.*

At the end of the week, Ms. Heatherwood invites students to share their plans. She starts by sharing her own:

1. *Follow a writing schedule, and continue to read works by inspiring and contemporary authors.*

2. *Create a complete outline of the novel by July.*

3. *Write and send out query letters when the novel is complete.*

4. *Keep sending query letters, and begin a new writing project.*

Next she asks for volunteers to read or simply describe their plans but lets her students know that they can keep them private if they so desire. At the end of class, she collects students' plans and later reads them attentively, writing suggestions and words of encouragement such as, "Damon, this is something I can picture you doing. Don't be afraid to go for it!"

Phase Six: What Small Steps Can I Take Right Now?

During this phase, students look at some things they can begin doing immediately that will set them on the path toward achieving their goals. This is referred to as taking *small steps.* Teachers should communicate to students that completing short-term goals (accomplished in a few days or weeks) can help them accomplish their long-term goal. In fact, accomplishing a long-term goal is nothing more than accomplishing a series of short-term goals. During this phase, students are asked to write down something they will accomplish in a week or two that is a small step toward their ultimate goals. The teacher collects these statements and returns them after the due date for the small step. The following vignette depicts the sixth phase of a personal project.

> *After Ms. Heatherwood has read and returned students' plans, she challenges them to set goals they can accomplish in the next week. She says that they will refer to this as a "small step." She hands out 3 × 5 index cards to the students and says, "Write out the phrase 'By next week, I will . . .'" She then shows them what she has written on her index card, "By next week, I will have signed up for the next fiction workshop with the Lighthouse Writers Workshop group and followed my writing schedule every day."*
>
> *She tells students that she will collect the cards and return them in one week. Damon decides to write, "By next week, I will have attended the first community service club meeting and followed the study schedule to prepare for the next math test."*

Phase Seven: How Have I Been Doing? What Have I Learned About Myself?

Generating small steps can occur multiple times. For example, a teacher can have students generate small steps for three or four weeks in a row. Each week, the teacher returns the small-steps statements to students, who examine how well things have gone and identify corrections they need to make in their behavior. The personal project will eventually come to an end, at least in terms of class time that is devoted to it—usually a quarter or semester. At that point, it is useful for students to take stock of what they have learned about themselves. The following vignette depicts the final phase of a personal project.

> *During the last few days of the personal project, Ms. Heatherwood challenges the class to answer the question "What have I learned about myself?" She shares that she asked this question of herself last night and concluded that she has learned how much she really loves writing and that she can be quite creative and productive when she dedicates herself to it. She also learned that she has a lazy side to her that she really needs to battle in order to accomplish her goal.*

She gives students some time to reflect in their journals. She says, "Be honest with yourself. You will probably notice some good things about yourself and some things you might want to change." Damon takes the challenge seriously. He writes, "I learned a lot about myself during the personal project. I learned that my dad and I can get along really well. I learned that even though I have a hard time motivating myself to go to the community service club, I really like getting outside of myself and helping other people. I also learned that my grades have really suffered all along just because I have been really lazy and afraid that even if I tried to get good grades, I would fail."

When all students have had enough time to write, she invites them to share what they have learned about themselves. To her surprise, quite a few students volunteer insights about themselves in a very honest and open manner. It seems that one student's candid observation inspires the same in another and so on.

As a final activity, Ms. Heatherwood invites students to fill out one more "small step" index card, but this time she sets the date for two months in the future. She collects the cards and promises that she will mail them home in two months so that they can check their progress. Finally, she wishes them good luck on their personal projects and reminds them that while the final goal they have set for themselves might take a number of years to accomplish, it will be worth the effort. They will accomplish many things along the way and learn a great deal about themselves.

Exercise 4.2 provides an opportunity to test your understanding of how connecting to students' life ambition goals can contribute to students' sense of self-efficacy. Answering these questions will require making connections and inferences that may not be obvious. In other words, the answers to these questions are not found explicitly in the text. (See page 113 for a reproducible of this exercise and page 175 for a reproducible answer sheet. Visit **marzanoresearch.com/classroomstrategies** to download all the exercises and answers in this book.)

Exercise 4.2
Connecting to Students' Life Ambitions

1. Why is it true that personal projects can intrinsically motivate students?
2. Explain the reasoning behind asking students in phase one to identify what they would try if they knew they wouldn't fail.
3. What are the roles of heroes and role models in the personal project?

Encouraging Application of Knowledge

As we saw in chapter 1, students tend to perceive tasks that are cognitively complex as important and engaging. Opportunities for choice also help students see content and the learning process as important. Finally, when students are able to use what they have learned to effect change in their communities directly, they are much more likely to answer affirmatively to the emblematic question "Is this important?"

Design Cognitively Challenging Tasks

Cognitively challenging tasks can stimulate higher-level thinking in students, but this doesn't happen automatically. The book *Designing and Teaching Learning Goals and Objectives* (Marzano, 2009) presents four types of knowledge utilization processes that can be used to design these cognitively challenging tasks. They are: decision making, problem solving, experimental inquiry, and investigation.

Decision making is a process of selecting from among two or more alternatives. The basic framework is as follows:

1. Identify the decision you need to make and the alternatives you are considering.

2. Generate and prioritize the criteria that the final decision needs to meet.

3. Apply the criteria to the alternatives and select which alternative best meets the criteria.

4. Based on your reaction to the selection, make your final decision, rethink the alternative, or modify your criteria.

Problem solving is a process of overcoming constraints or barriers that are making it difficult to achieve a specific goal. The following framework can help guide the process:

1. Identify the goal you are trying to achieve.

2. Identify the barriers or constraints that are blocking the achievement of the goals.

3. Consider alternative ways of overcoming the constraints or barriers.

4. Select and try the alternative that seems most likely to work.

5. Based on the results, proceed to achieve the goal, try a different alternative, or reframe the original goal.

Experimental inquiry is using what is known or understood to generate and then test an explanation of a physical or psychological phenomenon. The following framework can guide this process:

1. Identify what you are observing.

2. Use what you know to explain what you are observing.

3. Based on your explanation, make a prediction.

4. Construct an experiment or other activity to test your prediction.

5. Based on the results, decide if your explanation and prediction were confirmed, if you need to set up an alternative test, or if you need to offer a different explanation of the phenomenon.

Investigation is a process of clearing up confusions or disagreements related to a concept or an event. There are three major types of investigation based on whether your goal is to (1) define something, (2) create a probable scenario for a historical event about which there is general disagreement, or (3) offer a hypothetical scenario for a past or future event. The following framework can guide this process:

1. Identify the concept, historical event, or hypothetical event to be investigated.

2. Explain the areas of general agreement and the areas where there is disagreement.

3. Generate and defend what you did to clear up the disagreements as you created

    • The definition of the concept

    • A probable scenario for the historical event

    • The hypothetical scenario for a past or future event

Using these four processes, teachers can design cognitively challenging tasks. For example, as part of a high school unit on the histories and current events of third-world countries, a teacher could design a task similar to one of the following:

• Decision making—Some countries are considered third world because of a tyrannical, isolationist regime like the one in North Korea. Others are considered third world because of the near anarchy that reigns, such as in Somalia. Decide which situation offers a better life.

• Problem solving—Third-world countries are fraught with problems ranging from government corruption to lack of education to lack of clean drinking water. Choose a specific country and a specific problem and use the problem-solving guidelines to offer potential solutions.

• Experimental inquiry—Would you expect to find anyone in our city living in similar circumstances as those found in third-world countries? What similarities and differences do you predict you would find? Design a way to collect data that will help you test your hypothesis.

• Investigation—One of the major factors contributing to the third-world status of Somalia is its turbulent political history. Looking at events following the collapse of the Siad Barre regime in 1991, make a prediction about what the next decade in Somalia will bring.

These tasks not only call for complex thinking but they also address topics that have real-world significance. An elementary teacher or middle school teacher could build on the same four core reasoning processes and apply them to simpler content. For example, if a class had been studying nutrition and the food pyramid, the teacher might consider designing a task similar to one of the following:

• Decision making—A school district wants kids to eat less junk food. The administrators cannot decide whether to ban junk food at the school entirely, remove vending machines with any junk food, or just increase the attempts to convince kids to eat less junk food. Set up a process that could help them make the decision at the next board meeting.

• Problem solving—Our school district has been trying to offer more nutritional school lunches for a long time. Try to identify what is stopping progress and offer a solution.

• Experimental inquiry—All of the information given to kids about eating healthier food does not seem to be working. Do a little detective work to determine if you can figure out what might actually work.

- Investigation—Much disagreement resounds about whether or not sugar makes kids hyper. Offer and defend an answer to this question.

Provide Choice

As shown in chapter 1, choice has the potential of helping students perceive classroom activities as important. Teachers can build choice into many of the activities already discussed. For example, consider the previous discussion regarding comparisons to student interest. Choice is inherent in such tasks in that students select a topic of personal interest they will use as the basis of comparison. In this section, we consider four ways to provide choice: (1) choice of tasks, (2) choice of reporting formats, (3) choice of learning goals, and (4) choice of behaviors.

Choice of Tasks

Teachers can allow students to choose their tasks in many ways. Specifically, when assigning a task, a teacher might provide students with options from which they can choose, or they can guide students in designing their own tasks.

For more teacher-structured options, students would choose from among several teacher-designed tasks. For example, a language arts teacher who wants to employ a comparison activity might invite his students to compare a text they are reading in class to something of personal interest in one of the following ways:

- Comparing the psychological characteristics of one of the main characters to a topic of choice

- Comparing a sequence of events in the story to a topic of choice

- Comparing a cause-and-effect relationship in the text to a topic of choice

Likewise, a teacher can provide choice when assigning cognitively complex tasks. Consider the previous examples of the high school social studies teacher addressing third-world countries and the elementary teacher addressing nutrition. As opposed to designing and presenting one of those tasks, a teacher might present all four and allow students to choose the task that is most interesting to them.

If teachers want to use a more choice-oriented approach, they might provide students with the opportunity to use the core thinking processes to construct their own tasks. With this more open approach, students can use these guiding questions to create and engage in tasks that are meaningful to them. For example: in the social studies class addressing a unit on third-world countries, a student might not be so interested in a country or issue the teacher identified, but the fact that there are quite different ways of actually defining the term "third world" might intrigue him. This student might take on the investigation task of discovering the origins of each of those definitions. He might also choose which definition is best and justify his selection. To use another example, in the elementary nutrition unit, another student might observe that adults tend to preach about eating healthy despite the fact that they do not eat healthy themselves. She hypothesizes that other students in the school feel the same way. She conducts an experiment in which she creates a survey that will provide her with data to test her hypothesis.

Keep in mind that while the goal is for students to create their own tasks, they may still need some guidance. To this end, the teacher may employ the following questions:

- Relative to the topic we are studying, is there an important decision you want to examine?

- Relative to the topic we are studying, is there an important problem that you want to solve?

- Relative to the topic we are studying, is there an important hypothesis you would like to test?

- Relative to the topic we are studying, is there an important concept, past event, or hypothetical or future event you want to study?

The following vignette depicts a teacher providing students with choice regarding a task.

Mr. Michaels is doing a unit on the European Enlightenment. Once students have a general grasp of the content, he poses the following questions:

- *Relative to the European Enlightenment, is there an important decision you want to examine?*

- *Relative to the European Enlightenment, is there an important problem you want to solve?*

- *Relative to the European Enlightenment, is there an important hypothesis you want to test?*

- *Relative to the European Enlightenment, is there an important concept, past event, or hypothetical or future event you want to study?*

Kelly decides to choose the second option. She has grown up in a religious home, and though she does not want to abandon her religious beliefs, she finds she has been facing many of the spiritually based questions John Locke faced during his life. Most prominently, she is interested in the problem of how she can integrate both faith and reason into her life. She decides to use the work and biography of Locke to help her come to her own conclusions about this problem of coexistence.

Will chooses the last option. He wants to study how the French Revolution affected the momentum of the Enlightenment. "It is an interesting time for European Enlightenment because many of the principles of the Enlightenment were catalysts to the French Revolution, but overall the Revolution hurt the strength and momentum of the movement," he says.

Hoyt decides to choose the first option. He has been thinking about Voltaire's comment, "Those who can make you believe absurdities can make you commit atrocities." He thinks it seems particularly relevant in terms of modern-day cult-related events such as the Jonestown massacre and the Heaven's Gate mass suicide. He thinks he can design a questionnaire that he can use to test whether students in school believe Voltaire was correct.

Farrah decides to choose the third option. She has been introduced to the work of Mary Wollstonecraft during the unit on the Enlightenment. She learned about Wollstonecraft's many terrible romantic decisions, and she is curious about how those terrible decisions and their consequences affected her work and subsequent legacy in the woman's rights movement.

Choice of Reporting Formats

Providing choice of reporting format is a relatively simple way of providing choice to students. Options a teacher might offer include the following:

- A written report
- An oral report
- A dramatic presentation
- A debate
- A videotaped report
- A demonstration or simulation

Of these formats, written and oral reports are certainly the most common, probably because they apply to such a wide range of topics and subject areas. However, with a little planning, teachers can offer the other reporting formats to students. Teachers should consider the time it takes to get through each student's report when providing reporting-format options. Consequently, reporting options are usually reserved for comprehensive, long-term projects. The following vignette illustrates this type of choice in the classroom.

Ms. Vane challenges her language arts students with the following task: "We have read In Cold Blood *and discussed its importance both in subject matter and structure. Choose one of these elements, and discuss its long-term effects on art and society today. In other words, how are we still feeling the reverberations of this book today?" She gives her students the choice of reporting this task in one of the following ways: a written report, an oral report, a dramatic presentation, a debate, or a videotaped report. She is surprised at how many different and creative things her students come up with.*

Kelsey is one of Ms. Vane's shyer students. She does not feel comfortable in front of an audience, but she does like to write, so she chooses to fulfill the task with a traditional written report. Henry is active in political clubs in school, but he doesn't feel like he is a great writer, so he chooses an oral report. Donovan is active in theater and the arts, so he really likes the opportunity to create and perform a dramatic performance. His performance features a criminal on death row, and he really surprises Ms. Vane with his insight and depth. Micah and Darlene team up for a debate about In Cold Blood *and its influence on what is arguably violence-glorifying culture. Finally, Holly puts together a very creative videotape in which she plays a reporter covering a current event similar to the Clutter murders. She styles the report almost like it is a movie, commenting on Capote's influence in film and television genres.*

Choice of Learning Goals

One powerful way to provide choice is for teachers to allow students to generate their own personal learning goals within a unit of instruction. Quite obviously, when students are generating their own goals, there is a greater chance they will focus on subjects that interest them. This does not imply that the teacher will not have any learning goals for a unit. Certainly teacher-designed goals will always be an integral part of effective teaching. However, in addition to teacher-designed goals for a unit, teachers can ask students to create their own learning goals. It is important that student-generated learning goals are given credence in the final assessment of students for the unit. That is, the teacher would base the final grade for the unit on how well the student did relative to the teacher's learning goals and the student's learning goals. The following vignette depicts how a teacher might introduce student-designed learning goals.

Ms. Keller's French class is beginning a unit on contemporary life in France. She lets her students know that two learning goals will be the subjects of this unit—one goal on the topic of the French government and the other on the topic of class relations. Her students are surprised when she announces that they will also be able to choose a third learning goal based on a topic of their choice. "You might be curious about pop culture in France or about the different ways the French view Americans," she says. She facilitates a class discussion in which she writes students' suggested topics on the board. "Think about these suggestions for next class period," she says. "You can use one of these or come up with another, but once you decide on something, we will meet so you can tell me about your topic and we can set out a plan for success." She stresses that she will hold them accountable for their own learning goals just as much as she will for the other two goals in the unit.

Choice of Behaviors

Chapter 2 discussed the importance of students feeling accepted and supported in class so that they have a positive response to the question "How do I feel?" In that chapter, we emphasized establishing behaviors in the classroom that ensure all students are treated fairly and equitably. Teachers can build choice into this process. Specifically, at the beginning of the school year, students can design the standards for the behaviors that are expected in their classroom. To this end, Jonathan Erwin (2004) outlines a detailed process for creating a classroom constitution that provides students with choices as to how the classroom is run. An abbreviated version of Erwin's process follows; it is geared toward an elementary classroom, but teachers can adapt its basic premise to students of any age. For a more thorough discussion of his process, see *The Classroom of Choice* (Erwin, 2004). The point is simply to give students a voice in the classroom, so that they feel the rules of engagement are not simply being imposed on them.

Step 1: Identify desirable and undesirable behaviors and attitudes. First, students work independently to write a brief description of how they would want to be treated in the classroom. What would positive behaviors look and sound like, and what negative behaviors should be avoided? Next, students gather in small groups to create a composite list of agreed-upon positive and negative behaviors.

Step 2: Create symbols. Each group then creates pictures or symbols to represent each of the positive behaviors the class listed. For example, if kindness was listed, students might draw a picture of one student helping a student who has fallen on the playground.

Step 3: Give group presentations. Each group presents its list of positive and negative behaviors and their associated pictures. Additionally, the group members might talk briefly about why they chose the behaviors they included.

Step 4: Discuss the whole-class living space. The whole class discusses the presentations and reaches a consensus about which behaviors they do and do not want to see in the classroom. The teacher may guide students from statements like "no bullying" to more firm principles about respect so that the class can create a short list of guiding principles to post in the room. The pictures can be posted around the room as well.

Step 5: Compromise on classroom behaviors. After the guiding principles and their associated behaviors are articulated, the teacher engages students in a discussion of what they would be willing to give in order to ensure these principles are practiced in the classroom. In short, students discuss the idea that they will have to treat others the way they would like to be treated.

Step 6: Get a commitment. Each student is asked to commit to do his or her best to live up to these guiding principles. The teacher may also consider asking students to hold one another accountable for following them. A verbal or written commitment will work. Students can sign individual contracts, or they can sign the paper on which the overall guiding principles are written.

Step 7: Keep it alive. In order to keep the classroom constitution in effect, it is important for the teacher to refer to it frequently, especially early on in the school year. Making reference to it when the class is going well and principles are being upheld, as well as when they are not, will help students see the constitution as a true picture of how a class should act as opposed to just a list of rules (Erwin, 2004).

Present Real-World Applications

Thus far, the suggestions presented have dealt with techniques to help students view classroom content as important. Perhaps a more direct way to provide students with a sense that what they are doing in school is important is to provide tasks that serve a tangible goal beyond the confines of the classroom. Occasionally, an individual teacher can design and implement such an approach. More frequently, though, such an effort requires a schoolwide or districtwide emphasis. Here we briefly summarize three programs that have operationalized real-world applications: (1) Kepner Educational

Excellence Program, (2) service learning in the Fowler Unified School District, and (3) the National Novel Writing Month project in Battle Creek, Michigan.

Kepner Educational Excellence Program

Kepner Middle School in Denver, Colorado, is situated in one of the poorest neighborhoods in the city. Fifty-six percent of the nearby residents do not have a high school diploma, and 40 percent of the students attending Kepner are not English proficient. Though many of these students come from caring and hardworking families, the effects of generations of poverty have taken a toll.

Carrie Olson has been a teacher in Denver Public Schools since 1985. She is familiar with the damage poverty can do to young people, specifically to middle school students, who are at a critical point in their lives. In 1992, she was teaching her class about the Holocaust. The students were particularly moved by what they learned, and when they expressed interest in seeing the memorial set to open in Washington DC in the spring of 1993, she knew it was imperative that they go.

The cooperation necessary to make this goal a reality was intimidating, but the students were excited, and soon school administrators were behind the project. It was not long before parents and others in the community were on board as well. It was a rare thing to see in the Westwood neighborhood, and when this integration and hard work saw success, Ms. Olson knew she had stumbled onto something important. History had come alive for her students; each of them was more engaged than she had ever seen them, and their families had become engaged as well. It was the closest she had ever come as a teacher to breaking the cycle of generational poverty.

What began as a spontaneous success in Carrie Olson's class has become a full-fledged academic program: the Kepner Educational Excellence Program (KEEP). Sixth-grade students who participate make the trip to Washington DC, and now eighth graders have the chance to continue their world history studies by traveling to Europe. A seventh-grade project focusing on Colorado history will soon be implemented as well.

The students who choose to participate know the reward of the trip does not come easily. First, they must sit down with Ms. Olson or another of the participating teachers before the school year begins and set personalized academic goals. For students already making the honor roll, this may mean committing to peer tutoring. For students with poor grades, it may mean making Cs. Students can set behavioral goals as well, such as attending all classes every day or showing self-control by not disrupting class. Throughout the year, students meet with teachers to discuss progress on their goals and make any necessary adjustments.

Second, students must commit to forty hours of work that they fulfill before or after school or on weekends. Jobs entail working as a cashier at a concession stand or school café, recycling papers, or sweeping hallways and classrooms. Just like any other job, they are expected to arrive on time and maintain an appropriate demeanor and appearance. In lieu of an after-school job, they can participate in a sport or school activity to earn work hours. The work commitment gives students a sense of empowerment—they know they earned the trip. It also affords them the opportunity to learn workplace skills of immediate and lasting value.

In order to prepare students for the trip, they are also required to take an elective class with one of the participating teachers. In class, they learn about the culture and history of the place they will visit. On "travel Fridays" they also learn about the technicalities of traveling, such as what documents they will need and what kind of clothes and supplies to pack. Many students have never traveled more than a day's distance from home and need to prepare themselves for what to expect as well as what will be expected of them. Teachers of these courses make special efforts to include the parents and families of the students so that, in addition to being supported in their efforts at school, they are supported at home (Kepner Middle School, 2010).

Fowler Unified School District's Service Learning Program

California's Central Valley is a largely rural area made almost entirely of vineyards and packing plants. The large immigrant population, part of a small total population, makes for a strong community chiefly dependent on the earth for survival. Fowler Unified School District is a small school district there. It has seen high dropout rates in the past and well-below-average performances on state tests.

In the mid-1990s, district leaders began meeting with concerned parents and community members. They saw a strong need for curricular emphasis on character development. In response, district leaders created the "Big Ten"—ten character traits that teachers were to teach and practice in every classroom alongside the traditional academic content. The ten traits are caring, citizenship, courage, duty, fairness, honesty, respect, responsibility, trustworthiness, and work ethic. A few years into the program, teachers and district leaders found that simply teaching the Big Ten in the sterile environment of a classroom was not enough. In order to effect real change, they would need to take these lessons into the real world. After doing some research, they decided the best way to apply the Big Ten was through service. They brought in the Fresno County Office of Education for service-learning teacher training.

Ten years have passed since the initial dedication to service learning, and the program now encompasses every teacher and every student in the district. Middle and high school students even have volunteer-time requirements. At the elementary and middle school levels, teachers develop unique service-learning projects based on personal interests or experience. They range anywhere from two weeks to an entire semester, and teachers record each hour that students spend in service. The service projects are diverse in focus, ranging from the collection of sunscreen and lip balm for field-workers, to tutoring immigrants in preparation for citizenship exams, to creating and tending a garden that the entire school can use as a learning lab. At the high school level, students are expected to design their own service projects.

Typically, projects begin in the classroom. In one such project, third-grade students began an environmental service project by learning about the life cycles of trout. They learned about breeding and about sustainability requirements specific to the trout's environment. With donations from the Department of Fish and Game and other local conservation groups, they obtained thirty fertilized trout eggs and a twenty-gallon tank with a cooling system. The lessons then went beyond third-grade science requirements. Using their math skills, students monitored the water temperature, used formulas to predict when the eggs would hatch, and created timelines for release. After the fish were released into the San Joaquin River, students reviewed notes and wrote about the experience, thus refining language arts skills.

As a result of the project, the district has seen a vast improvement in dropout rates—less than 1 percent of students do not graduate, and scores on the state tests have improved by 10 percent. They have an overall attendance rate of 97 percent, much higher than other districts in surrounding areas (Morehouse, 2009).

National Novel Writing Month

In 2007, after hearing about National Novel Writing Month (NaNoWriMo), Luke Perry, a middle school language arts teacher in Battle Creek, Michigan, decided it would be the perfect challenge for his students. He had been noticing many of them seemed to have a very critical inner voice that led, in some cases, to a fear of words and language. Initially, he was met with resistance from colleagues, but, convinced that the sheer size of the challenge was exactly what his students needed to overcome such fears and become comfortable with writing, he proposed the challenge to his sixth-grade students—write a novel in one month.

At first, his students were hesitant as well; only twelve initially signed up, but as word spread, more and more students *and* teachers became interested. Before long, the principal even agreed to suspend the regular curriculum so that 115 students (roughly one-third of the student body) could take part in NaNoWriMo. Momentum for the project continued to grow. Students worked during class as well as before and after school and through lunch periods during the entire month in order to complete their novels. At the end of the month, the school hosted a reading party attended by students, parents, reporters, and even city council members.

It was such a success that the next year over 250 students throughout the entire district participated. Students who have taken part say that the project not only accomplished the goal of overcoming the fear of language and writing, but bolstered their overall confidence as well. One student, who went on to college, still remembers the project when he feels overwhelmed with course work. If he can write a novel in a month, he thinks, he can certainly handle finals (Pogash, 2009).

Exercise 4.3 provides some practice at identifying each of the four types of choice. It also provides an opportunity to test your understanding of how designing cognitively complex tasks and real-world applications helps students answer affirmatively to the question "Is this important?" Answering these questions will require making connections and inferences that may not be obvious. In other words, the answers to these questions are not found explicitly in the text. (See page 114 for a reproducible of this exercise and page 176 for a reproducible answer sheet. Visit **marzanoresearch.com/classroomstrategies** to download all the exercises and answers in this book.)

Exercise 4.3
Encouraging Application of Knowledge

---

1. Identify each of the following examples as one of the types of choice:

    A. Choice of task

    B. Choice of reporting format

    C. Choice of learning goal

    D. Choice of behaviors

    •   Mr. Lopez is beginning a unit on narrative writing. He tells his students they will be writing some short stories. Two of their learning goals will focus on creating sensory descriptions and on using their imaginations to come up with unique storylines. "But we can do a lot more with stories than just these things," Mr. Lopez tells them. "Think about what you would like to improve on in your own writing. Would you like to create a story that uses a lot of dialogue? Would you like to create a story that makes use of different points of view?" After thinking about what they would like to improve on, Mr. Lopez asks them to write their own goal so that they can keep track of their progress on all three goals for the unit.

    •   Ms. Knapton has had some discipline problems with her class. She knows she needs to address this problem, but she also knows that more severe punishment may backfire on her. She begins the next class by taking down the poster with the classroom rules and throwing it away. "Let's start over," she says. "Let's build our rules together, and maybe this way everyone will be happy." She thinks students who have been disruptive might suggest unrealistic rules, such as allowing teasing or speaking out of turn, but she also believes that reminding them that the behavior would be allowed for everyone will dissuade them from such suggestions.

- Ms. Acker's sociology class has been studying the bystander effect. She tells them they must write an essay to demonstrate their understanding of the topic, but says that the essay can focus on a number of different aspects of the bystander effect. "First, we do not always see the bystander effect in emergencies, but the fact that it happens at all is problematic. What can society at large do to help minimize the bystander effect? Second, we have discussed in class the idea that most people, when asked hypothetically, would say they would take action if someone was hurt in a public setting. Make a prediction about this and create a survey that tests the idea. Discuss your results. Third, there is no doubt that the bystander effect exists, but what is puzzling is why. Conduct an investigation and see if you can offer a logical explanation. Finally, no one gets to decide when and where a crime takes place, but suppose you could. Would you want to be in a large group, or would you want a more isolated situation where only one or two people might be able to help you? In which situation do you think your chances of survival would be greater?"

- Ms. Lane's science class has been studying the evolution of man's understanding of dinosaurs. They have been learning about man's discovery of more and more species, how closely dinosaurs were related to birds and, just recently, the discovery of a way to tell what color the fur or feathers of a dinosaur were. "For our final exam on this topic, each of you will provide an in-depth look at how our thinking of a particular dinosaur has changed." She gives them some options in terms of how they want to deliver their presentations. They can: (A) write an essay, (B) give an oral report, (C) conduct an interview with an expert on the topic, or (D) present a debate on the topic of whether or not our renderings of this species are now correct.

2. Explain why cognitively complex tasks help students affirmatively answer the question "Is this important?"

3. Considering your students and your community, what kinds of real-world applications might be most engaging and meaningful?

Analyzing Your Strengths and Weaknesses

In this chapter, we have presented a variety of recommendations across four general categories of strategies, all of which increase the chances that students will have a positive response to the question "Is this important?" Again, table 4.1 (page 110) provides the self-assessment scale introduced in chapter 2. Using the scale, rate yourself on each strategy listed. (See page 116 for a reproducible of this scale. Visit **marzanoresearch.com/classroomstrategies** to download all self-assessment scales in this book.)

Summary

This chapter began with a brief discussion regarding the third question in the attention and engagement model, "Is this important?" We discussed how asking students to make comparisons between their personal lives and classroom content can help them make important connections to what they are learning. We also discussed a seven-phase process for implementing personal projects, which is designed to inspire students to look into the future and identify realistic paths toward long-term goals. Finally, we discussed how teachers can encourage students to apply what they have learned by assigning cognitively complex tasks, giving them structured choices in the classroom, and providing opportunities for learning in the real world.

Table 4.1: Self-Assessment Scale for Chapter 4

	0 **Not Using** I never use this strategy.	1 **Beginning** I sometimes use this strategy, but I don't think I use it correctly.	2 **Developing** I use this strategy, but I do so mechanically.	3 **Applying** I use this strategy and monitor how well it works.	4 **Innovating** I know this strategy well enough that I have created my own version of it.
Connecting to Students' Lives					
Comparison tasks	0	1	2	3	4
Analogical reasoning tasks	0	1	2	3	4
Connecting to Students' Life Ambitions					
Personal projects	0	1	2	3	4
Encouraging Application of Knowledge					
Design cognitively challenging tasks	0	1	2	3	4
Provide choice	0	1	2	3	4
Present real-world applications	0	1	2	3	4

Exercise 4.1

Connecting to Students' Lives

Identify each of the following examples as one of the types of comparison activities:

A. Physical characteristic comparison

B. Process comparison

C. Sequence of events comparison

D. Cause-and-effect relationship comparison

E. Psychological characteristic comparison

F. Fame or notoriety comparison

G. Analogical reasoning

1. Mr. Moyer's science class has been studying the Manhattan Project as an example of a scientific advancement that is remembered in both positive and negative ways. "What else is like this?" he asks. "Choose something you are interested in to make the comparison." Zane compares the Manhattan Project to spiders. "Some people think the atomic bomb saved a lot of lives in the long run and was a good thing, but some people think it was morally corrupt and made the world a more dangerous place. I think this is like spiders because a lot of people think spiders are gross or scary, but I really like them. I think they can spin really beautiful webs; and without spiders, entire ecosystems would be totally wiped out. They have a complex reputation, too, I guess."

2. Mr. Okpik's social studies class has been studying North and South Korea in a unit about current events. They have been looking specifically at the recent activities at the 38th parallel. "One of South Korea's responses to North Korea sinking one of their warships was to broadcast a South Korean pop song across the border at the 38th parallel. The song was chosen because of its sultry tone and its lyrics, which tout rebellion and independence. Acts like this are often referred to as psychological warfare. What do you think South Korea was trying to accomplish? What else can you think of that has a similar aim? Choose something you are interested in to make the comparison," he says. Torin compares South Korea's broadcast to some of the taunting that happens at his baseball games. He says, "I'm a catcher, and when a batter first comes to the box I sometimes make comments at him. They are harmless, but I'm trying to rattle him, break his concentration. I think South Korea's broadcast was similar in that it was harmless—no one was injured or killed because of it. I think they did it to rattle the North Koreans, to tease them a little and send a message that they aren't afraid of them." He also notes that while those mental games can seem

kind of silly, they can also be quite effective. "I've been in the box as a batter before and been rattled by some of the comments the catcher has made to me," he says.

3. Ms. Kwon's science class has been studying migration. "Animals of various species have migration patterns they follow generation after generation. Can you think of something you know about and are interested in that has the same relationship?" she asks. Emma compares migration to her family's recent move to a new city. "We don't move around regularly like animals that migrate do, but animals basically migrate in order to get what they need, whether it's food or breeding grounds or a warmer climate. We moved because my mom got a job that she really wanted and because some of my cousins live here, too. So we came to a new place in order to get what we wanted," she says.

4. Ms. Philips wants the students in her mathematics class to understand the nature of inverse processes such as multiplication and division. She explains that multiplication and division use the same numerical concept but in opposite ways. She says, "What are some things you know of that have the same basic relationship? Choose something you are interested in, and fill in the following statement: Multiplication is to division as what is to what?" Brandy completes the statement with the words *toe loop* and *salchow*. She explains that she is an ice skater. Both the toe loop and the salchow are jumps where the skater spins a certain number of times in the air, but what makes them opposite is the takeoff. In the toe loop the skater takes off on the back foot, the foot the spin revolves around. In the salchow though, the skater leads with the other foot, the foot that creates the revolution. So the two jumps are essentially opposites, just like multiplication and division.

Exercise 4.2

Connecting to Students' Life Ambitions

1. Why is it true that personal projects can intrinsically motivate students?

2. Explain the reasoning behind asking students in phase one to identify what they would try if they knew they wouldn't fail.

3. What are the roles of heroes and role models in the personal project?

Exercise 4.3

Encouraging Application of Knowledge

1. Identify each of the following examples as one of the types of choice:

   A. Choice of task

   B. Choice of reporting format

   C. Choice of learning goal

   D. Choice of behaviors

   • Mr. Lopez is beginning a unit on narrative writing. He tells his students they will be writing some short stories. Two of their learning goals will focus on creating sensory descriptions and on using their imaginations to come up with unique storylines. "But we can do a lot more with stories than just these things," Mr. Lopez tells them. "Think about what you would like to improve on in your own writing. Would you like to create a story that uses a lot of dialogue? Would you like to create a story that makes use of different points of view?" After thinking about what they would like to improve on, Mr. Lopez asks them to write their own goal so that they can keep track of their progress on all three goals for the unit.

   • Ms. Knapton has had some discipline problems with her class. She knows she needs to address this problem, but she also knows that more severe punishment may backfire on her. She begins the next class by taking down the poster with the classroom rules and throwing it away. "Let's start over," she says. "Let's build our rules together, and maybe this way everyone will be happy." She thinks students who have been disruptive might suggest unrealistic rules, such as allowing teasing or speaking out of turn, but she also believes that reminding them that the behavior would be allowed for everyone will dissuade them from such suggestions.

   • Ms. Acker's sociology class has been studying the bystander effect. She tells them they must write an essay to demonstrate their understanding of the topic, but says that the essay can focus on a number of different aspects of the bystander effect. "First, we do not always see the bystander effect in emergencies, but the fact that it happens at all is problematic. What can society at large do to help minimize the bystander effect? Second, we have discussed in class the idea that most people, when asked hypothetically, would say they would take action if someone was hurt in a public setting. Make a prediction about this and create a survey that tests the idea. Discuss your results. Third, there is no doubt that the bystander effect exists, but what is puzzling is why. Conduct an investigation and see if you can offer a logical explanation. Finally, no one gets to decide when and where a crime takes place, but suppose you could. Would you want to be in a large group, or would you want a more isolated situation where only one or two people might be able to help you? In which situation do you think your chances of survival would be greater?"

- Ms. Lane's science class has been studying the evolution of man's understanding of dinosaurs. They have been learning about man's discovery of more and more species, how closely dinosaurs were related to birds and, just recently, the discovery of a way to tell what color the fur or feathers of a dinosaur were. "For our final exam on this topic, each of you will provide an in-depth look at how our thinking of a particular dinosaur has changed." She gives them some options in terms of how they want to deliver their presentations. They can: (A) write an essay, (B) give an oral report, (C) conduct an interview with an expert on the topic, or (D) present a debate on the topic of whether or not our renderings of this species are now correct.

2. Explain why cognitively complex tasks help students affirmatively answer the question "Is this important?"

3. Considering your students and your community, what kinds of real-world applications might be most engaging and meaningful?

Self-Assessment Scale for Chapter 4

	0 **Not Using** I never use this strategy.	**1** **Beginning** I sometimes use this strategy, but I don't think I use it correctly.	**2** **Developing** I use this strategy, but I do so mechanically.	**3** **Applying** I use this strategy and monitor how well it works.	**4** **Innovating** I know this strategy well enough that I have created my own version of it.
Connecting to Students' Lives					
Comparison tasks	0	1	2	3	4
Analogical reasoning tasks	0	1	2	3	4
Connecting to Students' Life Ambitions					
Personal projects	0	1	2	3	4
Encouraging Application of Knowledge					
Design cognitively challenging tasks	0	1	2	3	4
Provide choice	0	1	2	3	4
Present real-world applications	0	1	2	3	4

Chapter 5

CAN I DO THIS?

How students answer the emblematic question "Can I do this?" very much defines their sense of self-efficacy. Self-efficacy is quite possibly the most important factor affecting engagement. Even if students feel good ("How do I feel?"), are interested in what is occurring ("Am I interested?"), and believe it to be important ("Is this important?"), they will probably not engage fully if they believe the task is impossible. In other words, if a student's answer to the question "Can I do this?" is no, most, if not all, engagement is lost. In this chapter we address four strategies to enhance students' sense of self-efficacy: (1) tracking and studying progress, (2) using effective verbal feedback, (3) providing examples of self-efficacy, and (4) teaching self-efficacy.

Tracking and Studying Progress

To develop a sense of self-efficacy, students can track their progress and then examine the relationship between their behavior and their academic achievement. A comprehensive approach to developing self-efficacy through tracking and studying progress would include tracking academic progress over time, setting personal academic goals, and examining effort and preparation.

Track Academic Progress Over Time

First, students chart their progress on a specific learning goal. For example, a mathematics teacher might have students track how many problems of a specific type they can solve in a specific amount of time, or a language arts teacher might have students track how many spelling words they answer correctly on their weekly tests. Figure 5.1 (page 118) depicts a student's chart for spelling test scores.

The scores graphed in figure 5.1 are percentage scores for each test. Using percentage scores works well when the assessments address a very specific skill area like spelling, solving a specific type of mathematics problem, using a specific type of punctuation, and the like. When the content is more general and less skill based, the percentage score may not accurately reflect a student's growth. This is because assessments that address general informational knowledge tend to focus on different aspects of that knowledge at different difficulty levels from assessment to assessment. In these cases, a student may receive a lower score on a specific assessment than he or she received on the earlier assessment, but still knows more than he or she previously did. This is because the second assessment addresses more complex content than the first (for a detailed discussion see *Formative Assessment and Standards-Based Grading*, Marzano, 2010). Consequently, for general information knowledge we recommend a rubric or scale like that in table 5.1 (page 118).

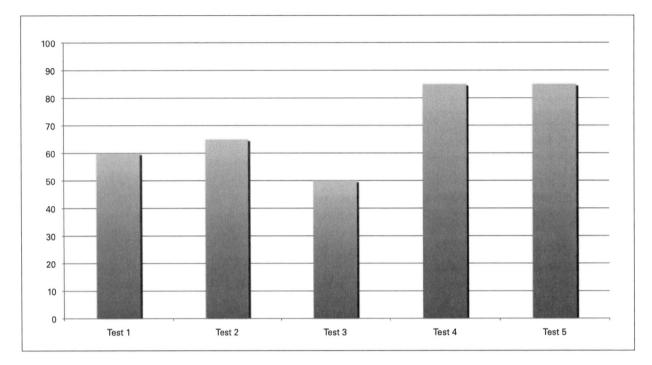

Figure 5.1: Spelling test scores.

Table 5.1: Scale for Heritable and Nonheritable Traits

Score 4.0	Students will be able to discuss how heritable traits and nonheritable traits affect one another.
Score 3.0	Students will be able to differentiate heritable traits from nonheritable traits in real-world scenarios.
Score 2.0	Students will be able to recognize accurate statements about and isolated examples of heritable and nonheritable traits.
Score 1.0	With help, partial success at score 2.0 content and score 3.0 content
Score 0.0	Even with help, no success

Source: Marzano (2010, p. 45). Copyright 2007 Marzano & Associates. All rights reserved.

The scale in table 5.1 is based on the generic form in table 5.2.

Table 5.2: Generic Form of the Scale

Score 4.0	More complex content
Score 3.0	Target learning goal
Score 2.0	Simpler content
Score 1.0	With help, partial success at score 2.0 content and score 3.0 content
Score 0.0	Even with help, no success

Source: Marzano (2010, p. 45). Copyright 2007 Marzano & Associates. All rights reserved.

As shown in table 5.2, the fulcrum of the scale is the 3.0 content, which represents the target learning goal for a specific unit or set of lessons—in table 5.1, it is differentiating between heritable and nonheritable traits. Score 4.0 typically represents application of the score 3.0 content in a way that demonstrates inferences that go beyond what was addressed in class—in table 5.1, it is discussing how heritable and nonheritable traits affect one another. Score 2.0 represents simpler content that is related to the target goal (score 3.0)—in table 5.1, it is recognizing accurate statements about heritable and nonheritable traits. Score 1.0 does not involve new content. Rather, it indicates that the student does not accurately address content independently but can demonstrate partial understanding with some help from the teacher. Finally, score 0.0 indicates that even with help, the student does not demonstrate even partial knowledge.

Many teachers prefer an adaptation of the scale that uses half-point scores, which allows for more precision (see Marzano, 2010, for a more detailed discussion). For example, the scale depicted in table 5.3 will allow teachers and students to assign a score to performances in which a student has demonstrated mastery of the simpler content (score 2.0) and some but not all of the target content (score 3.0). That score would be a 2.5.

Table 5.3: Complete Scale

Score 4.0	More complex content
Score 3.5	In addition to score 3.0 performance, partial success at score 4.0 content
Score 3.0	Target learning goal
Score 2.5	No major errors or omissions regarding score 2.0 content, and partial success at score 3.0 content
Score 2.0	Simpler content
Score 1.5	Partial success at score 2.0 content, and major errors or omissions regarding score 3.0 content
Score 1.0	With help, partial success at score 2.0 content and score 3.0 content
Score 0.5	With help, partial success at score 2.0 content but not at score 3.0 content
Score 0.0	Even with help, no success

Source: Marzano (2010, p. 48). Copyright 2007 Marzano & Associates. All rights reserved.

When students track their progress using the type of scale depicted in table 5.3, their personal progress charts look like the one in figure 5.2 (page 120).

As shown in figure 5.2, the student has kept track of her progress across four assessments. The student began with a score of 1.5 and ended with a score of 2.0 but had a high score of 2.5. By asking students to track their progress over time, teachers are encouraging them to see assessments not as isolated tests that can permanently influence their overall grade but as connected measurements of their learning and progress over time.

Set Personal Academic Goals

In addition to tracking their progress, students can be asked to set personal goals for their individual progress and strategize how they would accomplish their goals. To this end, the form in figure 5.3 (page 120) is very useful.

Notice that the form in figure 5.3 has a place for the student's performance goal relative to the content being addressed. In this case, the student wishes to achieve a 4.0 by the end of the unit. The form also has a section for the student to record his or her answer to the question "What will I do to accomplish my goal?" In this case, Avery has recorded that for ten minutes each night she will work on her presentation of how heritable and nonheritable traits affect each other. Finally, there is a section on the form where students answer "How well am I doing?" Students should fill out this section on a regular basis—perhaps daily. The teacher might provide a few minutes at the end of class each day for students to record their perceptions of their progress. The teacher might also provide some guidance to this end, asking students to identify "Those things that are helping you succeed" and "Those things that are getting in your way." In this case, Avery has noted that she has to stop watching television so much because it is keeping her from her plan. The following vignette depicts the use of the student goal-setting form in the classroom.

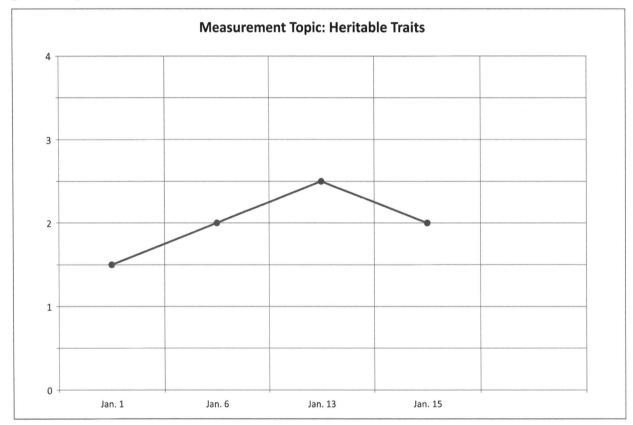

Figure 5.2: Personal progress chart for the goal of heritable traits.

Name: *Avery DeMarco*

My Goal: *A score of 4.0 by the end of the unit.*

What Will I Do to Accomplish My Goal? *I will work on my presentation of how heritable and nonheritable traits affect each other for at least ten minutes each night.*

How Well Am I Doing? *I'm not keeping up with my plan to work ten minutes each night. I have to stop watching TV so much.*

Figure 5.3: Student goal-setting form.

Mandy has already earned a 2.0 for a learning goal in her social studies class on the topic of civic responsibility. She writes the following performance goal: "By the end of the unit, I would like to have earned a 3.5." She knows she has some work to do in order to accomplish this goal. She writes, "I will review my class notes once a week, answer the review questions in the textbook, and attend the review session after school to prepare for tests." Once every few days, Mandy's teacher asks the students to write a sentence or two about how they feel they are progressing. Mandy writes, "I did review my class notes and I answered some of the review questions in the textbook, but I did not answer all of them. I think I am progressing, but I could probably work a little harder to make sure I meet my goal." When identifying what helps and hinders her, Mandy writes, "Setting a goal helps me stay on track; so does showing my mom my goal-setting form so she can remind me about what I need to do. Keeping my assignments and notes organized helps me, too—it's much easier to review them when they are organized. I've had a lot of dance practice lately in preparation for a recital, and that can get in the way of studying. Also, sometimes I have the television on while I study, and I think that might distract me more than I thought. Another thing that hinders me is that I don't like this topic as much as some of the others we have studied. It's hard to dedicate myself when I don't find the topic interesting."

Examine Effort and Preparation

As the final activity, teachers can direct students to track their effort and preparation along with their academic progress. To this end, teachers can use a scale like that in table 5.4.

Table 5.4: Scale for Effort and Preparation

Score 4.0	To be sure I accomplish my goal, I'm trying harder and preparing more than I think is necessary.
Score 3.0	I'm trying hard enough and preparing well enough to accomplish my goal.
Score 2.0	I'm trying hard but not preparing as well as I could.
Score 1.0	I'm not trying very hard or preparing very well.
Score 0.0	I'm not really trying or preparing at all.

Notice that the scale in table 5.4 links effort and preparation. This is because with academic content, trying hard and paying attention in class is not all that is required to accomplish complex learning goals. Rather, students typically have to study, read, and do homework outside of class to prepare. With a scale like that in table 5.4, students can plot their level of effort along with their academic performance. This is depicted in figure 5.4 (page 122).

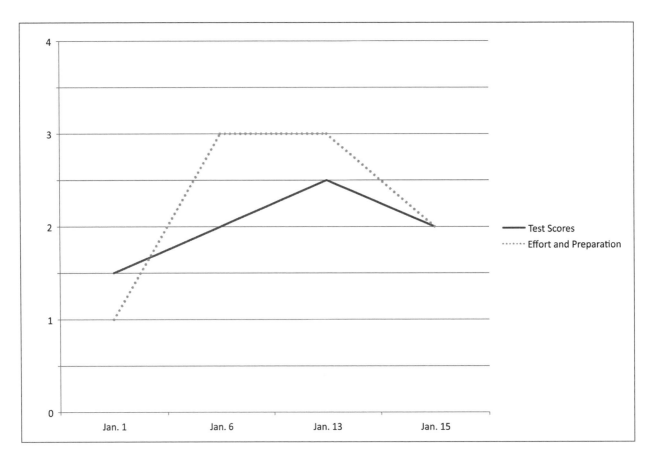

Figure 5.4: Tracking effort and preparation.

Figure 5.4 contains two lines. The solid line tracks the student's academic achievement and is, of course, the same line shown in figure 5.2 (page 120). The dotted line tracks the student's effort and preparation. This line was derived from the student's self-rating using the effort and preparation scale shown in table 5.4 (page 121). Here the student's first score was a 1, indicating that the student was not trying very hard or preparing very much. The second and third scores are 3, indicating that the student was trying hard enough and preparing well enough to accomplish his or her goal. The fourth score dropped to a 2, indicating that the student was trying hard enough by attending class but not preparing as well as he or she could. The purpose of having students track effort and preparation along with their academic performances is to heighten their awareness about the connection between the two, thus enhancing their own sense of self-efficacy. Students can benefit even more from understanding this connection if the teacher also actively engages them in frank discussions about the relationship between effort and performance. The following vignette depicts how a student can track effort and preparation in the classroom.

Wendy set a goal at the beginning of a mathematics unit on ratio and proportion—she wanted to earn a score of 3.5 by the end of the unit. She felt that completing the homework assignments and weekly challenge problems and studying thirty minutes each day for a week would be enough effort and preparation to reach that goal. For the next three weeks, she tracked both her test scores and her effort and preparation scores. Just before the final test for the unit, her teacher points out to

> *her that the highest score she has achieved so far for the unit was a 3.0 and that her effort score was higher during that time as well. She asks Wendy what that might indicate. "It proves that when I work hard I do better," she says. "Right," her teacher says. "So if you want to reach your goal of receiving a 3.5, what should you do before our final test?" Wendy says that it is clear she needs to put in quite a bit of effort and preparation, and that if she does, she has a good shot at reaching her goal.*

Exercise 5.1 provides an opportunity to test your understanding of how tracking and studying progress is connected with students' sense of self-efficacy. Answering these questions will require making connections and inferences that may not be obvious. In other words, the answers to these questions are not found explicitly in the text. (See page 141 for a reproducible of this exercise and page 178 for a reproducible answer sheet. Visit **marzanoresearch.com/classroomstrategies** to download all the exercises and answers in this book.)

Exercise 5.1
Tracking and Studying Progress

> 1. How does tracking student progress relate to the growth theory of competence?
> 2. What does asking students to develop a plan for their goal and tracking effort and preparation add to the utility of having students track their progress?

Using Effective Verbal Feedback

As described in chapter 1, Dweck's concept of self-theories is one of the most useful in describing the nature of self-efficacy and how it is developed. The distinction she makes between the fixed mind-set and the growth mind-set forms the basis for many of the suggestions made in this chapter.

In this section, we consider the subtle but important influence teachers can have on students' development toward the fixed or growth mind-sets through verbal feedback. Certain types of feedback tend to reinforce the fixed theory, and others tend to reinforce the growth theory. While it is certainly true that the type of verbal feedback the teacher provides does not cause a student to develop a specific self-theory, it can predispose students to one theory or another. Most importantly, verbal feedback within a given classroom is completely under the control of the classroom teacher. Therefore, all classrooms should become places in which verbal feedback reinforces the growth model.

Types of Verbal Feedback to Avoid

A rather obvious type of verbal feedback to avoid is one that references permanent characteristics of students. For example, if a teacher provides feedback to a student that he or she is bad or inferior, this reinforces the fixed theory of competence—students either have it or they don't. The same caution applies for verbal feedback that refers to students being good. It, too, communicates the message that a student either has it or doesn't. Finally, any type of normative reference can reinforce the fixed theory. Therefore, if a teacher tells a student that he or she is doing better or worse than another student, the teacher might unwittingly reinforce the fixed theory. Another type of verbal feedback to avoid is that which references intelligence or talent. For example, a middle school teacher should avoid saying things like "You solved all of those mathematics problems very quickly, see how smart you are?" Again, references to fixed characteristics, whether positive or negative, can reinforce the fixed theory of competence.

The following vignette illustrates a potentially harmful effect of verbal feedback that reinforces the fixed theory.

> *Ms. Ranjan's elementary class is taking turns reading aloud for story hour. Jane reads a few sentences aloud, and Ms. Ranjan says, "Thank you, Jane." Dennis reads next. He reads more articulately than Jane does, as he and his mother read aloud every night. Ms. Ranjan says, "That was great, Dennis, you are so smart!" During the next story hour, Ms. Ranjan notices Jane is having more trouble with her reading. She is fidgeting and seems to stumble over words she didn't stumble over before. When Ms. Ranjan talks with Jane and her father at the next parent teacher conference, Jane says she doesn't want to read aloud because she isn't smart like Dennis. She just wants to be left alone.*

Types of Verbal Feedback to Use

While teachers should avoid certain types of verbal feedback, they should take advantage of other types. We first consider how to provide verbal feedback for tasks that are done well. Then, we consider verbal feedback for tasks done poorly.

As we have already seen, any reference to fixed traits regarding students is not advisable. However, reference to how a student engages in a task can be very useful. This type of feedback usually makes reference to effort or preparation. For example, a teacher might say, "You did a very nice job on this assignment. It's clear that you did a lot of work on this." Similarly, a teacher might say, "It's clear that you prepared well for this." When a task is done well, statements such as the following are advisable:

- You tried very hard on this; nice job.

- You put a lot of effort into this; way to go.

- You were very focused; keep it up.

- You were well prepared; it sure paid off.

- You really thought this through; this is excellent work.

- You came well informed; very good.

- You were ready for this; nice work.

As these examples indicate, praising the effort students make and the quality of the work avoids any statements about their long-term characteristics. When providing feedback on tasks done well, it is also advisable to identify the aspects of the task that were done well. The following vignette depicts how teachers can accomplish this.

> *Ms. Blue is discussing Horace's recent essay on Eleanor Roosevelt with him during a student-teacher conference. She says, "It's clear that you really worked hard on this. You have a well-organized essay here, and it is very well developed—especially the part about her influence as a First Lady. It appears as though you took a lot of time to do some careful research about her time in the White House; nice job."*

Providing verbal feedback on a task that was done poorly involves some of the same techniques that are used when providing feedback on tasks done well. For example, it is always appropriate to comment on aspects of the task that were done well. It is also appropriate and useful to provide feedback on aspects of the task that could have been done better. The following vignette depicts how teachers can accomplish this approach.

> *Mr. Hartswick is discussing Lance's recent performance on a science test with him after class one day. "You did well on the questions that dealt with vocabulary," she notes. "You were well prepared for those terms, but you seemed to have the most trouble with the section on the limbic system. You didn't really describe how that system works and what its function is. Maybe we can schedule a time to go over that again so that the next time it comes up on a test you will feel better prepared."*

Verbal feedback on a task done poorly might also include comments on effort and preparation when appropriate. If a student demonstrated effort or preparation on a task, it should be acknowledged even though the task did not turn out well. However, if a student's lack of effort or preparation was clearly a factor on the outcome of the task, the teacher should bring it to the student's attention. However, he or she must tell them in a way that does not communicate that lack of effort or preparation implies anything permanent about the student. In general, students should receive feedback regarding lack of effort or preparation when it is clearly an issue. This feedback should help students make a link between their lack of effort and their performance in a way that makes them want to try harder or prepare better in the future—it should not make them embarrassed about not putting enough effort or preparation into the particular task at hand. To illustrate, consider the previous example with Mr. Hartswick and Lance. If Lance's relatively poor performance on the science test was caused in part by lack of effort, Mr. Hartswick might have said something like, "How well did you prepare for the test, Lance? You usually seem pretty well prepared for most everything we do." Bringing up the issue as a question focuses on the problem but does not imply any characteristics about the student or label the student.

Table 5.5 (page 126) summarizes the recommendations about verbal feedback regarding successful and unsuccessful performances.

One final comment should be made about providing verbal feedback. In this section, we have provided guidelines about what to do and what not to do. We caution that the reader does not translate these guidelines into rules to follow in a verbatim fashion. Rather than focusing on the words and phrases that are used, teachers should keep the message underlying their words in mind. That message should always be that if students try hard and prepare well, they can accomplish great things. Teachers can communicate this message through actions as well as words. If this message is clear and consistent, the guidelines presented in this section might be altered or perhaps even violated in certain situations but still produce the intended result.

Table 5.5: Recommendations for Verbal Feedback

	Successful Student Performance	Unsuccessful Student Performance
Specific Aspects of the Task	Teacher points out aspects of the task that were done well.	Teacher points out aspects of the task that were done well and aspects that were done poorly.
Student Effort and Preparation	Teacher comments on student's obvious effort and preparation.	Teacher comments positively about student's effort and preparation or questions student about his or her lack of effort and preparation.

Exercise 5.2 provides some practice at identifying different uses of verbal feedback. (See page 142 for a reproducible of this exercise and page 179 for a reproducible answer sheet. Visit **marzanoresearch .com/classroomstrategies** to download all the exercises and answers in this book.)

Exercise 5.2
Using Effective Verbal Feedback

Each of the following classroom scenarios can be classified in one of three ways:

  A. The teacher is using feedback in ways that should be avoided.

  B. The teacher is using verbal feedback effectively with a student who has done well on a task.

  C. The teacher is using verbal feedback effectively with a student who has not done well on a task.

1. Ms. Redmond is walking around the gym as her physical education students are playing three different games of volleyball. She calls out to different students according to what she sees. Arnold is a student who has struggled with sports in the past. She notices that he is putting in more effort than usual today, but that his performance is not much better. When he is taking a time-out, she approaches him and says, "You're really getting into it today, Arnold." After acknowledging his effort, she gives him a few pointers. "When you serve, try watching the ball throughout your underhand swing; watch it until it crosses the net. You can get a good idea of how much power you need in your swing that way."

2. Ms. Bowles's art history class has been studying the work of Jackson Pollock and its influence on abstract expressionism. The class is discussing the role of chaos in his work. Brandon says, "Ms. Bowles, I just don't get it. I mean, it's just splatter. Couldn't I spill something on the floor and call it chaos?" Ms. Bowles has encountered comments like this from Brandon before. In her mind, he never seems to appreciate anything the class studies. She says, "No, Brandon, you couldn't. I guess you just don't have an appreciation of abstract art."

3. Mr. Norris's science class is learning about human anatomy. He administered a pretest to get a feel for what his students knew at the beginning of the unit, and he is now looking at the first official test of the unit. He notices that Felicia started off with very little knowledge, less than most of the students in the class, but that her score on the first test is very high. During a private meeting with her, he says, "You really did well on this test. You answered every question about the skeletal system correctly. It looks like you really prepared for this. You learned a lot too." He shows her the pretest score so that she can see how much she has learned.

Providing Examples of Self-Efficacy

It is significant for students to discuss self-efficacy and study it firsthand through correlating their effort and preparation with achievement; however, everyone needs a reminder of just how powerful a strong sense of self-efficacy can be in terms of shaping one's future. In this section, we consider using inspiring stories and quotations as ways of providing students with examples of the power of self-efficacy.

Stories

Literature and history are replete with examples of people whose lives have demonstrated the power of efficacy. Teachers can present stories of such people to students on a regular basis. Consider the following three stories, each of which demonstrates the power of self-efficacy.

Will Allen

Will Allen grew up on a farm outside Washington DC. His father was a construction worker from a family of thirteen children who never learned to read. Allen was initially interested in basketball, and after receiving a scholarship from the University of Miami, he played professionally in Europe until he was twenty-eight. He then moved his family to Milwaukee, Wisconsin, because his wife's family owned some farmland there. No one was utilizing that land, so he began to grow food, and like his parents had done, he insisted his three children participate in running the farm. At first, he merely grew food for his family and sold the excess at farmers' markets or donated it to a local food pantry. In 1993, he bought a plant nursery in hopes of growing food year round. He invited local teenagers to his farm and taught them about growing food. He then partnered with a sustainable-agriculture charity to create the Growing Power organization. Growing Power now has over forty acres run by both employees and volunteers. The farm consists of six greenhouses and eight hoophouses in which herbs and vegetables are grown. Chickens, goats, ducks, and turkeys are all raised on the farm, as are tilapia and perch. Even beehives thrive there. In 2008, the MacArthur Foundation awarded Allen the "genius grant" and $500,000. He hopes to ultimately build an entirely sustainable community where people from around the world can come and learn how to create similar communities (Miner 2008; Royte, 2009).

Suraya Pakzad

In 1988, the Taliban were in power in Afghanistan, and under Taliban rule, women were not allowed to receive an education; they were not even allowed to learn how to read. Suraya Pakzad, though, began using privately donated books to teach girls and young women to read in her home city of Herat. She founded a group called Voice of Women, which operated in secret until the fall of the Taliban. Voice of Women now openly shelters Afghan women and provides job training and counseling. Many of the women she shelters have recently been released from jail or have escaped violent marriages they were forced into as girls. Though Voice of Women is now able to work for women's rights in the open, Pakzad still faces daily death threats. These threats are hardly idle—in a period of two years (2006–2008) a prominent female police officer, the director of the Ministry of Women's Affairs, and a female journalist have been murdered in Afghanistan because they advocated so openly for women's rights. Despite the danger, Pakzad is now speaking at workshops throughout Afghanistan and was a recipient of the International Women of Courage Award (Hosseini, 2009).

Roland Fryer

Roland Fryer was raised in Daytona Beach, Florida, in a tough, drug-infested urban neighborhood. With the support of his grandmother, he earned an athletic scholarship to the University of Texas. It was in college that he really began to excel. Not only did he graduate as a mathematics major, he also earned a PhD by the age of thirty and became a tenured professor at Harvard University. He was the youngest African American ever to have done so. He did not stop there, though. He created the Education Innovation Laboratory at Harvard, which specializes in research and development in the field of education. To improve the quality and rigor of education, he now partners with school districts to help administrators, teachers, and students understand the factors affecting low performance in urban areas. He even visits with students personally to encourage them to invest in their own futures through education (Rhee, 2009).

Teachers can use a number of resources to gather similar stories, such as the following:

- *Time* magazine online, www.time.com. *Time* is famous for its personal profiles. This site even has a section where featured celebrities answer ten questions from an online audience. The yearly top–one hundred lists, such as the "100 Most Influential People," are inspirational personal story sources as well.

- *Kids With Courage: True Stories About Young People Making a Difference* by Barbara A. Lewis (1992). This book and others like it feature the personal stories of young people who faced many life obstacles, acted heroically in dangerous situations, or fought ambitiously for social or environmental causes.

- *It's Our World, Too! Stories of Young People Who Are Making a Difference* by Phillip M. Hoose (1993). This book offers personal stories and specific strategies for young people who want to become involved or make a difference but do not know how. For example, it has a chapter featuring ten tools for change—ten ways to help attract attention and begin to effect change.

- *Dare to Dream! 25 Extraordinary Lives* by Sandra McLeod Humphrey (2005). This book tells the brief biographies of twenty-five famous and influential people such as Abraham Lincoln, Maya Angelou, Jackie Robinson, and Eleanor Roosevelt.

In addition to these sources, teachers may use clips from movies such as the following:

- *Rudy*
- *A Beautiful Mind*
- *October Sky*
- *Oliver Twist*
- *Glory*

- *Mr. Holland's Opus*
- *The Pursuit of Happyness*
- *Apollo 13*
- *Philadelphia*
- *Babe*

Stories that exemplify self-efficacy can help teachers reinforce the growth perspective in a variety of ways. Quite obviously they fit well within the personal projects discussed in chapter 4. While students work on their personal projects, the teacher can provide stories about people who have overcome great odds to accomplish impressive goals. After a section of a story has been read, the teacher might lead a discussion on how the specifics of the story relate to students' personal projects.

Even if personal projects are not being employed, teachers can treat stories as vehicles to stimulate discussions about efficacy. Many classes have downtime at the end of class; the teacher could fill the remaining time with stories that inspire discussion.

If stories of people with a strong sense of self-efficacy are used systematically in class, students can discern common traits among those who accomplish great things even in the face of significant obstacles. To this end, the matrix in table 5.6 can be helpful.

Table 5.6: Efficacy Trait Matrix

Person With Strong Sense of Efficacy	Trait 1	Trait 2	Trait 3	Trait 4
Person 1				
Person 2				
Person 3				
Person 4				

When a few stories have been read and discussed, the teacher can organize students into small groups. Each group lists traits that seem to be associated with self-efficacy and then examines how each trait relates to each person. Groups then share their matrices and conclusions. Additionally, the class can generate a list of traits inspirational people display and post it prominently. The following vignette depicts the use of stories.

> Mr. Klein often finishes his lesson five minutes before class ends so that he or students can share inspirational stories. Sometimes he shares stories about soldiers who demonstrated bravery in the midst of battle; sometimes he shares stories about professional athletes who overcame poverty or abuse. Whatever the story, the theme is always about overcoming obstacles and fulfilling dreams. He does not have time to open up a discussion after telling every one of the stories, but he finds that students talk about them with him and with one another outside of class. Sometimes he finds that students are reminded of them in surprising ways during lessons. On the occasions he sets aside more time for a class discussion, students talk about the stories that most affected them and why. He finds he doesn't have to try very hard to make his students see a connection between these stories and the large or small obstacles they face in their own lives both in and out of class.

Quotations

Quotations can be another powerful tool in providing examples of efficacy. Like stories, teachers can easily include quotations in the context of personal projects. For example, on a daily basis, or at least systematically, the class can discuss the meanings of the quotations as they relate to personal projects.

Even if personal projects are not being employed, a class can discuss quotations and their meanings during downtime.

In addition to simply discussing quotations, students can keep a list of quotes that are the most meaningful to them. They might also research the stories behind the quotes. For example, a particular student might want to find out the context in which Franklin Delano Roosevelt said, "When you get to the end of your rope, tie a knot and hang on." Finally, the teacher can ask students to collect their own quotes about efficacy. The class might post a list of quotes on the bulletin board and periodically update it. The following vignette exemplifies the use of quotations in the classroom.

> *Ms. Kristof begins many classes with a quote, asking her students to write each one down in their notebooks. On busier days, the quotes are simple or funny, like one from Walt Whitman: "If you done it, it ain't bragging." These quotes are effective, but they do not require a lot of discussion. On the days before an exam, she offers directly applicable quotes, like one from Winston Churchill: "If you're going through hell, keep going." The students laugh, but they are encouraged, too. Finally, on days where she has more time, she begins with a quote like one from Muhammad Ali that says, "I am the greatest; I said that even before I knew I was."*
>
> *She asks them to imagine themselves saying something like that: "What would you be the greatest at, if you could be the greatest at anything in the world?" Once she has them thinking about their own dreams, she asks them what they think Ali's statement means in terms of the role of confidence in success, noting, "Even when he hadn't proven himself to himself, much less anyone else, he still said he was the greatest. How do you think that helped him?" Finally, she asks them to think about what they say to themselves about their own abilities: "Do you say you're the greatest? If you don't, what do you say?"*

Figure 5.5 provides selected quotations organized into five categories: (1) perseverance, (2) change, (3) greatness and following hopes and dreams, (4) opposition, and (5) optimism.

Perseverance

"Genius is eternal patience."—Michelangelo

"The man on the top of the mountain did not fall there."—Anonymous

"If you find a path with no obstacles, it probably doesn't lead anywhere."—Anonymous

"The man who can drive himself further once the effort gets painful is the man who will win."—Roger Bannister

"Without a struggle, there can be no progress."—Frederick Douglass

"Genius is 99 percent perspiration and 1 percent inspiration."—Thomas A. Edison

---

Figure 5.5: Selected quotations that help teach about efficacy.

"In the middle of difficulty lies opportunity."—Albert Einstein

"Success seems to be largely a matter of hanging on after the others have let go."—William Feather

"Pain is temporary. It may last a minute, or an hour, or a day, or a year, but eventually it will subside and something else will take its place. If I quit, however, it lasts forever."—Lance Armstrong

"I hated every minute of training, but I said, 'Don't quit. Suffer now and live the rest of your life as a champion.'"—Muhammad Ali

"I've failed over and over and over again in my life and that is why I succeed."—Michael Jordan

"When you get to the end of your rope, tie a knot and hang on."—Franklin Delano Roosevelt

"I am always doing that which I cannot do, in order that I may learn how to do it."—Pablo Picasso

"Don't fear mistakes, there are none."—Miles Davis

"Happiness does not lie in happiness but in the achievement of it."—Fyodor Dostoevsky

"I've got to keep breathing. It'll be my worst business mistake if I don't."—Steve Martin

"Perseverance is failing nineteen times and succeeding the twentieth."—Julie Andrews

"People of mediocre ability sometimes achieve outstanding success because they don't know when to quit. Most men succeed because they are determined to."—George E. Allen

"The difference between perseverance and obstinacy is that one comes from a strong will and the other from a strong won't."—Henry Ward Beecher

"Ambition is the path to success. Perseverance is the vehicle you arrive in."—Bill Bradley

"Most of the important things in the world have been accomplished by people who have kept on trying when there seemed to be no help at all."—Dale Carnegie

"When you reach for the stars you might not reach them, but you won't come up with a handful of mud either."—Leo Burnett

"All great masters are chiefly distinguished by the power of adding a second, a third, and perhaps a fourth step in a continuous line. Many a man has taken a first step. With every additional step you enhance immensely the value of the first."—Ralph Waldo Emerson

"History has demonstrated that the most notable winners usually encountered heartbreaking obstacles before they triumphed. They won because they refused to become discouraged by their defeats."—Bertie C. Forbes

"Perseverance is a great element of success. If you only knock long enough and loud enough at the gate, you are sure to wake up somebody."—Henry Wadsworth Longfellow

"If you're going through hell, keep going."—Winston Churchill

"The story of America isn't about people who quit when things got tough. It's about people who kept going, who tried harder, who loved their country too much to do anything less than their best."—Barack Obama

"It's not whether you get knocked down; it's whether you get up."—Vince Lombardi

"Do not wait for leaders; do it alone, person to person."—Mother Teresa

"I know God will not give me anything I cannot handle. I just wish that He didn't trust me so much."—Mother Teresa

Continued on next page →

"Anxiety is the handmaiden of creativity."—T. S. Eliot

"Success is going from failure to failure without a loss of enthusiasm."—Winston Churchill

Change

"Change will not come if we wait for some other person or some other time. We are the ones we've been waiting for. We are the change that we seek."—Barack Obama

"Change is inevitable, growth is intentional."—Glenda Cloud

"Change does not roll in on the wheels of inevitability, but comes through continuous struggle. And so we must straighten our backs and work for our freedom. A man can't ride you unless your back is bent."—Martin Luther King Jr.

"Are you doing what you're doing today because you want to do it, or because it's what you were doing yesterday?"—Dr. Phil McGraw

"They always say time changes things, but you actually have to change them yourself."—Andy Warhol

"Loyalty to petrified opinion never yet broke a chain or freed a human soul."—Mark Twain

"Any change is resisted because bureaucrats have a vested interest in the chaos in which they exist."—Richard Nixon

"The world is before you, and you need not take it or leave it as it was when you came in."
—James Baldwin

"Never doubt that a small group of thoughtful, committed citizens can change the world. Indeed, it is the only thing that has."—Margaret Mead

"The chains of habit are too light to be felt until they are too heavy to be broken."—Warren Buffett

"If you want to truly understand something, try to change it."—Kurt Lewin

"Adapt or perish, now as ever, is nature's inexorable imperative."—H. G. Wells

"Though no one can go back and make a brand new start, anyone can start from now and make a brand new ending."—Anonymous

"It is not possible to step into the same river twice."—Heraclitus

"To change is difficult. Not to change is fatal."—Ed Allen

Greatness and Following Hopes and Dreams

"A different world cannot be built by indifferent people."—Anonymous

"I am the greatest; I said that even before I knew I was."—Muhammad Ali

"All of us failed to match our dreams of perfection. So I rate us on the basis of our splendid failure to do the impossible."—William Faulkner

"The future belongs to those who believe in the beauty of their dreams."—Eleanor Roosevelt

"There are those who look at things the way they are, and ask why. . . . I dream of things that never were, and ask why not?"—Robert Kennedy

"Every artist was first an amateur."—Ralph Waldo Emerson

"My mother said to me: 'If you are a soldier, you will become a general. If you are a monk, you will become the Pope.' Instead, I was a painter, and became Picasso."—Pablo Picasso

"Do not let what you cannot do interfere with what you can do."—John R. Wooden

"I've dreamt in my life dreams that have stayed with me ever after, and changed my ideas: they've gone through and through me, like wine through water, and altered the color of my mind."—Emily Brontë

"A man is not old until regrets take the place of dreams."—John Barrymore

"Not knowing when the dawn will come, I open every door."—Emily Dickinson

"Dream no small dreams for they have no power to move the hearts of men."—Johann Wolfgang von Goethe

"The dream was always running ahead of me. To catch up, to live for a moment in unison with it, that was the miracle."—Anaïs Nin

"My dreams were all my own; I accounted for them to nobody; they were my refuge when annoyed—my dearest pleasure when free."—Mary Shelley

"To achieve the impossible, one must think the absurd; to look where everyone else has looked, but to see what no one else has seen."—Unknown

"Decide that you want it more than you are afraid of it."—Bill Cosby

"If you done it, it ain't bragging."—Walt Whitman

"If everyone is thinking alike, then somebody isn't thinking."—George S. Patton

"Imagination rules the world."—Napoleon Bonaparte

"It's a poor sort of memory that only works backwards."—Lewis Carroll

"Don't be afraid to see what you see."—Ronald Reagan

"You can't put a limit on anything. The more you dream, the further you get."—Michael Phelps

"History will be kind to me for I intend to write it."—Winston Churchill

"At the age of six I wanted to be a cook. At seven I wanted to be Napoleon. And my ambition has been growing ever since."—Salvador Dali

Opposition

"No one can make you feel inferior without your consent."—Eleanor Roosevelt

"There may be times when we are powerless to prevent injustice, but there must never be a time when we fail to protest."—Elie Wiesel

"The only thing necessary for the triumph of evil is for good men to do nothing."—Edmund Burke

"We must build dikes of courage to hold back the flood of fear."—Martin Luther King Jr.

"I used to think anyone doing anything weird was weird. Now I know that it is the people that call others weird that are weird."—Paul McCartney

"If you break your neck, if you have nothing to eat, if your house is on fire, then you got a problem. Everything else is just inconvenience."—Robert Fulghum

Continued on next page →

"Smooth seas do not make skillful sailors."—African proverb

"I don't know the key to success, but the key to failure is trying to please everybody."—Bill Cosby

"You cannot lead from the crowd."—Margaret Thatcher

"If my critics saw me walking over the Thames, they would say it was because I couldn't swim."—Margaret Thatcher

"In the practice of tolerance, one's enemy is the best teacher."—Dalai Lama

"I've learned that you shouldn't go through life with a catcher's mitt on both hands; you need to be able to throw something back."—Maya Angelou

"Everything negative—pressure, challenges—it's all an opportunity for me to rise."—Kobe Bryant

"Difficulty is the excuse history never accepts."—Edward R. Murrow

"Do the best you can in every task, no matter how unimportant it may seem at the time. No one learns more about a problem than the person at the bottom."—Sandra Day O'Connor

Optimism

"When you were born, you cried and the world rejoiced. . . . Live your life so that when you die, the world cries and you rejoice."—Cherokee saying

"Don't worry about the world coming to an end today. It's already tomorrow in Australia."—Charles M. Schwab

"A pessimist is one who makes difficulties of his opportunities and an optimist is one who makes opportunities of his difficulties."—Harry Truman

"In the long run, the pessimist may be proved right, but the optimist has a better time on the trip."—Daniel L. Reardon

"We do survive every moment, after all, except the last one."—John Updike

"If you worried about falling off the bike, you'd never get on."—Lance Armstrong

"It's not the load that breaks you down, it's the way you carry it."—Lena Horne

"There is hope for the future because God has a sense of humor, and we are funny to God."—Bill Cosby

"You cannot climb uphill by thinking downhill thoughts."—Anonymous

"Change your thoughts and you change the world."—Norman Vincent Peale

"And your very flesh shall be a great poem."—Walt Whitman

Source: Marzano, Paynter, & Doty (2003) and BrainyMedia (2010)

Exercise 5.3 provides an opportunity to test your understanding of developing students' efficacy through using stories and quotations. Answering these questions will require making connections and inferences that may not be obvious. In other words, the answers to these questions are not found explicitly in the text. (See page 143 for a reproducible of this exercise and page 181 for a reproducible answer sheet. Visit **marzanoresearch.com/classroomstrategies** to download all the exercises and answers in this book.)

Exercise 5.3
Providing Examples of Self-Efficacy

1. What is the relationship between stories and developing a sense of efficacy?
2. How might quotations be used in ways that stories cannot be easily used?
3. What are stories from your own life or lives of people close to you that might inspire efficacy in students?

Teaching Self-Efficacy

A final approach to developing a sense of efficacy is to teach students directly about it. We saw in chapter 1 that simply teaching students about the elasticity of the human brain and reinforcing the notion that hard work and practice enhance competence can result in improved achievement. Teachers can use a number of resources to provide such information to students. Selected resources are summarized as follows:

- *Talent Is Overrated: What* Really *Separates World-Class Performers From Everybody Else* by Geoff Colvin (2008). This book discusses in-depth why ideas of innate talent and intelligence are not valid and are not major contributors to great performance. It also discusses how and why the right mind-set and deliberate practice are major contributors to great performance.

- *Think Smart: A Neuroscientist's Prescription for Improving Your Brain's Performance* by Richard Restak (2009). This book explains the anatomy of the brain and how each part works. It also outlines specific strategies for increasing intelligence, such as ensuring proper nutrition, using technology beneficially, and maximizing creativity. Finally, it highlights some things that inhibit intelligence.

- *The Talent Code: Greatness Isn't Born. It's Grown. Here's How.* by Daniel Coyle (2009). This book discusses the role of myelin in brain function and overall performance; it also explains how to produce more of the neural substance to increase intelligence and performance and offers some stories of average people who achieved greatness.

- *The Road to Excellence: The Acquisition of Expert Performance in the Arts and Sciences, Sports, and Games* edited by K. Anders Ericsson (1996). This book discusses in-depth the concept and application of "deliberate practice." More than innate abilities, this book argues that deliberate practice is behind high achievement in any field.

To a great extent, some of the strategies already discussed in this chapter will help teach students about efficacy and its potential power in their lives. Certainly, when students track their progress and their effort and preparation, they will learn valuable lessons. Similarly, the discussions that ensue from reading stories and examining quotations will add to students' understanding of the nature of self-efficacy.

Here we consider directly teaching students about the two theories found in Dweck's (2006) research: the fixed theory and the growth theory. We've organized directly teaching about efficacy into three phases: (1) distinguishing between growth and fixed theories, (2) having students identify their personal theories, and (3) keeping the conversation alive.

Distinguish Between Growth and Fixed Theories

A teacher might begin by simply explaining to students that research indicates that our beliefs about competence greatly influence how we approach challenging situations. Teachers can and should use the labels *growth theory* and *fixed theory* with students. The following vignette depicts how a teacher might present this information to students.

> *Ms. Gareth begins class one week by displaying a few silly illustrations and pictures—some of them are of weight lifters and bodybuilders, and others are of cartoon characters like Olive Oil from* Popeye. *She asks her students to pick out the characters who are the strongest. Of course, the task is not difficult for the students, and Ms. Gareth asks why it was so easy. "You can see who is strong and who isn't," Valery says. "It's obvious." Ms. Gareth agrees that it isn't hard to pick out the people with the biggest muscles in the images.*
>
> *"Look at this guy," she says, displaying a photo of an Olympic speed skater. "How do you think he grew so strong? Do you think he was born with legs so big?" Her students think it is pretty obvious that the skater wasn't born strong. He had to train really hard for a long time to be in the kind of shape he is in. She asks, "If you trained as long and as hard as this skater trained, would you be as strong as he is?"*
>
> *"I would be," Darren says, "but it really takes a lot of work to become that strong. Most people don't work that hard."*
>
> *"That's true," Ms. Gareth says. "So, it's fair to say that the harder people work, the stronger they grow?" The class agrees that this is a reasonable thing to say. "What about being smart? Does it work the same way?"*
>
> *"I don't think so," Jesse says. "Your brain doesn't get bigger. You learn more the older you get, but you don't get smarter."*
>
> *"So you think each person is born with a fixed amount of smarts?" Ms. Gareth asks.*
>
> *"Maybe not completely, but it doesn't work the way the rest of your body works."*
>
> *Harry disagrees, "My brother went to college after he got out of high school, and he flunked out his first year, but it was because he wasn't trying—all he did was ski. He went back to college a few years later, and he did fine. He realized he wanted a degree."*

As the days go by, Ms. Gareth continues the conversation, each time making finer and finer distinctions between the growth theory and the fixed theory. She even introduces the terms growth theory and fixed theory, and students begin to use these terms in their discussion.

Have Students Identify Their Personal Theories

Once the distinction between the two theories has been made, students can determine whether they have a growth theory or a fixed theory. To this end, students aged ten and older can answer the following questions in figure 5.6 designed by Carol Dweck (2000).

Read each of the following sentences and then circle the number that shows how much you agree with it. There are no wrong answers.

*1. You have a certain amount of intelligence, and you really can't do much to change it.

1	2	3	4	5
Strongly Agree	Agree	Mostly Agree	Mostly Disagree	Strongly Disagree

*2. Your intelligence is something about you that you can't change very much.

1	2	3	4	5
Strongly Agree	Agree	Mostly Agree	Mostly Disagree	Strongly Disagree

*3. You can learn new things, but you can't really change your basic intelligence.

1	2	3	4	5
Strongly Agree	Agree	Mostly Agree	Mostly Disagree	Strongly Disagree

4. No matter who you are, you can change your intelligence a lot.

1	2	3	4	5
Strongly Agree	Agree	Mostly Agree	Mostly Disagree	Strongly Disagree

5. You can always greatly change how intelligent you are.

1	2	3	4	5
Strongly Agree	Agree	Mostly Agree	Mostly Disagree	Strongly Disagree

6. No matter how much intelligence you have, you can always change it quite a bit.

1	2	3	4	5
Strongly Agree	Agree	Mostly Agree	Mostly Disagree	Strongly Disagree

---

Figure 5.6: Self-theory survey.

*These three items can be used alone.

Source: Dweck (2000, p. 177). Used with permission.

In figure 5.6 (page 137), scores of "mostly agree" to "strongly agree" on items one, two, and three indicate a fixed theory, and scores of "mostly agree" to "strongly agree" on items four, five, and six indicate a growth theory. Students can complete these questions or similar ones to help determine their personal theories. It is important to remember that although people tend toward one dominant theory, they can have different theories in each aspect of life. Thus, a student might have a growth theory about himself in athletics but a fixed theory regarding school. Consequently, students might complete the form twice—once while thinking about something at which they excel and again while thinking about something at which they do poorly. The following vignette depicts the use of the self-theory survey in class.

> *Mr. Panjir hands out a questionnaire to each of his students as they come into class. He asks them to fill it out in the next few minutes, but to do it while thinking about something they are really good at or something they like a lot. "Chris, I know you are really into soccer. Lonnie, I know you really like to play the guitar. Think about anything you are good at while filling this out, and put what you were thinking of in the top right-hand corner of the questionnaire." When the class has completed the task, he hands out another copy of the same questionnaire. "I'd like you to fill it out again, this time thinking about something you struggle with. It can be something inside or outside of school," he says. "And do just what you did last time; write what you were thinking of on the top right-hand corner of the page." After students have filled out the questionnaires, Mr. Panjir leads the students in a discussion of the growth theory and the fixed theory and how those theories affect their lives.*

Keep the Conversation Alive

Once distinctions have been made about the growth and fixed theories and students attain some self-awareness regarding their self-theories, a teacher can periodically pose questions such as the following to keep the conversation alive in class:

- How is your understanding of your self-theory affecting you in school?

- What insights have you gained based on your understanding of the growth theory and the fixed theory?

- What are you doing to enhance your belief in the growth theory?

Students might answer these questions in their journals or learning logs. These answers should be kept private, but the teacher might invite class discussion from volunteers, particularly if the teacher keeps a log or journal and answers the questions himself or herself. The following vignette depicts the use of questions regarding the theories.

> *Ms. Law asks her students to write in their private journals once a week in response to a question she poses. Her students have been learning about the growth theory versus the fixed theory, so this week she asks, "What is your theory? Were you surprised to find out which theory you held? How do you think this theory affects*

your performance in school?" Grayson thinks about each question, and as he writes in his journal, he realizes that although he began with a fixed theory, he might change his mind. "I always thought I was good at music and nothing else, like my brain was hardwired for one thing. But since we have been learning about influential people who had to work really hard and fail many times before they succeeded, I am thinking about things differently. I guess I thought high-achieving people were just smart and things came naturally and easily to them, but they really had to work. If they really had to work, then maybe I could achieve more if I worked harder, too."

Exercise 5.4 provides an opportunity to test your understanding of developing students' efficacy through directly teaching about efficacy. Answering these questions will require making connections and inferences that may not be obvious. In other words, the answers to these questions are not found explicitly in the text. (See page 144 for a reproducible of this exercise and page 182 for a reproducible answer sheet. Visit **marzanoresearch.com/classroomstrategies** to download all the exercises and answers in this book.)

Exercise 5.4
Teaching Self-Efficacy

1. What are the defining characteristics of the growth theory and the fixed theory?
2. What is the importance of keeping the efficacy conversation alive?

Analyzing Your Strengths and Weaknesses

In this chapter, we have presented a variety of suggestions across four general categories of strategies, all of which increase the chances that students will have a positive response to the question "Can I do this?" Table 5.7 (page 140) provides the self-assessment scale introduced in chapter 2. Using the scale in table 5.7, rate yourself on each strategy listed. (See page 145 for a reproducible of this scale. Visit **marzanoresearch.com/classroomstrategies** to download all self-assessment scales in this book.)

Summary

This chapter began with a discussion of the fourth and perhaps most important question in the attention and engagement model "Can I do this?" If students are to meet any challenge, large or small, they must feel they have the ability to succeed. We discussed subtle approaches to increasing students' efficacy such as using specific and task-based verbal feedback, as well as more direct approaches such as inviting students to track both their academic progress over time and their perceived levels of effort and preparation. Scales that clearly define learning goals and data displays such as line and bar graphs highlight the correlation between effort and achievement. When students begin to see this relationship, they are more likely to set and work toward academic goals. Inspirational biographies of and quotes from people (both famous and not) who succeeded in the face of nearly insurmountable odds can indirectly teach students about efficacy as well. Finally, we discussed the direct strategy of teaching students about efficacy and the relationship between effort and competence.

Table 5.7: Self-Assessment Scale for Chapter 5

	0 **Not Using** I never use this strategy.	1 **Beginning** I sometimes use this strategy, but I don't think I use it correctly.	2 **Developing** I use this strategy, but I do so mechanically.	3 **Applying** I use this strategy and monitor how well it works.	4 **Innovating** I know this strategy well enough that I have created my own version of it.
Tracking and Studying Progress					
Track academic progress over time	0	1	2	3	4
Set personal academic goals	0	1	2	3	4
Examine effort and preparation	0	1	2	3	4
Using Effective Verbal Feedback					
Types of verbal feedback to avoid	0	1	2	3	4
Types of verbal feedback to use	0	1	2	3	4
Providing Examples of Self-Efficacy					
Stories	0	1	2	3	4
Quotations	0	1	2	3	4
Teaching Self-Efficacy					
Distinguish between growth and fixed theories	0	1	2	3	4
Have students identify their personal theories	0	1	2	3	4
Keep the conversation alive	0	1	2	3	4

Exercise 5.1

Tracking and Studying Progress

1. How does tracking student progress relate to the growth theory of competence?

2. What does asking students to develop a plan for their goal and tracking effort and preparation add to the utility of having students track their progress?

Exercise 5.2

Using Effective Verbal Feedback

Each of the following classroom scenarios can be classified in one of three ways:

    A. The teacher is using feedback in ways that should be avoided.

    B. The teacher is using verbal feedback effectively with a student who has done well on a task.

    C. The teacher is using verbal feedback effectively with a student who has not done well on a task.

1. Ms. Redmond is walking around the gym as her physical education students are playing three different games of volleyball. She calls out to different students according to what she sees. Arnold is a student who has struggled with sports in the past. She notices that he is putting in more effort than usual today, but that his performance is not much better. When he is taking a time-out, she approaches him and says, "You're really getting into it today, Arnold." After acknowledging his effort, she gives him a few pointers. "When you serve, try watching the ball throughout your underhand swing; watch it until it crosses the net. You can get a good idea of how much power you need in your swing that way."

2. Ms. Bowles's art history class has been studying the work of Jackson Pollock and its influence on abstract expressionism. The class is discussing the role of chaos in his work. Brandon says, "Ms. Bowles, I just don't get it. I mean, it's just splatter. Couldn't I spill something on the floor and call it chaos?" Ms. Bowles has encountered comments like this from Brandon before. In her mind, he never seems to appreciate anything the class studies. She says, "No, Brandon, you couldn't. I guess you just don't have an appreciation of abstract art."

3. Mr. Norris's science class is learning about human anatomy. He administered a pretest to get a feel for what his students knew at the beginning of the unit, and he is now looking at the first official test of the unit. He notices that Felicia started off with very little knowledge, less than most of the students in the class, but that her score on the first test is very high. During a private meeting with her, he says, "You really did well on this test. You answered every question about the skeletal system correctly. It looks like you really prepared for this. You learned a lot too." He shows her the pretest score so that she can see how much she has learned.

Exercise 5.3

Providing Examples of Self-Efficacy

1. What is the relationship between stories and developing a sense of efficacy?

2. How might quotations be used in ways that stories cannot be easily used?

3. What are stories from your own life or lives of people close to you that might inspire efficacy in students?

Exercise 5.4

Teaching Self-Efficacy

1. What are the defining characteristics of the growth theory and the fixed theory?

2. What is the importance of keeping the efficacy conversation alive?

Self-Assessment Scale for Chapter 5

	0 **Not Using** I never use this strategy.	1 **Beginning** I sometimes use this strategy, but I don't think I use it correctly.	2 **Developing** I use this strategy, but I do so mechanically.	3 **Applying** I use this strategy and monitor how well it works.	4 **Innovating** I know this strategy well enough that I have created my own version of it.
Tracking and Studying Progress					
Track academic progress over time	0	1	2	3	4
Set personal academic goals	0	1	2	3	4
Examine effort and preparation	0	1	2	3	4
Using Effective Verbal Feedback					
Types of verbal feedback to avoid	0	1	2	3	4
Types of verbal feedback to use	0	1	2	3	4
Providing Examples of Self-Efficacy					
Stories	0	1	2	3	4
Quotations	0	1	2	3	4
Teaching Self-Efficacy					
Distinguish between growth and fixed theories	0	1	2	3	4
Have students identify their personal theories	0	1	2	3	4
Keep the conversation alive	0	1	2	3	4

Chapter 6

PLANNING FOR HIGH ENGAGEMENT

In chapter 1, we provided a model that made a distinction between attention and engagement. *Attention* was described as a function of how a student answers the first two emblematic questions:

- How do I feel?

- Am I interested?

Engagement was defined as a function of how a student answers the last two emblematic questions:

- Is this important?

- Can I do this?

In chapters 2–5, we presented a variety of strategies organized within the framework of these questions. Although the four emblematic questions are useful in terms of organizing classroom strategies in a manner that is consistent with the research and theory, they are not the best framework for planning on a day-to-day basis.

Creating a classroom in which students are highly engaged doesn't happen automatically. On a daily basis, teachers should consider specific engagement strategies to use prior to every unit of instruction. To this end, in this chapter we have organized the strategies presented in chapters 2–5 into three categories: (1) daily strategies, (2) opportunistic strategies, and (3) extended strategies, which go beyond the traditional structure of the classroom. A form with these planning questions is provided in appendix D (page 201).

Daily Strategies

Teachers should use four categories of strategies described in previous chapters on a daily basis: (1) using effective pacing, (2) demonstrating intensity and enthusiasm, (3) building positive teacher-student and peer relationships, and (4) using effective verbal feedback.

Using Effective Pacing

Pacing is an important part of every lesson, regardless of the grade level or content. It affects students' answers to the question "How do I feel?" As we have seen in chapter 2, there are four things to consider when planning for effective pacing: (1) administrative tasks, (2) transitions, (3) seatwork, and

(4) presentation of new content. Asking oneself the following questions on a daily basis can be a useful reminder:

- Do I have appropriate routines in place for the administrative tasks I will be using today?

- Am I aware of the transition between activities I will use today, and do I have a plan for how to address those transitions?

- Do I have activities planned for students who finish their seatwork early?

- What will I do to remain aware of moving too slowly or too quickly when presenting new content?

Demonstrating Intensity and Enthusiasm

Demonstrating intensity and enthusiasm is important when establishing a positive tone in class. Such a tone also affects how students answer the question "How do I feel?" Every lesson, teachers should consider two things when planning for intensity and enthusiasm: (1) places in the content for which intensity and enthusiasm can be legitimately displayed and (2) the manner of intensity and enthusiasm displayed. To this end, the following planning questions are useful to consider:

- Which aspects of the content addressed today am I particularly enthusiastic about?

- How will I demonstrate my enthusiasm?

  - Sharing personal stories
  - Giving verbal and nonverbal signals
  - Reviving the zest for teaching

Building Positive Teacher-Student and Peer Relationships

Effective teacher-student and peer relationships are at the core of a supportive tone in the classroom. Relationships affect how students answer the question "How do I feel?" Teachers should consider three things when planning for effective relationships: (1) ensuring fair and equal treatment of all students, (2) showing interest in and affection for students, and (3) identifying and using positive information about students. To this end, the following planning questions are useful:

- What can I do today to ensure fair and equitable treatment for all students?

  - Ensure students are not teased or bullied
  - Establish expectations for fair and equitable treatment

- How can I show interest in and affection for students in class today?

  - Simple courtesies
  - Physical contact and physical gestures
  - Attending to needs and concerns

- How can I gather positive information to use in building relationships?

  - Structured opportunities to highlight students' interests and accomplishments
  - Parents and guardians
  - Fellow teachers

Using Effective Verbal Feedback

Verbal feedback is part of almost every lesson. Effective feedback helps students affirmatively answer the question "Can I do this?" Its effectiveness is important because verbal feedback helps set the stage for the self-theories the students will cultivate. To this end, the following planning questions are useful:

- During what activities today could I provide feedback to students?

- What are some phrases I should avoid when providing feedback?

- What are some phrases I should use when providing feedback?

The following vignette depicts a teacher using one or more of the daily strategies for the purpose of enhancing attention and engagement.

Ms. Rhodes is planning the next lesson for her elementary EL class, and she wants to make sure the lesson captures their attention and engages them as much as possible. Because the next lesson is on Monday she knows she will spend a few minutes at the start of class building relationships with her students by discussing any important events over the weekend or the previous week. She knows how important it is that students feel accepted by her and by their peers. They are accustomed to this routine and often bring in photos, ticket stubs, concert programs—anything that is symbolic of a recent discovery or accomplishment to hang on the display board she set up in the back of the classroom. Before planning the rest of the lesson, she reads over the learning goals for the unit she is currently teaching and makes a mental note of how the class seems to be progressing. While she has noticed that, generally speaking, her students can properly identify items in isolation (a drawing of a single house or item of clothing), they have trouble identifying objects in a more complex setting. In order to help them progress, she decides to use an activity that will allow her to provide feedback easily. She spends some time thinking through the ways to provide feedback so that it reinforces the growth theory of competence. She has also noticed that her students do well in collaborative settings, so she will ask them to gather in the home groups they are already familiar with. This too should help students feel accepted by their peers. She plans an activity in which students will look at various colored drawings, each depicting a complex scene, and work together to pick out the items she calls out. For example, she might ask them to find all of the drawings in which a dog appears.

In order to challenge them a bit more, she plans a third activity, one which will require students to independently identify objects or events in a video clip. She plans to do these activities in a back-to-back fashion, thus maintaining a lively pace throughout class. She prepares for the lesson by obtaining the drawings and videotape and designating the items she will ask them to identify. She also brings her timer, which helps her students move from one activity to the next without getting off task. This will help keep the action moving throughout the class.

Opportunistic Strategies

Typically, a teacher can look for opportunities within upcoming lessons where engagement strategies will naturally fit as opposed to trying to make them fit into every lesson. Twelve types of strategies fall into this category: (1) incorporating physical movement, (2) using humor, (3) using games and inconsequential competition, (4) initiating friendly controversy, (5) presenting unusual information, (6) questioning to increase response rates, (7) connecting to students' lives, (8) connecting to students' life ambitions, (9) encouraging application of knowledge, (10) tracking and studying progress, (11) providing examples of self-efficacy, and (12) teaching self-efficacy.

Incorporating Physical Movement

Physical movement affects how students answer the question "How do I feel?" Because physical movement does not naturally relate to all content, forethought is necessary to determine how and when it will be employed. The following questions are useful when planning for physical movement:

- How can I introduce physical movement today?

- What techniques will best fit into today's lesson?

  - Movement to lift energy

  - Movement that furthers understanding of content

  - Movement for the whole class or school

Using Humor

Humor also affects how students answer the question "How do I feel?" Many times, humorous situations come up in class quite naturally. When these situations occur, teachers can utilize them to encourage a positive affective tone. In addition to spontaneous opportunities for humor, teachers can and should plan humorous activities. They can use the following questions when planning for the use of humor:

- Could I incorporate humor into any of the addressed content?

- What strategies will I use?

  - Self-directed humor

  - Funny headlines or quotes

  - Movie clips and media entertainment

  - A class symbol for humor

Using Games and Inconsequential Competition

Games and inconsequential competition help stimulate interest, and teachers can embed them in lessons in a variety of ways. They affect how students answer the question "Am I interested?" Commonly, games are used as review activities for content that has been previously addressed. The following questions are useful when planning for games and inconsequential competition:

- Is there content that has been addressed that can be effectively reviewed using games?

- What types of games best fit this content?

Initiating Friendly Controversy

Friendly controversy helps stimulate interest in the content. These activities affect how students answer the question "Am I interested?" Given the complexity of friendly controversy tasks, they typically require a good deal of planning. Questions like the following can stimulate effective use of these strategies:

- Could I incorporate friendly controversy into any of the addressed content?

- What strategy will I use to stimulate friendly controversy?

  - Class vote

  - Debate model

  - Town hall meeting

  - Legal model

  - Perspective analysis

Presenting Unusual Information

Unusual information can help students positively respond to the question "Am I interested?" With some forethought, teachers can embed unusual information in a variety of lessons. The following questions can be useful when planning for the use of unusual information:

- Could I use unusual information in any of the addressed content?

- How will I use unusual information?

  - To introduce a lesson

  - To allow students to research and collect interesting facts

  - By inviting guest speakers

Questioning to Increase Response Rates

Teachers continuously ask questions in class. As we saw in chapter 3, asking questions does not necessarily gain the attention of all students; however, when designed well, questions can positively affect how students respond to the question "Am I interested?" To ensure that response rates are high when questions are asked, teachers must structure questioning activities thoughtfully. The following questions can help when planning:

- What content should I ask questions about?

- What techniques should I use to increase the effectiveness of my questions?

  - Call on students randomly

  - Paired response

  - Wait time

  - Response chaining

- Choral response
- Simultaneous individual response

Connecting to Students' Lives

As we saw in chapter 4, activities that foster comparisons to students' lives help students attach importance to content being addressed in class. These activities help students respond positively to the question "Is this important?" However, not all content lends itself to these types of activities. The following questions aid in planning for comparison activities:

- Could I incorporate comparisons with students' lives in any of the addressed content?
- What categories will I use for the comparisons?
  - Physical characteristics
  - Processes
  - Sequence of events
  - Cause-and-effect relationships
  - Psychological characteristics
  - Fame or notoriety
  - Analogies

Connecting to Students' Life Ambitions

Personal projects help connect learning to students' life ambitions. In essence, they affect how students answer the question "Is this important?" However, personal projects don't automatically fit into traditional subject areas. The following questions can help facilitate their use:

- Are there specific units or courses in which I can use personal projects?
- How long will the projects last?
- How much time will I spend each week on the projects?

Encouraging Application of Knowledge

Cognitively challenging tasks and choice can help students affirmatively answer the emblematic question "Is this important?"

When teachers design *cognitively challenging tasks* that require students to apply information in authentic ways, it helps students perceive classroom activities as important. The following questions help when designing cognitively challenging tasks:

- Does the content being addressed lend itself to authentic applications to real-world issues?
- Is there a problem that can be solved or studied using the content?
- Is there a decision that can be made or studied using the content?
- Is there a hypothesis that can be tested or studied using the content?
- Is there an issue that can be investigated using the content?

Choice helps students generate a positive response to the question "Is this important?" Teachers can offer students the following types of choices:

- Choice of task

- Choice of reporting format

- Choice of learning goals

- Choice of behaviors

The following questions help in planning for offering choice:

- Am I allowing students to make choices using cognitively complex processes?

- What choices of response formats could I offer to students?

- How might I provide choice in learning goals?

- How will I provide choice in behavior?

Tracking and Studying Progress

Tracking and studying student progress can reinforce efficacy and help students respond positively to the question "Can I do this?" However, tracking student progress requires a great deal of planning and preparation. For example, it requires teachers to design scales for achievement and effort. To that end, teachers must address content over time so that students can track their own progress. The following questions are useful when planning for tracking and studying student progress:

- Can students track their progress over time on any of the addressed content?

- How will I design the scale for students to track their progress?

- How will I facilitate students' personal goal-setting and development of strategies to attain these goals?

- How will I design the scale for students to track their effort?

Providing Examples of Self-Efficacy

In chapter 5, we saw that providing examples of self-efficacy can help foster a growth theory and generate a positive response to the question "Can I do this?" Teachers can provide examples in the form of stories and quotations. With thoughtful planning, these can be integrated into regular classes. To this end, the following planning questions can be useful:

- Are there specific units or courses that can provide examples of self-efficacy?

- How can I use stories in these situations?

- How can I use quotations in these situations?

Teaching Self-Efficacy

Chapter 5 also discussed how teaching about self-efficacy can help students respond positively to the question "Can I do this?" Teachers should ask the following questions to help integrate teaching self-efficacy into classroom instruction:

- Can I teach efficacy through any content that has been covered or will be covered?

- What sources will I use to teach about efficacy?

- How will I make the distinction between the growth theory and the fixed theory?

- How will I facilitate students identifying their own self-theories?

- How will I maintain an active conversation about the two perspectives?

The following vignette depicts a teacher using one or more of the opportunistic strategies for the purpose of enhancing attention and engagement.

> *Ms. Ariaga is planning an upcoming lesson that associates attention and engagement. Two days ago, Ms. Ariaga presented her students with four tasks: (1) a decision-making task, (2) a problem-solving task, (3) an experimental inquiry–based task, and (4) an investigatory task. She gave them two days to think about which of the tasks they would like to complete, and now she is planning the next lesson to help students make a choice that helps them view their projects as important. She also wants them to collaborate with other students and brainstorm different ways of completing the task they have chosen. For example, students who chose the problem-solving task might brainstorm different possible solutions and discuss the merits of each. She decides to incorporate physical movement into the lesson by having students vote with their feet. She knows that students like this activity. She will display a poster board with a number (1–4) in each of the room's four corners. Students will stand in the corner associated with the task they have chosen. That way, students will have declared the tasks they chose and gathered in the collaborative group in one step. Finally, she plans for using a bit of humor when the class gathers as a group once again. Comedians like Will Ferrell often portray characters who make outrageous or inflammatory statements that could never be proven true. She decides to show a clip from one of his movies to make her students laugh, but also to introduce the discussion about valid and invalid research sources.*

Extended Strategies

Some of the strategies presented in previous chapters fall outside the structure of typical lessons. These include whole-class or whole-school activities (see chapter 2, page 21) and real-world applications (see chapter 4, page 87). Obviously, an individual teacher cannot design and implement a schoolwide program on his or her own. However, a teacher can implement elements of a schoolwide program in his or her class to determine the feasibility of such a program. Additionally, an individual teacher can work with other like-minded teachers to generate interest in a schoolwide program. The following planning questions can be useful when developing a schoolwide program:

- Does a schoolwide program need to be developed to enhance the engagement of our students?

- What are some things I can do in my classroom to try out aspects of the program?

- Who are some other teachers I might work with to generate interest in a schoolwide program?

Summary

This chapter focused on using the strategies presented in chapters 2–5 to plan for high engagement. Teachers can use some of the strategies on a daily basis, and others with some planning or as opportunities arise. Finally, some of the strategies transcend the traditional structure of a classroom. Implementation of these strategies can be very powerful, but the strategies require careful planning and, in some cases, collaboration with other teachers and administrators. Each strategy, in addition to being classified by its best use, was accompanied by a set of planning questions designed to help teachers effectively plan for high engagement.

EPILOGUE

This book has been about classroom practices that can positively affect students' attention and engagement. Our basic premise has been that both of these psychological phenomena are directly under the control of the classroom teacher. Consequently, there is no reason any student should be systematically bored, inattentive, or disengaged in any class at any grade level. Using the strategies presented in this book, teachers can plan for specific activities that positively affect students' answers to the four emblematic questions: (1) "How do I feel?," (2) "Am I interested?," (3) "Is this important?," and (4) "Can I do this?" In short, this book provides K–12 classroom teachers with the tools necessary to make their classrooms places of learning, high energy, positive feelings, and even fun.

At a deeper level, this book is about fairly radical change in the perspective of teaching. Specifically, the third and fourth emblematic questions ("Is this important?" and "Can I do this?") open new vistas to classroom teachers, schools, and districts. Rather than focusing solely on academic content, K–12 curriculum can also address students' self-awareness regarding what they consider important and how their personal theories of competence positively or negatively influence their lives. Ultimately, such awareness may be some of the more important and influential learnings students take from their K–12 experiences.

APPENDIX A

ANSWERS TO EXERCISES

Answers to Exercise 2.1
Using Effective Pacing

1. *What is the relationship between pacing, working memory, and attention?*

    Whatever a student is paying attention to occupies his or her working memory. For information to stay in working memory, students must consciously focus on it. Additionally, there is always a battle between working and permanent memory—that is, what is occurring in class and what has occurred in the outside world. If pacing is slow in class, students can easily tire of the content being addressed. In such cases, they will turn their attention (fill working memory) to content from permanent memory that might have nothing to do with what is occurring in class.

2. *What are some limitations of pacing strategies in terms of keeping students' attention?*

    Effective pacing cannot hold students' attention in and of itself. At best, it simply decreases the chances a student will become distracted. Effective pacing might be considered a necessary but insufficient condition to trigger and maintain students' attention.

3. *Which aspects of pacing are you effective at, and which aspects are you ineffective at?*

    Answers will vary.

Answers to Exercise 2.2

Incorporating Physical Movement

1. *Mr. Rush's language arts class has been reading poetry. In order to help the students begin to think about the abstract concepts in the poems and to lift the energy level in the room, he asks his students to stand. "I'm going to call out a word, and I want you to do something with your body that you think represents its meaning." When he begins by calling out the word* beauty, *his students are a bit hesitant, but as the exercise continues they begin to have more fun with it and create many different poses.*

   This classroom scenario depicts the use of movement that furthers understanding. Specifically, it depicts the use of physical representations. Each pose the students strike represents the term Mr. Rush calls out; students are thinking abstractly through conveying abstract movements with their bodies.

2. *Students in Mr. Ulrick's first class of the day are often still tired and lethargic. In order to energize them a bit, he often asks them to stand in the beginning of class and do some simple exercises that are designed to wake up both sides of the brain.*

   This classroom scenario depicts the use of movement to lift energy. Specifically, Mr. Ulrick is employing stretch breaks. Because Mr. Ulrick's students are still tired and not at their best in the morning, he wants to energize them so he leads them through some stretches.

3. *Ms. Rollin's choir class has been looking at potential songs for an end-of-year performance. She has put together four possible programs students can choose from. She gives them the song list for each of the four programs at the end of class one day, giving each program a number 1–4. She asks them to think overnight about which program they like best and why. Before class the next day, she places four posters, each with a number (1–4) in different places around the room. When class begins she asks them to stand under the number that represents the program they have chosen. She then asks students under each number to explain why they like that program the best. However, simply liking or disliking the songs in each program is not sufficient. She asks each of them to provide technical justifications, using vocabulary and concepts they have learned throughout the year to articulate their opinions. She finds that while they have not had many in-depth discussions about music in the past, many of her students are able to speak technically and articulately and even have strong opinions. Finally, she gives them a chance to change their votes after having heard the opinions of some classmates.*

   This classroom scenario depicts the use of movement that furthers understanding. Specifically, Ms. Rollin is asking her students to vote with their feet. By asking them to articulate their opinions using technical vocabulary and concepts, she is able to elicit a discussion in which students apply what they have learned, thus deepening their understanding of music.

4. *Mr. Holmes is having a review session for an upcoming social studies test on different governmental systems in place throughout the world. He tells his students to gather the notes they have on each of the different systems and the countries in which they are employed. He calls out two names randomly and those students pair up. When everyone is paired he says, "You have five minutes to share your notes with one another. You can glean new information that might be on the test this way, and you can clear up any mistakes you may have in your notes." After the five minutes are up, he calls out names in random pairs again and students repeat the process with a new partner.*

This classroom scenario depicts the use of movement that furthers understanding. Specifically, students are using give one, get one to move around the room, find their assigned partner, and then share classroom notes.

Answers to Exercise 2.3

Demonstrating Intensity and Enthusiasm and Using Humor

1. *Ms. Amnell is a language arts teacher, and when she is teaching creative writing to her students, she finds they sometimes have a hard time thinking of original ideas. To help them along, she brings in short clips from films the students have probably never seen. Sometimes the clip is of a brief conversation between two people, sometimes it is an explosion or an alien ship landing on earth. All clips are humorous in some way. Students must use the clip as the beginning of a narrative piece. Ms. Amnell finds that when they have a beginning, especially a funny beginning they wouldn't have thought of on their own, students show a lot of imagination.*

   This classroom scenario depicts the use of humorous movie clips. The clips she uses might not contain content information, but they are designed to provide students with a springboard from which they can begin creative writing.

2. *Mr. Dermot tells his students that he has an imaginary brother named Leon Swankis. He tells his class about some of his adventures with Leon. It seems Leon is always getting Mr. Dermot in trouble. Sometimes he means well, but it is usually better when Mr. Dermot follows his own plan instead of listening to Leon's ideas. Every day when class lets out, he reminds his students: "If you meet Leon, don't listen to him! He'll get you into trouble!" Throughout the year, he finds that students adopt Leon as their symbol for trouble, and their stories of him can be quite outlandish and funny. Some of them meet Leon, and though Leon tried to get them in trouble, they didn't listen to him. Occasionally, a student does find himself or herself in trouble, whether it be in class or in school or even at home. If the student talks to Mr. Dermot about it, he will ask, "Was Leon there?" The student usually smiles and nods, affirming Leon was there. "I've told you, you can't listen to Leon," Mr. Dermot says. "You have to listen to yourself."*

   This classroom scenario depicts the use of a humorous class symbol. Leon Swankis is always in trouble, and so, while he is humorous, he also provides Mr. Dermot's students with opportunities to discuss mistakes they have made and even ways to learn how to avoid mistakes in the future.

3. *Ms. Mason is an art teacher who happens to enjoy magic shows. When she demonstrates a technique in class, she uses the exaggerated and theatrical hand movements magicians use. She has the serious demeanor of a magician, and when the demonstration is complete, she holds out her arms and says, "Ta-da! Magic!" When students execute a technique particularly well or produce*

something they are really proud of, she does the same thing, telling them in a dramatic voice that what they have done is nothing short of magic!

This classroom scenario depicts the use of verbal and nonverbal signals for the purpose of demonstrating enthusiasm. By exhibiting a theatric demeanor, the mood in Ms. Mason's class changes, becoming more like a magic show than a classroom.

4. *Mr. Starr has been teaching science for over fifteen years. Sometimes teaching the same or similar content can get old and feel stale. When he feels uninspired about teaching, he takes the time to read science-based magazines and articles about new advancements and breakthroughs. Thinking about how many discoveries are being made in science today—and the ramifications of those discoveries—re-energizes him about teaching science.*

This classroom scenario depicts a teacher reviving the zest for teaching. As with any other profession, teachers occasionally get stuck in a rut. Mr. Starr is trying to get out of a rut by recalling what it was that originally fed his passion for science and for teaching.

Answers to Exercise 2.4

Building Positive Teacher-Student and Peer Relationships

1. *Mr. Briggs usually gets the chance to talk with his students' families at the school's Back to School Night. However, Rodney's mother did not attend Back to School Night, so Mr. Briggs calls her at home on an evening Rodney said she would be home. She tells him that Rodney has recently been diagnosed with Asperger's syndrome, and that while they are doing what they can to get him all the help he needs, he still has a bit of a hard time socially at school. "He loves math," she says. "He loves chess, too. Puzzles of any kind fascinate him." After learning this information, Mr. Briggs watches out for Rodney. Sometimes he makes eye contact with Rodney so he knows he is as important as the other students; sometimes they have lunch together and do puzzles. When a fellow teacher decides to form a chess club, Mr. Briggs talks to Rodney and encourages him to join. He also talks to Rodney's mother once a week to get updates and see if there is anything else he can do to help.*

   This classroom scenario depicts a teacher building a relationship with a student by eliciting information from the student's parents, attending to the student's special needs, and showing affection through eye contact. Had Mr. Briggs not spoken with Rodney's mother he might not have known about Rodney's condition. The knowledge helps him understand and attend to Rodney's needs by spending some alone time with him and suggesting the chess club. It also lets him know that Rodney might need more encouragement and support than other students during class, so Mr. Briggs should make frequent eye contact to show affection.

2. *After greeting her students by name as they come into class, Ms. Landis asks her students, as she does every Monday, if there is anything they would like to change about their personal profiles. The personal profiles are placed around the room and feature photos of each student as well as pictures or illustrations of hobbies, pets, friends, or anything else the student finds important. After taking a few minutes to allow students to add to or change their profiles, the class gets into small groups to continue work on a class project. Ms. Landis circulates the room to monitor progress, and when a student has questions or comments she kneels beside his or her chair to talk. She finds that some of her more soft-spoken students will open up a little more if she is closer and at eye level with them.*

This classroom scenario depicts the use of a teacher building relationships with students through the use of a structured opportunity for students to highlight their accomplishments. It also illustrates a teacher showing affection through physical proximity. By encouraging her students to display profiles about themselves, Ms. Landis helps the whole class get to know one another, and by kneeling next to shyer students, she is letting them know she is interested in what they have to say.

3. *While in search of information about his new students, Mr. Heim asks another teacher about a student named Li. The teacher says Li is a bully and will likely try to hurt other students. During a private meeting with Li, Mr. Heim asks him to share a little bit about himself. Li tells him that the last school year was his first at this school, and it was tough for him. Mr. Heim asks why, and Li tells him that he didn't know anyone when he moved here and that where he comes from, kids have to prove they are tough to make friends and be respected. "I don't think it's like that here," Li says, "but it took me a while to figure it out. Now most of the kids are afraid of me." Mr. Heim tells Li he will do what he can to help him make some friends, and later shares his conversation with the teacher he originally spoke with. "He is not a bully," Mr. Heim says. "He just didn't know how to fit in. The rules at his old school don't apply here. I think we should give him a chance before making assumptions; negative presumptions will only make life harder for him."*

This classroom scenario depicts the use of a teacher building a relationship with a student through eliciting information about him from other teachers. Mr. Heim is also listening to Li's concerns and extinguishing a negative conversation about Li with another teacher. Mr. Heim finds out about Li's reputation from another teacher but listens to what Li has to say about his own past behavior. After listening, Mr. Heim is better able to respond to the teacher who told him about Li's reputation and turns the conversation to a positive instead of negative tone.

4. *Ms. Ballard is a physical education teacher. In the beginning of the year, she likes to initiate a class discussion in which she asks students what their favorite sports are and what kinds of games and sports they would like to learn. Over the course of the year, she tries to fit in as many requests as possible, asking the students who made the requests to assist during that unit. She uses high and low fives to encourage her assistants as well as all of her other students and sometimes uses elaborate handshakes she and the students make up.*

This classroom scenario depicts a teacher building relationships with students through the use of physical gestures and class discussions designed to allow students to share information about themselves. Ms. Ballard's students know she is interested in what they like and dislike because she initiates a class discussion about it and does her best to accommodate students' requests. They also know she supports them because she offers encouraging gestures like the high five.

The Highly Engaged Classroom © 2011 Marzano Research Laboratory • marzanoresearch.com
Visit **marzanoresearch.com/classroomstrategies** to download this page.

5. *Mr. Fuentes learns from Gage's mother that he recently lost a grandfather to whom he was very close. Mr. Fuentes knows Gage won't want to talk much about it at school, but he wants to show that he recognizes his student is going through a hard time. When he sees Gage in the hallway or as he is coming or going from class, Mr. Fuentes simply puts his hand on Gage's shoulder and gives him a smile.*

This classroom scenario depicts a teacher building a relationship with a student by using appropriate physical contact and eliciting information from the student's parent. Had he not spoken with Gage's mother, Mr. Fuentes may not have known his student was going through a tough time. Mr. Fuentes can now simply put his hand on Gage's back or give a smile to offer subtle support.

Answers to Exercise 3.1

Using Games and Inconsequential Competition

1. *Why do academic games stimulate attention?*

   Games stimulate situational interest—usually, triggered situational interest and maintained situational interest. Most academic games provide students with clues or hints to questions without providing them with the exact answers. Such situations typically activate the natural human tendency to fill in missing information or to establish closure around something that is incomplete. When a competition is added to academic games, mild pressure provides another stimulus for attention. It is important, however, that competition is just for fun—it is inconsequential. Winning or losing a game should have no effect on students' grades or test scores. Games should be used as a lighthearted way to review and analyze information.

2. *What would be appropriate teacher behavior if many students did poorly on the questions in an academic game?*

   Games must maintain an academic focus. They can be used as a form of feedback to teachers. If a large number of students do poorly on an academic game, it might be an indication that review or re-teaching of the content is necessary. Games should always be debriefed to determine what students know well. Additionally, games can always be used as a quick review of content.

3. *What are some ways you have used games in the past?*

   Answers will vary.

Answers to Exercise 3.2

Initiating Friendly Controversy

1. *Compare the defining features of the debate model, the town hall–meeting model, and the legal model.*

   The debate model asks students to take a position on a specific issue and use evidence, logic, and persuasive techniques in order to persuade an audience. Students must also find ways to defeat the arguments the opposition proposes. The town hall meeting does not focus so intently on persuasion. Instead, its purpose is to encourage students to look at an issue from a variety of different perspectives. In addition to learning about how a single issue can affect many different people, the town hall–meeting model also requires students to argue from the point of view of a role that is assumed and may be very different from their own. Finally, the legal model focuses on complex analysis of a text. In addition to analyzing different perspectives, students are required to scrutinize how judicial decisions affect public policy.

2. *What is unique about perspective analysis as compared to other approaches described in this section?*

   The focus of the perspective analysis is for a person to identify his or her own perspective and the logic underlying that perspective. Of course, this is similar to the other approaches discussed in the section, each of which has this characteristic to one degree or another. The unique feature of the perspective analysis is that it requires students to examine the underlying logic of their own positions and contrast it with the underlying logic of a differing position. Where some of the other models might require students to argue from an opposing position to that of their own, they do not require students to analyze the logic of an opposing position.

Answers to Exercise 3.3

Presenting Unusual Information

1. *What is the underlying dynamic behind using unusual information to capture students' attention?*

   Unusual information taps into the natural human tendency to pay attention to anything that is unexpected, suspenseful, or out of the ordinary. Even if unusual information is only tangentially related to the content being studied, it still helps elicit triggered situational interest and can lead to maintained situational interest.

2. *How might the use of unusual information facilitate class participation and cooperation?*

   Students can use the challenge of finding unusual (but true and relevant) information about a particular topic as an opportunity for collaboration. Collaboration can take the form of creating an overall class project such as an online wiki or a catalog of outrageous or unusual facts. Additionally, one class can inherit the work of past classes and contribute to a growing legacy for classes yet to come. The challenge of finding the most unusual (but true and relevant) information might also stimulate some friendly competition among students as well as present opportunities for humor.

3. *How have you utilized unusual information in the past? Are there specific topics you teach that could use unusual information?*

   Answers will vary.

Answers to Exercise 3.4

Questioning to Increase Response Rates

1. *Mr. Severs is beginning a social studies unit about current events, and he would like to get an idea of what his students already know about the national and global stages. He prepares a number of questions about recent political happenings. At the start of class, he hands out voting devices in alphabetical order. When each student has one, Mr. Severs asks his first question. "Which of these people is not a member of President Obama's cabinet? Is it (A) Hillary Clinton, (B) William Reilly, (C) Janet Napolitano, or (D) Rahm Emanuel?" He gives his students a few moments to think about the question and vote for the answer they think is correct. When all of the votes are in, he shows everyone a bar graph depicting how the class voted. He asks more questions as class goes on, each time showing the class the results and explaining the correct answer. When class is over, he takes a deeper look at the individual responses of each student. Now he knows that, in general, his class doesn't know much about current events, but he has three or four students who do appear to keep up.*

This classroom scenario depicts the use of simultaneous individual response through a voting technology. Mr. Severs is using a technological voting system that allows all students to vote for which answer they think is correct, and then he is able to show the class the results. He is also able to gather feedback about individual students.

2. *Ms. Palmer has drawn names in order to pair students up in the beginning of her language arts class. During the lesson she asks a few questions about the book they have been reading and gives the students a set amount of time to construct a reply. After her first question, "How did Jacob respond when he didn't make the Olympic team the first time?" she waits a few minutes and then calls on Jared and Kendra. "He was really depressed about it, and he stopped training and went to work for his dad's restaurant," Jared says. Ms. Palmer asks Kendra how she might respond in the same situation. "I would be really upset too. Gymnastics is a sport that traditionally really young athletes compete in. I might have stopped training too, but I would have gone to college instead of working for my dad. I probably would have moved on from athletics." Ms. Palmer then asks another pair to discuss the outcome of Jacob's next Olympic quest. After one student responds, she asks the other student how he feels about Jacob's decision to continue his quest given that he did eventually make the team but did not win a medal.*

This classroom scenario depicts a teacher who is using paired response. Ms. Palmer pairs her students before beginning the activity. She then asks a question and gives each pair of students time to collaborate. When she calls on one pair of students, one student responds to the question directly and another student elaborates by discussing how he or she might feel in a similar circumstance.

3. *Mr. Vinci has four students who are quite interested in various aspects of photography and will consistently volunteer to answer his questions or show the class the photos they took for the previous assignment. Although he appreciates their enthusiasm, he has noticed that many of his other students will refrain from volunteering because they know these four students will. He institutes a new policy in response. At the beginning of every class, he gathers the photos from the last assignment, and when he asks a question, he selects a photo at random. The student who took the photo is called on to answer the question. He finds that doing this also means that more photos taken by his students are shown in class.*

    This classroom scenario depicts a teacher who is calling on students randomly. Because Mr. Vinci calls on whichever student took the selected photo, all students must be alert and prepared to answer each of his questions.

4. *Ms. Montrose likes to get an idea of how confident students feel in what they are learning in the days and weeks before an exam. If they are confident, they are more likely to do well, and if they are not, Ms. Montrose can offer some personal one-on-one time prior to the exam. As the last activity in class one day, she asks the class how well they feel they understand the topic: "Give me a thumbs up if you think you understand this well enough to get an A on the test; hold your thumb out to the side if you think you are getting better but are not quite ready for a test yet, and give me a thumbs down if you don't feel you understand this material very well at all." Once they have signaled their feelings, she reminds them before the bell rings that she is available for extra help before and after school by appointment.*

    Ms. Montrose is using simultaneous individual response. Specifically she is using hand signals to get an idea of how confident her students are about the content. All students are responding, and additionally, Ms. Montrose gets a better idea of how well students think they know the material and which students might need her help before the exam.

Answers to Exercise 4.1

Connecting to Students' Lives

1. *Mr. Moyer's science class has been studying the Manhattan Project as an example of a scientific advancement that is remembered in both positive and negative ways. "What else is like this?" he asks. "Choose something you are interested in to make the comparison." Zane compares the Manhattan Project to spiders. "Some people think the atomic bomb saved a lot of lives in the long run and was a good thing, but some people think it was morally corrupt and made the world a more dangerous place. I think this is like spiders because a lot of people think spiders are gross or scary, but I really like them. I think they can spin really beautiful webs; and without spiders, entire ecosystems would be totally wiped out. They have a complex reputation, too, I guess."*

Mr. Moyer is asking his students to base their comparisons on characteristics of fame or notoriety. Zane compares the complex legacy of the Manhattan Project to spiders because he is interested in them. He notes that while he finds spiders interesting and important, some people just view them as gross or scary.

2. *Mr. Okpik's social studies class has been studying North and South Korea in a unit about current events. They have been looking specifically at the recent activities at the 38th parallel. "One of South Korea's responses to North Korea sinking one of their warships was to broadcast a South Korean pop song across the border at the 38th parallel. The song was chosen because of its sultry tone and its lyrics, which tout rebellion and independence. Acts like this are often referred to as psychological warfare. What do you think South Korea was trying to accomplish? What else can you think of that has a similar aim? Choose something you are interested in to make the comparison," he says. Torin compares South Korea's broadcast to some of the taunting that happens at his baseball games. He says, "I'm a catcher, and when a batter first comes to the box I sometimes make comments at him. They are harmless, but I'm trying to rattle him, break his concentration. I think South Korea's broadcast was similar in that it was harmless—no one was injured or killed because of it. I think they did it to rattle the North Koreans, to tease them a little and send a message that they aren't afraid of them." He also notes that while those mental games can seem kind of silly, they can also be quite effective. "I've been in the box as a batter before and been rattled by some of the comments the catcher has made to me," he says.*

Mr. Okpik's student makes a comparison based on psychological characteristics. Torin compares South Korea's psychological intent of implying superiority or strength through taunting North Korea with the pop-song broadcast to his actions as a catcher on the baseball team.

3. *Ms. Kwon's science class has been studying migration. "Animals of various species have migration patterns they follow generation after generation. Can you think of something you know about and are interested in that has the same relationship?" she asks. Emma compares migration to her family's recent move to a new city. "We don't move around regularly like animals that migrate do, but animals basically migrate in order to get what they need, whether its food or breeding grounds or a warmer climate. We moved because my mom got a job that she really wanted and because some of my cousins live here, too. So we came to a new place in order to get what we wanted," she says.*

Ms. Kwon has asked her students to make a comparison based on the characteristics of a particular process—migration. Emma points out that her comparison of the process is based on purpose rather than pattern, but she has clearly articulated the purpose of both migration as a whole and her family's recent move.

4. *Ms. Philips wants the students in her mathematics class to understand the nature of inverse processes such as multiplication and division. She explains that multiplication and division use the same numerical concept but in opposite ways. She says, "What are some things you know of that have the same basic relationship? Choose something you are interested in, and fill in the following statement: Multiplication is to division as what is to what?" Brandy completes the statement with the words* toe loop *and* salchow. *She explains that she is an ice skater. Both the toe loop and the salchow are jumps where the skater spins a certain number of times in the air, but what makes them opposite is the takeoff. In the toe loop the skater takes off on the back foot, the foot the spin revolves around. In the salchow though, the skater leads with the other foot, the foot that creates the revolution. So the two jumps are essentially opposites, just like multiplication and division.*

Brandy completes Ms. Philips's analogical reasoning statement. Ms. Philips begins the comparison by stating the relationship between multiplication and division, and Brandy completes the analogy by filling in the names for two ice skating jumps that have the same relationship.

The Highly Engaged Classroom © 2011 Marzano Research Laboratory • marzanoresearch.com
Visit **marzanoresearch.com/classroomstrategies** to download this page.

Answers to Exercise 4.2

Connecting to Students' Life Ambitions

1. *Why is it true that personal projects can intrinsically motivate students?*

   Assuming that the human mind is organized in a hierarchy of goals, any time students are working on high-level goals within their personal hierarchies, they are probably highly engaged. The personal project is designed to tap into high-level goals for each student. The students' personal project selections have no constraints. Consequently, students should choose personal projects that they consider valuable and select goals about which they are truly excited.

2. *Explain the reasoning behind asking students in phase one to identify what they would try if they knew they wouldn't fail.*

   The purpose of the activity is to help students recognize goals they have for themselves that they may have suppressed because they believe the goals to be impossible to accomplish. As we saw in chapter 1, this can happen at a very early age if students have not cultivated the belief that they can accomplish complex goals with necessary effort.

3. *What are the roles of heroes and role models in the personal project?*

   Heroes and role models represent concrete examples of people who have achieved the type of goal to which students aspire. The fact that others have accomplished their goals helps students perceive their goals as much more reasonable and possible. Also, as students learn about the lives of their role models and heroes, they might glean ideas and insights that will help them with their goals.

Answers to Exercise 4.3

Encouraging Application of Knowledge

1. Identify each of the following examples as one of the types of choice:

   A. Choice of task

   B. Choice of reporting format

   C. Choice of learning goal

   D. Choice of behaviors

   - *Mr. Lopez is beginning a unit on narrative writing. He tells his students they will be writing short stories. Two of their learning goals will focus on creating sensory descriptions and on using their imaginations to come up with unique storylines. "But we can do a lot more with stories than just these things," Mr. Lopez tells them. "Think about what you would like to improve on in your own writing. Would you like to create a story that uses a lot of dialogue? Would you like to create a story that makes use of different points of view?" After thinking about what they would like to improve on, Mr. Lopez asks them to write their own goal so that they can keep track of their progress on all three goals for the unit.*

     This classroom scenario depicts the use of choice regarding learning goals. Students have all been assigned a specific task and reporting format. Though they have also been assigned two specific learning goals, each student has been given an opportunity to choose his or her third learning goal.

   - *Ms. Knapton has had some discipline problems with her class. She knows she needs to address this problem, but she also knows that more severe punishment may backfire on her. She begins the next class by taking down the poster with the classroom rules and throwing it away. "Let's start over," she says. "Let's build our rules together, and maybe this way everyone will be happy." She thinks students who have been disruptive might suggest unrealistic rules, such as allowing teasing or speaking out of turn, but she also believes that reminding them that the behavior would be allowed for everyone will dissuade them from such suggestions.*

     This classroom scenario depicts the use of choice regarding behavior. Students are being asked to design a system of expectations about how everyone will be treated.

   - *Ms. Acker's sociology class has been studying the bystander effect. She tells them they must write an essay to demonstrate their understanding of the topic, but says that the essay can focus on a number of different aspects of the bystander effect. "First, we do not always see the bystander effect in emergencies, but the fact that it happens at all is problematic. What can society at large do to help minimize the bystander effect? Second, we have discussed in class the idea that most people, when asked hypothetically, would say they would take action if someone was hurt in a public setting. Make a prediction about this and create a survey that tests the idea. Discuss your results. Third, there is no doubt that the bystander effect exists, but what is puzzling is why. Conduct an investigation and see if you can offer a logical explanation. Finally, no one gets to decide when and where a crime takes place, but suppose you could. Would you want to be in a large group, or would you want a more isolated situation where only one or two people might be able to help you? In which situation do you think your chances of survival would be greater?"*

This classroom scenario depicts the use of choice regarding tasks. The students are studying the bystander effect, and they will write an essay to demonstrate their understanding of the topic; however, they have been given a choice of various cognitively complex tasks from which to choose.

- *Ms. Lane's science class has been studying the evolution of man's understanding of dinosaurs. They have been learning about the discoveries of more and more species, how closely dinosaurs were related to birds, and, just recently, a way to tell the color of the fur or feathers of a dinosaur. She announces, "For our final exam on this topic, each of you will provide an in-depth look at how our thinking of a particular dinosaur has changed." She gives them some options in terms of how they want to deliver their presentations. They can: (A) write an essay, (B) give an oral report, (C) conduct an interview with an expert on the topic, or (D) present a debate on the topic of whether or not our renderings of this species are now correct.*

This classroom scenario depicts the use of choice regarding reporting formats. All students are working on the same learning goals and are tasked with looking at the evolution of theories on dinosaurs, but each student is allowed to choose how he or she presents the relevant information.

2. *Explain why cognitively complex tasks help students affirmatively answer the question "Is this important?"*

Cognitively complex tasks ask students to go beyond memorization or regurgitation of information and apply what they have learned in challenging ways. Making decisions, solving problems, or conducting experiments or investigations are authentic tasks that help students make connections to issues of personal concern.

3. *Considering your students and your community, what kinds of real-world applications might be most engaging and meaningful?*

Answers will vary.

Answers to Exercise 5.1

Tracking and Studying Progress

1. *How does tracking student progress relate to the growth theory of competence?*

   In school, students very seldom have the opportunity to observe their progress over time relative to a specific learning goal in class. This might not automatically help foster the growth perspective, but it does establish a foundation for interacting about the growth perspective and the general notion of efficacy. As students observe their improving scores, they can interact with the teacher and each other about the reasons for their progress.

2. *What does asking students to develop a plan for their goal and tracking effort and preparation add to the utility of having students track their progress?*

   Adding these two components makes discussions of the growth perspective more concrete and substantive. As students develop their plans and analyze their progress, discussion can occur between the teacher and students about the characteristics of efficacy. Students can be invited to share what they are learning about themselves and about the nature of efficacy. As students progress in their understanding of efficacy, they can also report on the changes in their behavior.

Answers to Exercise 5.2

Using Effective Verbal Feedback

1. *Ms. Redmond is walking around the gym as her physical education students are playing three different games of volleyball. She calls out to different students according to what she sees. Arnold is a student who has struggled with sports in the past. She notices that he is putting in more effort than usual today, but that his performance is not much better. When he is taking a time-out, she approaches him and says, "You're really getting into it today, Arnold." After acknowledging his effort, she gives him a few pointers. "When you serve, try watching the ball throughout your underhand swing; watch it until it crosses the net. You can get a good idea of how much power you need in your swing that way."*

   This is an example of a teacher giving appropriate and specific feedback to a student on a task that was done poorly. Ms. Redmond begins her discussion with Arnold by commenting positively on his level of effort. However, she also gives him some very specific feedback on an element of his performance that was lacking. This feedback was given appropriately, increasing the likelihood that Arnold will want to try his serve again as opposed to decreasing his level of effort.

2. *Ms. Bowles's art history class has been studying the work of Jackson Pollock and its influence on abstract expressionism. The class is discussing the role of chaos in his work. Brandon says, "Ms. Bowles, I just don't get it. I mean, it's just splatter. Couldn't I spill something on the floor and call it chaos?" Ms. Bowles has encountered comments like this from Brandon before. In her mind, he never seems to appreciate anything the class studies. She says, "No, Brandon, you couldn't. I guess you just don't have an appreciation of abstract art."*

   This is an example of inappropriate verbal feedback. Ms. Bowles's frustration with Brandon might be quite understandable, but her feedback was not effective. In fact, she was promoting the fixed theory of intelligence by making reference to "an appreciation for abstract art." This statement implies that Brandon either has an appreciation or does not.

3. *Mr. Norris's science class is learning about human anatomy. He administered a pretest to get a feel for what his students knew at the beginning of the unit, and he is now looking at the first official test of the unit. He notices that Felicia started off with very little knowledge, less than most of the students in the class, but that her score on the first test is very high. During a private meeting*

1 of 2

with her, he says, "You really did well on this test. You answered every question about the skeletal system correctly. It looks like you really prepared for this. You learned a lot too." He shows her the pretest score so that she can see how much she has learned.

This is an example of appropriate praise and verbal feedback for a task that was done well. Mr. Norris pointed out what was done well about the test, and pointed out how much knowledge Felicia had gained. He also commented on apparent effort and preparation.

The Highly Engaged Classroom © 2011 Marzano Research Laboratory • marzanoresearch.com
Visit **marzanoresearch.com/classroomstrategies** to download this page.

Answers to Exercise 5.3
Providing Examples of Self-Efficacy

1. *What is the relationship between stories and developing a sense of efficacy?*

   The concept of overcoming formidable odds to achieve a goal might be quite foreign to some students, particularly those who have spent years operating from a fixed-theory perspective. In such cases, students probably need concrete examples of the power of efficacy. Stories provide those concrete examples.

2. *How might quotations be used in ways that stories cannot be easily used?*

   Since quotations require very little class time, they can be used quite frequently as a brief reminder of the power of a strong sense of efficacy. Additionally, they frequently stimulate students to research the context in which the quotes were stated.

3. *What are stories from your own life or lives of people close to you that might inspire efficacy in students?*

   Answers will vary.

Answers to Exercise 5.4
Teaching Self-Efficacy

1. *What are the defining characteristics of the growth theory and the fixed theory?*

The growth theory is rooted in the idea that intelligence increases with effort—that we can always get smarter by working harder. The fixed theory is rooted in the idea that intelligence is a fixed trait—something we cannot really change no matter how hard we work. The differences between these theories are profound because a student who believes he can become more and more intelligent is far more likely to take on challenging tasks and to learn from, rather than be embarrassed by, failure. Students who hold a fixed theory, however, will likely shy away from challenges to avoid failure and will also likely shy away from putting in substantial effort. For them, if you are intelligent then success should come easily.

2. *What is the importance of keeping the efficacy conversation alive?*

Unfortunately, a fixed theory is one that tends to be deeply ingrained in students. Changing from a fixed theory mind-set to a growth theory mind-set is difficult and time consuming. Students with fixed theories need consistent reminders about the growth theory. They also need consistent encouragement if they are to believe success both inside and outside the classroom is possible.

APPENDIX B

WHAT IS AN EFFECT SIZE?

Reports on educational research use terms such as *meta-analysis* and *effect size* (ES). While these terms are without doubt useful to researchers, they may confuse or even frustrate the practitioner. So what does meta-analysis mean exactly? What is an ES? A meta-analysis is a summary, or synthesis, of relevant research findings. It looks at all of the individual studies done on a particular topic and summarizes them. This is helpful to educators in that a meta-analysis provides more and stronger support than does a single analysis (a meta-analysis is literally an analysis of analyses).

An average ES tells us about the results across all of the individual studies examined. For example, let us say the purpose of the meta-analysis is to examine multiple studies regarding the effect of attention and engagement strategies on student achievement (that is, the effect of X on Y). An average ES reports the results of all the included studies to tell us whether or not these strategies improve student achievement and, if so, by how much.

Exactly how does a meta-analysis work, and how is an ES calculated? Empirical research is highly detailed and often uses idiomatic language; however, in the following steps, we have made efforts to demystify the processes of meta-analysis and ES calculation.

1. *Researchers survey the wide field of educational studies available with an eye for what is relevant to their meta-analysis.* They create keyword lists to help determine the breadth and depth of the search. Published articles, unpublished articles, dissertations, book chapters, and online and other electronic databases are considered for inclusion. Quite simply, they construct a database of all relevant studies.

2. *After an initial examination of the relevant studies, researchers have an idea of the rigor of each study. They craft their own inclusion criteria by asking which studies are good enough to include and which studies should be excluded.* They also pay close attention to the similarities and differences between the studies. Strong results will be based on studies with common purposes and variables. In other words, researchers want to include the studies that are most analogous. For example, if one study defines student achievement in terms of standardized test scores, and another defines student achievement in terms of students' self-reported learning, it is unlikely researchers would include both studies in the same meta-analysis.

3. *Once researchers have identified the studies they will use for a meta-analysis, they examine the results of each study.* Specifically, they look at the ESs of each study in order to mathematically calculate an average ES for the overall meta-analysis. The process behind calculating the ES is quite detailed, but basically it is computed by determining the difference between the mean (average) of the experimental group (the group that has had the benefit of a particular educational practice), and the mean of the control group (the group that has not had the benefit of a particular educational practice), and then dividing the difference by the standard deviation. In simple terms, a *standard deviation* is the average distance each score is from the mean. For example, if the mean of a group of scores is 60, and the standard deviation is 5, then the average distance the scores are from 60 is 5.

To illustrate how an ES is computed, let's assume that one class of science students is the experimental group; their class received attention and engagement-based instruction and took a test on the science content addressed during a specific unit. Another class served as the control group; those students did not receive attention or engagement-based instruction for that unit and took the same test. The experimental group had a mean score of 85 on the test, and the control group had a mean score of 75. The standard deviation for the test given to both groups was 20. The ES for this study would be (85 - 75)/20 or 0.50. This means that the average score in the experimental group is 0.50 of a standard deviation larger than the mean score of the control group.

An advantage of the ES is that a researcher can readily and accurately interpret it in terms of average percentile gain. A percentile gain effectively translates an ES into a language we can understand. How this is done requires a somewhat detailed explanation. Briefly though, an ES is equivalent to a point on the normal distribution, and once you have a point on the normal distribution, you can determine the expected percentile gain (or loss) for someone at the fiftieth percentile. "Conversion of Effect Size to Percentile Gain" lists expected percentile gains for various ESs. If the ES for attention and engagement strategies is 0.50, for example, a teacher could predict that students in the classroom will improve by 19 percentile points. That is, practitioners would predict students scoring at the fiftieth percentile on achievement tests to score at the sixty-ninth percentile after strategies that enhance attention and engagement had been introduced. In general, the higher the ES, the better.

When an average effect size for an educational practice is calculated using a number of studies in a meta-analysis, practitioners can be even surer that the average ES and its associated percentile gain are accurate. Although terms such as *meta-analysis, average effect size,* and *percentile gain* may look daunting at first, they are ultimately employed to describe the widest array of the strongest research and translate the findings into meaningful language for the classroom teacher or school administrator.

Conversion of Effect Size to Percentile Gain

Effect Size	Percentile Gain	Effect Size	Percentile Gain	Effect Size	Percentile Gain	Effect Size	Percentile Gain
0.01	0	0.26	10	0.51	19	0.76	28
0.02	1	0.27	11	0.52	20	0.77	28
0.03	1	0.28	11	0.53	20	0.78	28
0.04	2	0.29	11	0.54	21	0.79	29
0.05	2	0.3	12	0.55	21	0.8	29
0.06	2	0.31	12	0.56	21	0.81	29
0.07	3	0.32	13	0.57	22	0.82	29
0.08	3	0.33	13	0.58	22	0.83	30
0.09	4	0.34	13	0.59	22	0.84	30
0.1	4	0.35	14	0.6	23	0.85	30
0.11	4	0.36	14	0.61	23	0.86	31
0.12	5	0.37	14	0.62	23	0.87	31
0.13	5	0.38	15	0.63	24	0.88	31
0.14	6	0.39	15	0.64	24	0.89	31
0.15	6	0.4	16	0.65	24	0.9	32
0.16	6	0.41	16	0.66	25	0.91	32
0.17	7	0.42	16	0.67	25	0.92	32
0.18	7	0.43	17	0.68	25	0.93	32
0.19	8	0.44	17	0.69	25	0.94	33
0.2	8	0.45	17	0.7	26	0.95	33
0.21	8	0.46	18	0.71	26	0.96	33
0.22	9	0.47	18	0.72	26	0.97	33
0.23	9	0.48	18	0.73	27	0.98	34
0.24	9	0.49	19	0.74	27	0.99	34
0.25	10	0.5	19	0.75	27		

1 of 2

Effect Size	Percentile Gain	Effect Size	Percentile Gain	Effect Size	Percentile Gain	Effect Size	Percentile Gain
1	34	1.25	39	1.5	43	1.75	46
1.01	34	1.26	40	1.51	43	1.76	46
1.02	35	1.27	40	1.52	44	1.77	46
1.03	35	1.28	40	1.53	44	1.78	46
1.04	35	1.29	40	1.54	44	1.79	46
1.05	35	1.3	40	1.55	44	1.8	46
1.06	36	1.31	40	1.56	44	1.81	46
1.07	36	1.32	41	1.57	44	1.82	47
1.08	36	1.33	41	1.58	44	1.83	47
1.09	36	1.34	41	1.59	44	1.84	47
1.1	36	1.35	41	1.6	45	1.85	47
1.11	37	1.36	41	1.61	45	1.86	47
1.12	37	1.37	41	1.62	45	1.87	47
1.13	37	1.38	42	1.63	45	1.88	47
1.14	37	1.39	42	1.64	45	1.89	47
1.15	37	1.4	42	1.65	45	1.9	47
1.16	38	1.41	42	1.66	45	1.91	47
1.17	38	1.42	42	1.67	45	1.92	47
1.18	38	1.43	42	1.68	45	1.93	47
1.19	38	1.44	43	1.69	45	1.94	47
1.2	38	1.45	43	1.7	46	1.95	47
1.21	39	1.46	43	1.71	46	1.96	48
1.22	39	1.47	43	1.72	46	1.97	48
1.23	39	1.48	43	1.73	46	1.98	48
1.24	39	1.49	43	1.74	46	1.99	48

Note: Effect sizes over 2.00 correspond to percentile gains of 49.

APPENDIX C

SAMPLE UNUSUAL INFORMATION

Language Arts

Elementary School

1. The phrases *only choice*, *freezer burn*, and *act naturally* are all oxymorons.

2. The question "Do geese see God?" is a palindrome.

3. *Pinocchio* means *pine eye* in Italian.

4. Dav Pilkey created *Captain Underpants* when he was in second grade (Hatty, 2003).

5. In antiquity, people in Asia and Europe threw old shoes at newly married couples instead of rice or confetti (Panati, 1987).

Middle School

1. Even famous writers had humble beginnings: Amy Tan wrote horoscopes, Henry David Thoreau made pencils, Charles Bukowski was a mail carrier, and L. Frank Baum bred chickens (Barrett & Mingo, 2003; Platt, 2006).

2. Ernest Hemingway's mother dressed him up as a girl when he was young and tried to pass him off as his older sister's twin. She even called him Ernestine in public (Platt, 2006).

3. Ian Fleming was once in espionage training, but he failed when he lost his nerve and could not bring himself to shoot anyone. Ironic considering he later created the famous character James Bond (Platt, 2006).

4. During the process of trying to publish *War of the Worlds*, H. G. Wells was not met with unanimous approval. One publisher said, "An endless nightmare. I do not believe it would take. . . . I think the verdict would be 'Oh don't read that horrid book'" (Barrett & Mingo, 2003).

5. E. B. White was distraught over the death of Charlotte in *Charlotte's Web*. In fact, while he was recording a reading of the book, he had to read that section nineteen times before he could get through it without crying (Barrett & Mingo, 2003).

High School

1. The phrase "the bends" came from the late 1800s when fashionable ladies wore bustles under their skirts to try to accentuate their backsides. They also walked with their upper bodies tilted forward, and this became known as the "Grecian bends." Not long after, when the Brooklyn Bridge was being built, men had to scuba dive to build the underwater foundations. They didn't know about the problem of decompression sickness and when they came out of the water they would lean forward in pain just like the fashionable ladies (Schwarcz, 2003).

2. Anne Sexton once faked her own death to punish a boyfriend for being late for a date; he found her lying in the snow with what looked like blood on her head. They were both hysterical, but only Anne thought it was funny (Platt, 2006).

3. Not every writer admires his peers. In fact, some are known to be quite vicious. T. S. Eliot once said of Henry James, "Henry James had a mind so fine that no idea could violate it" (Barrett & Mingo, 2003, p. 65). Even worse, William Faulkner once said of Mark Twain, "Mark Twain was a hack writer who would have been considered fourth rate in Europe, who tried out a few of the old proven 'sure-fire' literary skeletons with sufficient local color to intrigue the superficial and the lazy" (Barrett & Mingo, 2003, p. 61).

4. The FBI was keeping track of Allen Ginsberg. Among other things, they accused him of being "emotionally unstable [and] potentially dangerous" (Barrett & Mingo, 2003).

5. When John Steinbeck entertained guests, he had an unusual way of keeping the beer cold—he kept it at the bottom of the swimming pool (Platt, 2006).

References

Barrett, E., & Mingo, J. (2003). *It takes a certain type to be a writer: And hundreds of other facts from the world of writing.* York Beach, ME: Conari Press.

Hatty, M. (2003). *Interview: USA weekend.* Accessed at www.pilkey.com/int2.php on March 12, 2010.

Panati, C. (1987). *Extraordinary origins of everyday things.* New York: Perennial Library.

Platt, C. S. (2006). *Real cheesy facts about authors: Everything weird, dumb, and unbelievable you never learned in school.* Birmingham, AL: Crane Hill.

Schwarcz, J. (2003). *Dr. Joe and what you didn't know: 177 fascinating questions and answers about the chemistry of everyday life.* Toronto, Ontario, Canada: ECW Press.

Mathematics

Elementary School

1. Look at the following puzzle. Why are some letters on top of the line and some on the bottom?

    A E F H I K L M N T V W X Y Z

    B C D G J O P Q R S U

    Give up? All the letters made with straight lines are on top, and all the letters with curved lines are on bottom (Coolmath, 2009).

2. Pick any number from 1 to 10 (including 1 or 10). Multiply it by 9. Now add the two digits of your answer together (using a 0 with 9). Did you get 9? I bet you did! (Coolmath, 2009).

3. You won't ever find a light-year on a calendar. Why? Because a light-year measures distance and speed instead of time. A light-year is the distance light can travel in one year.

4. Since the year 2000, the U.S. Mint produced more than twenty-eight billion coins per year (The United States Mint, U.S. Department of the Treasury, 2010).

5. Infinity goes on forever, and while a number doesn't represent infinity, you can see it. How? Hold a small mirror in front of a large mirror. You'll see a mirror inside of a mirror forever (Pappas, 1997).

Middle School

1. Math is not a skill we learn like riding a bike or driving. Rather, man seems to be born with an innate mathematical ability. Even babies show basic math skills (Zimmer, 2009).

2. There is a Nobel Prize for peace, literature, physics, chemistry, and medicine, but not for mathematics. It is rumored that Alfred Nobel had a personal dislike of one of the world's foremost mathematicians at the time and did not want the prize awarded to him, but this has never been proven. No one really knows why mathematics was excluded (Pappas, 1997).

3. If you ever find yourself in the U.S. Capitol building, be careful what you say. As John Quincy Adams discovered, the parabolic ceiling (domed hall) creates unique acoustics. Specifically, the way noise bounces off the domed ceiling creates focal points, and if you happen to stand in one of them, you can clearly hear conversations taking place on the other side of the room. Since Adams's desk happened to sit in one of those focal points, he was able to easily eavesdrop on many private conversations that took place in that room (Pappas, 1989).

4. Numbers affect time itself—or at least how we perceive time. Julius Caesar instituted a calendar during his reign, but it was just a little bit wrong—his measurements were off by eleven minutes a year. No one noticed at the time, but 1,628 years later, the spring equinox was calculated to be in the middle of winter. Pope Gregory XIII implemented a more mathematically correct model, and deleted ten days from the year. In other words, everyone went to sleep one night and woke up ten days later! Understandably, this upset many people; riots even broke out. Many refused to accept the change initially, which meant more chaos for years to come—all because of an eleven-minute miscalculation per year (Beyer, 2003).

5. Lewis Carroll wasn't just a fiction author. He was also a self-taught mathematician. When he couldn't sleep at night, he would write and solve mathematical problems that included algebra, geometry, analytical geometry, and trigonometry. He even published seventy-two of them in a book titled *Pillow Problems* (Pappas, 1989).

High School

1. Arne Beurling was a Swedish mathematician and professor of mathematics. In 1940, the mathematician broke the German code used for strategic military communications. This accomplishment is considered one of the greatest achievements in the history of cryptography. Using only teleprinter tapes and ciphertext, he deciphered the code that the Germans believed impossible to crack in just two weeks. Beurling created a device using a cable that enabled Sweden to decipher German teleprinter traffic passing through Sweden from Norway. When Beurling was asked how he broke the code, he replied, "A magician does not reveal his secrets" (School of Mathematics and Statistics, 2005).

2. *Game theory* is a branch of mathematics that attempts to predict the behavior of a person or people based on potential harms and benefits among opposing individuals. Usually game theory is used in economics, but in 2002 Sasha Dall, a mathematics ecologist, used game theory to successfully predict animal behavior. Specifically, he noticed that young ravens scout food alone but then invite other birds to join in. It is an odd behavior; why would ravens do this? Dall applied game theory and came to a prediction: they do this to ward off territorial adult ravens and to secure dominance over younger or weaker birds. Within a year, Dall's own observations and those of behavioral ecologist Jonathan Wright proved the prediction correct (Grant, 2009).

3. It is a matter of dispute as to who invented calculus. In fact, Sir Isaac Newton in England and Gottfried Leibniz in Germany were both responsible for the accomplishment, but neither man nor the countries each came from were satisfied with that conclusion. Leibniz was the first to publish his theories nationally, and this came as quite a surprise to Newton. He and some of his

patriots sought to discredit Leibniz by accusing him of having stolen the work from Newton—of course there was never much evidence to support the claims. In 1711, Leibniz appealed to the Royal Society in England, asking that they settle the dispute. The society voted in favor of Newton, but that was because he had chosen the committee members and drafted the final report himself. It wasn't until both men died that those with impartial views were able to blend the nuances of both men's work and create a unified calculus (Pappas, 1997).

4. The Fibonacci sequence appears in nautilus shells, pinecones, many flowers, and cacti. In 2004, two mathematicians working for the University of Arizona discovered that the structure of the cacti is based on the Fibonacci sequence, and that this particular structure helps the plant carry out the necessities of survival while expending minimum energy. The mathematicians postulated that this discovery might be relevant to medical science. By applying "mathematical models of pattern formation" the mathematicians believe scientists could discover the key to things like tumor formation (Stone, 2004).

5. Think human rights issues are only found in social studies? Wrong. Hypatia is known as the first woman of note in mathematics. She became the head of the Neoplatonist school in Alexandria around 400 CE and was known as an excellent teacher and lecturer. In addition to being a woman, she was a pagan during a time of intolerance for anything other than Christianity. To make matters even worse, she was known for publicly opposing the policies of the Roman Empire. She was obviously a threat, specifically to Cyril, the patriarch of Alexandria, who is thought to have galvanized a fanatical Christian mob to murder her in 415 CE (Hypatia, 2010).

References

Beyer, R. (2003). *The greatest stories never told: 100 tales from history to astonish, bewilder, and stupefy.* New York: HarperCollins.

Coolmath. (2009). *Coolmath4kids.* Accessed at www.coolmath4kids.com/math_puzzles/a1-alphabetsoup_sol.html on March 15, 2010.

Grant, A. (2009). Animal intelligence: Darwin plays game theory—and wins. *Discover Magazine.* Accessed at http://discovermagazine.com/2009/jun/04-game-theory-meets-darwin on March 12, 2010.

Hypatia. (2010). In *Encyclopædia Britannica.* Chicago: Encyclopædia Britannica Online. Accessed at www.britannica.com/EBchecked/topic/279463/Hypatia on March 10, 2010.

Pappas, T. (1989). *The joy of mathematics: Discovering mathematics all around you* (Rev. ed.). San Carlos, CA: Wide World/Tetra.

Pappas, T. (1997). *Mathematical scandals.* San Carlos, CA: Wide World/Tetra.

School of Mathematics and Statistics. (2005). *Arne Carl-August Beurling.* Accessed at www-history.mcs.st-and.ac.uk/Biographies/Beurling.html on March 18, 2010.

Stone, A. (2004). Fibonacci cactus. *Discover Magazine.* Accessed at http://discover magazine.com/2004/jul/fibonacci-cactus0708 on May 27, 2010.

The United States Mint, U.S. Department of the Treasury. (2010). *Historian's corner: Coin production.* Accessed at www.ustreas.gov/education/faq/coins/production .shtml on May 27, 2010.

Zimmer, C. (2009). The brain: Humanity's other basic instinct: Math. *Discover Magazine.* Accessed at http://discovermagazine.com/2009/nov/17-the-brain-humanity.s-other -basic-instinct-math on March 12, 2010.

Science

Elementary School

1. Arabella and Anita were spiders, but they were also astronauts! A high school student named Judy Miles wondered if spiders could spin webs in space, so she suggested to NASA that they find out. NASA actually liked her idea! On August 5, 1973, Arabella and Anita were launched into space aboard the *Skylab 2.* They didn't do so well with webs at first; the spiders were disoriented and spun sloppy webs. But by day three, they had adjusted and spun webs like always. They were finer, but scientists had expected that. Who knew that spiders really *can* spin webs in space? (Smithsonian Center for Education and Museum Studies, 2010).

2. Male red-eyed tree frogs shake their bums to threaten each other (Discover Magazine, 2010).

3. Parent robins feed their chicks about one hundred meals each day (DLTK, 2009).

4. An adult human has 206 bones, but children have 300 bones (High-Tech Productions, 2010).

5. We blink roughly 4.2 million times each year (High-Tech Productions, 2010).

Middle School

1. It would take one thousand Earths to fill Jupiter, but it rotates so quickly that one day only lasts about ten hours. Because of this and other factors, it isn't totally round. It bulges at the equator and is flatter at the poles (Gierasch & Nicholson, 2004).

2. Nine percent of all human beings ever born are alive at this moment (Wilford, 1981).

3. Kids have sixty thousand miles of blood vessels, and adults have about one hundred thousand miles of blood vessels (if you were to put them end to end) (The Franklin Institute, 2010).

4. Many Greek philosophers around 500 BC began to study the properties of light. It was first imagined that human beings are able to see because the eye sent out a ray of light that illuminated the world (Light, 2010).

5. Have you ever heard of a spider that can eat a snake? The goliath bird-eating tarantula can. It can grow up to a foot in length, and can also eat mice, frogs, and toads (Smithsonian National Zoological Park, n.d.).

High School

1. The Chinese may have invented gunpowder as early as 100 BC, but they meant for it to be an elixir for immortality (Xinzhen, 2008).

2. Dead skin accounts for about a billion tons of dust in the atmosphere. A person's skin sheds about fifty thousand cells every minute (Markey, 2007).

3. Phosphorus was discovered in 1669 by Hennig Brand, a German merchant whose hobby was alchemy. Brand allowed fifty buckets of urine to stand until they putrefied and "bred worms." He then boiled the urine down to a paste and heated it with sand, thereby distilling elemental phosphorus from the mixture. (Phosphorus, 2010).

4. Behrad Khamesee is a microbiologist who created a flying robot roughly the size of a pencil eraser. It is operated wirelessly, and it has a tiny little pair of grippers. Ultimately, Khamesee hopes to advance his tiny robot to the point that it can fly around in the human body. He notes many possible purposes for this, one being that it could deliver drugs to targeted places in the body. Just imagine swallowing a little robot instead of a pill (Mayer, 2010)!

5. A moth exists in Madagascar that targets sleeping birds. It uses its barbed proboscis to pry open the bird's eyelids and drink its tears. Talk about a weird way to drink (Moseman, 2010)!

References

Discover Magazine. (2010). Tree frogs shake their bums to send threatening vibes. *Discover Magazine.* Accessed at http://blogs.discovermagazine.com/notrocketscience/2010/05/20/tree-frogs-shake-their-bums-to-send-threatening-vibes/ on May 27, 2010.

DLTK. (2009). *American robin.* Accessed at www.kidzone.ws/animals/birds/american-robin.htm on March 12, 2010.

The Franklin Institute. (2010). *Blood vessels: Tubular circulation.* Philadelphia: Author. Accessed at www.fi.edu/learn/heart/vessels/vessels.html on March 12, 2010.

Gierasch, P. J., & Nicholson, P. D. (2004). Jupiter. In *World book online reference center.* Washington, DC: World Book at NASA. Accessed at www.nasa.gov/worldbook/jupiter_worldbook.html on March 12, 2010.

High-Tech Productions. (2010). *Fun science facts you didn't know.* Accessed at www.hightechscience.org/funfacts.htm on March 12, 2010.

Light. (2010). In *Encyclopædia Britannica.* Chicago: Encyclopædia Britannica Online. Accessed at www.britannica.com/EBchecked/topic/340440/light on March 18, 2010.

Markey, S. (2007). 20 things you didn't know about skin: Flesh-based ID tags, people with no fingerprints, and more. *Discover Magazine.* Accessed at http://discover magazine.com/2007/feb/20-things-skin on March 12, 2010.

Mayer, H. (2010). The latest trend in aircraft: Really, really tiny. *Discover Magazine.* Accessed at http://discovermagazine.com/2010/mar/04-latest-trend-in-aircraft-really-tiny-microflier on March 12, 2010.

Moseman, A. (2010). How animals suck: 9 creatures that slurp creatively. *Discover Magazine.* Accessed at http://discovermagazine.com/photos/02-how-animals-suck-9-creatures-with-inventive-slurping-techniques on March 12, 2010.

Phosphorus (P). (2010). In *Encyclopædia Britannica.* Chicago: Encyclopædia Britannica Online. Accessed at www.britannica.com/EBchecked/topic/457568/phosphorus on March 12, 2010.

Smithsonian Center for Education and Museum Studies. (2010). *Secrets of the Smithsonian: Spiders in space.* Accessed at www.smithsonianeducation.org/students/secrets_of_the_Smithsonian/spiders_in_space.html on March 12, 2010.

Smithsonian National Zoological Park. (n.d.). *Goliath bird-eating tarantula.* Accessed at http://nationalzoo.si.edu/Animals/PhotoGallery/Invertebrates/4.cfm on March 12, 2010.

Wilford, J. N. (1981). 9 percent of everyone who ever lived is alive now. *New York Times.* Accessed at www.nytimes.com/1981/10/06/science/9-percent-of-everyone-who-ever-lived-is-alive-now.html on March 12, 2010.

Xinzhen, L. (2008). The mother of invention: China's four great ancient inventions have left their mark on local and global development. *Beijing Review, 35,* 46–47. Accessed at http://media.web.britannica.com/ebsco/pdf/34/34233360.pdf on March 12, 2010.

Social Studies

Elementary School

1. The shortest war in history was between the United Kingdom and Zanzibar in 1896—it lasted thirty-eight minutes (Lagan, 2009).

2. Louis Braille invented Braille when he was just thirteen years old! He perfected the system by the time he was fifteen (Beyer, 2003).

3. In 1836, Mexican General Santa Anna held a state funeral for his leg (Burns & Ives, 2001).

4. Gertrude Ederle was the first woman to swim the English Channel. She did it in 1926, at a time when only five men had risen to the challenge. Her time was roughly fourteen and a half hours, which was better than the fastest man by roughly two hours (Smithsonian National Museum of American History, n.d.)!

5. In the eighteenth century, people didn't use clocks to tell time! They used the sun, the stars, and information in an almanac instead (Smithsonian National Museum of American History, 2007).

Middle School

1. Eratosthenes (276–196 BC) was the first to use the word *geography,* and he measured—quite closely—the circumference of the Earth using little more than a shadow and a well (Davis, 1992).

2. Almost as many Americans fought *for* Britain in the Revolutionary War as fought *against* it. In 1780, there were nine thousand soldiers in Washington's army and eight thousand loyalist soldiers in the British army (Shenkman, 1988).

3. The *Mayflower* was originally headed for Virginia when a storm blew the ship all the way up to Massachusetts. Instead of making their way back down the coast though, the crew members landed at Plymouth Rock. Why? They had run out of beer. One of the first things they did upon landing was create a brewhouse (Beyer, 2003).

4. Bjarni Herjólfsson was trying to find Greenland when a series of storms blew his boat off course. When the weather cleared, he and his crew spotted land, but because it had neither mountains nor glaciers, he knew it wasn't Greenland. His crew desperately wanted him to land, but he didn't. He simply wanted to go home. Later, he told a friend the story of that trip. That friend was Leif Eriksson, and the land Herjólfsson ignored was the Americas (Beyer, 2003).

5. When Europe discovered coffee in the late 16th century, the Vatican believed it to be satanic. Pope Clement VIII tasted it and found it delicious. It is rumored that he lamented the infidels should be the only ones drinking it, so he gave coffee a papal blessing (Beyer, 2003).

High School

1. Shortly before the collapse of the Confederacy, Jefferson Davis authorized a diplomat to inform Britain and France that the Confederacy would emancipate the slaves in exchange for official recognition as an independent country (Shenkman, 1988).

2. In 1938, Hitler was voted *Time* magazine's Man of the Year. Stalin was voted Man of the Year in 1939 (*Time,* 2010).

3. In 1533, the Inca Empire was six million strong, and it was nearly twice the size of Texas. It also had an army of almost eight thousand men and a large supply of gold. Francisco Pizarro was a simple Spanish conquistador traveling with 150 men, but Pizarro was not intimidated. He persuaded the Incan Emperor Atahualpa to meet with him, and when the emperor arrived, Pizarro and his small army attacked. The ambush killed thousands and Pizarro captured Atahualpa. The surprise threw the Incans into disarray, and eventually Pizarro and his 150 men reduced the entire empire to ruins (Beyer, 2003).

4. In 1856, sixty Arab chieftains gathered in the French colony of Algeria. Why? The chieftains were from a local tribe who used magic tricks, such as fire-eating, to convince their followers to overthrow the French. The tricks proved the tribesmen had supernatural powers that could help them defeat the French and establish new leadership. The French asked famed magician Jean Eugène Robert-Houdin to perform for the chieftains to prove France was more powerful. During the performance, Robert-Houdin caught a bullet and made a member of the audience disappear, among other tricks. The audience was stunned. But Robert-Houdin didn't stop there. He sent out translators to explain how the tribesmen performed their tricks, thus stripping the chieftains of their "magic." The rebellion was squashed (Beyer, 2003).

5. It is quite possible that three cigars helped secure the Union victory in the American Civil War. How? When the Indiana regiment of the Union army stopped to rest in a place the Confederates had been a few days prior, a few soldiers discovered an envelope. Inside were three cigars wrapped in a piece of paper. While smoking, one of the soldiers idly opened that piece of paper and found the marching orders for General Lee's army. Clearly a Confederate had lost the envelope along the way. The orders were sent to General McClellan. As a result, the Confederates lost the Battle of Antietam—a key victory for the Union and the bloodiest single-day battle in the history of the United States (Beyer, 2003).

References

Beyer, R. (2003). *The greatest stories never told: 100 tales from history to astonish, bewilder, and stupefy.* New York: HarperCollins.

Burns, K. (Executive Producer), & Ives, S. (Director). (2001). *New perspectives on the west: Antonio López de Santa Anna* [Television documentary]. New York and Washington, DC: Public Broadcasting Service. Accessed at www.pbs.org/weta/thewest/people/s_z/santaanna.htm on March 12, 2010.

Davis, K. C. (1992). *Don't know much about geography: Everything you need to know about the world but never learned.* New York: Morrow.

Lagan, D. (2009). *The shortest war in history.* Accessed at www.militaryhistory.org/2009/09/the-shortest-war-in-history on March 12, 2010.

Shenkman, R. (1988). *Legends, lies, and cherished myths of American history.* New York: Harper Perennial.

Smithsonian National Museum of American History. (2007). *On time: How America has learned to live by the clock.* Accessed at http://americanhistory.si.edu/ontime/marking/index.html on March 12, 2010.

Smithsonian National Museum of American History. (n.d.). *Gertrude Ederle: First woman to swim the English Channel.* Accessed at http://americanhistory.si.edu/sports/exhibit/firsts/ederle/index.cfm on March 10, 2010.

Time. (2010). Person of the year: 1930s. *Time.* Accessed at www.time.com/time/personoftheyear/archive/covers/1930.html on March 12, 2010.

APPENDIX D

PLANNING QUESTIONS

Planning Questions

Daily Strategies	
Pacing	**What Will I Do?**
Do I have appropriate routines in place for the administrative tasks I will be using today?	
Am I aware of the transitions between activities I will use today and the plan for how to address those transitions?	
Do I have activities planned for students who finish their seatwork early?	
What will I do to remain aware of moving too slowly or too quickly when presenting new content?	
Intensity and Enthusiasm	**What Will I Do?**
Which aspects of the content addressed today am I particularly enthused about?	
How will I demonstrate my enthusiasm? • Personal stories • Verbal and nonverbal signals • Reviving the zest for teaching	
Teacher-Student and Peer Relationships	**What Will I Do?**
What can I do today to ensure fair and equitable treatment for all students? • Ensure students are not teased or bullied • Establish expectations for fair and equitable treatment	
Are there ways of showing interest in and affection for students that I will use in class today? • Simple courtesies • Using physical contact and physical gestures • Attending to students' needs and concerns	
How can I gather positive information to use in building relationships? • Structured opportunities to highlight students' interests and accomplishments • Parents and guardians • Fellow teachers	
Verbal Feedback	**What Will I Do?**
During what activities today could I provide praise and feedback to students?	
What are some phrases I should avoid when providing praise and feedback?	
What are some phrases I should use when providing praise and feedback?	

1 of 4

Opportunistic Strategies	
Physical Movement	**What Will I do?**
What opportunities are there today to introduce physical movement?	
What techniques will best fit into today's lesson? • Movement to lift energy • Movement that furthers understanding of content • Movement for the whole class or school	
Humor	**What Will I Do?**
Can I incorporate humor into any of the addressed content?	
What strategies will I use? • Self-directed humor • Funny headlines or quotes • Movie clips and media entertainment • A class symbol for humor	
Games and Inconsequential Competition	**What Will I Do?**
Is there content I can effectively review using games?	
What types of games best fit this content?	
Friendly Controversy	**What Will I Do?**
Could I incorporate friendly controversy into any of the addressed content?	
What strategy will I use to stimulate friendly controversy? • Class vote • Debate model • Town hall meeting • Legal model • Perspective analysis	
Unusual Information	**What Will I Do?**
Could I incorporate unusual information into any of the addressed content?	
How will I use unusual information? • To introduce a lesson • To allow students to research and collect interesting facts • By inviting guest speakers	
Questions and Response Rates	**What Will I Do?**
What content should I ask questions about?	

2 of 4

What techniques should I use to increase the effectiveness of my questions? • Call on students randomly • Use paired response • Use wait time • Use response chaining • Invite choral response • Use simultaneous individual response	
Students' Lives	**What Will I Do?**
Could I incorporate comparisons to students' lives in any of the addressed content?	
What categories will I use for the comparisons? • Physical characteristics • Processes • Sequences of events • Cause-and-effect relationships • Psychological characteristics • Fame or notoriety • Analogies	
Students' Life Ambitions	**What Will I Do?**
Are there specific units or courses I can use personal projects in?	
How long will the projects last?	
How much time will I spend each week on the projects?	
Application of Knowledge	**What Will I Do?**
Does the content being addressed lend itself to authentic applications to real-world issues?	
Is there a problem that can be solved or studied using the content?	
Is there a decision that can be made or studied using the content?	
Is there a hypothesis that can be tested or studied using the content?	
Is there an issue that can be investigated using the content?	
Am I allowing students to make choices using cognitively complex processes?	
What choices of response formats could I offer to students?	
How might I provide choice in learning goals?	
How will I provide choice in behavior?	

3 of 4

Progress	What Will I Do?
Can students track their progress over time on any of the addressed content?	
How will I design the scale students will use to track their progress?	
How will I facilitate students' setting of personal goals and development of strategies to attain these goals?	
How will I design the scale students will use to track their effort?	

Examples of Self-Efficacy	What Will I Do?
Are there specific units or courses that could provide examples of efficacy?	
How can I use stories in these situations?	
How can I use quotations in these situations?	

Self-Efficacy	What Will I Do?
Can I teach efficacy through any content that has been covered or will be covered?	
What sources will I use to teach efficacy?	
How will I make the distinction between the growth theory and fixed theory?	
How will I facilitate students identifying their own perspective?	
How will I keep the conversation about the two perspectives going in class?	

REFERENCES AND RESOURCES

Alberti, R. E., & Emmons, M. L. (1982). *Your perfect right: A guide to assertive living* (4th ed.). San Luis Obispo, CA: Impact.

Ames, C. (1984). Competitive, cooperative, and individualistic goal structures: A cognitive motivational analysis. In R. Ames & C. Ames (Eds.), *Research on motivation in education: Vol. 1, Student motivation* (pp. 177–207). Orlando, FL: Academic Press.

Anderson, J. R. (1995). *Learning and memory: An integrated approach.* New York: Wiley.

Arlin, M. (1979). Teacher transitions can disrupt time flow in classrooms. *American Education Research Journal, 16,* 42–56.

Armento, B. J. (1978). *Teacher behavior and effective teaching of concepts.* Paper presented at the annual meeting of the American Association of Colleges for Teacher Education, Chicago, IL. (ERIC Document Reproduction Service No. ED153949)

Aronson, J., Fried, C. B., & Good, C. (2002). Reducing the effects of stereotype threat on African American college students by shaping theories of intelligence. *Journal of Experimental Social Psychology, 38,* 113–125.

Association for Supervision and Curriculum Development. (2009). *21st century skills: Promoting creativity and innovation in the classroom* [DVD]. Alexandria, VA: Author.

Barrett, E., & Mingo, J. (2003). *It takes a certain type to be a writer: And hundreds of other facts from the world of writing.* York Beach, ME: Conari Press.

Bettencourt, E. M., Gillett, M. H., Gall, M. D., & Hull, R. E. (1983). Effects of teacher enthusiasm training on student on-task behavior and achievement. *American Educational Research Journal, 20,* 435–450.

Beyer, R. (2003). *The greatest stories never told: 100 tales from history to astonish, bewilder, and stupefy.* New York: HarperCollins.

Blackwell, L. S., Trzesniewski, K. H., & Dweck, C. S. (2007). Implicit theories of intelligence predict achievement across an adolescent transition: A longitudinal study and an intervention. *Child Development, 78,* 246–263.

Boekaerts, M. (2009). Goal-directed behavior in the classroom. In K. R. Wentzel & A. Wigfield (Eds.), *Handbook of motivation at school* (pp. 105–122). New York: Routledge.

BrainyMedia. (2010). *BrainyQuote*. Accessed at www.brainyquote.com on March 12, 2010.

Broadhurst, A. R., & Darnell, D. K. (1965). An introduction to cybernetics and information theory. *Quarterly Journal of Speech, 51*, 442–453.

Brophy, J. E. (2004). *Motivating students to learn* (2nd ed.). Mahwah, NJ: Erlbaum.

Buckner, R. L., & Barch, D. (1999). Images in neuroscience: Memory 1—Episodic memory retrieval. *American Journal of Psychiatry, 156*, 1311.

Burns, K. (Executive Producer), & Ives, S. (Director). (2001). *New perspectives on the west: Antonio López de Santa Anna* [Television documentary]. New York and Washington, DC: Public Broadcasting Service. Accessed at www.pbs.org/weta/thewest/people/s_z/santaanna.htm on March 12, 2010.

Cahill, L., Gorski, L., & Le, K. (2003). Enhanced human memory consolidation with post-learning stress: Interactions with the degree of arousal at encoding. *Learning and Memory, 10*(4), 270–274.

Carleton, L. A., & Marzano, R. J. (2010). *Vocabulary games for the classroom*. Bloomington, IN: Marzano Research Laboratory.

Coats, W. D., & Smidchens, U. (1966). Audience recall as a function of speaker dynamism. *Journal of Educational Psychology, 57*, 189–191.

Cohen, I., & Goldsmith, M. (2003). *Hands on: How to use brain gym in the classroom*. Ventura, CA: Edu-Kinesthetics.

Colcombe, S. J., & Kramer, A. F. (2003). Fitness effects on the cognitive function of older adults: A meta-analytic study. *Psychological Science, 14*, 125–130.

Colvin, G. (2008). *Talent is overrated: What really separates world-class performers from everybody else*. New York: Portfolio.

Coolmath. (2009). *Coolmath4kids*. Accessed at www.coolmath4kids.com/math_puzzles/a1-alphabetsoup_sol.html on March 15, 2010.

Coloroso, B. (2003). *The bully, the bullied, and the bystander: From preschool to high school—How parents and teachers can help break the cycle of violence*. New York: HarperResource.

Covington, M. V., & Teel, K. M. (1996). *Overcoming student failure: Changing motives and incentives for learning*. Washington, DC: American Psychological Association.

Coyle, D. (2009). *The talent code: Greatness isn't born. It's grown. Here's how*. New York: Bantam Books.

Cross, S. E., & Markus, H. R. (1994). Self-schemas, possible selves, and competent performance. *Journal of Educational Psychology, 86*, 423–438.

Csikszentmihalyi, M. (1990). *Flow: The psychology of optimal experience*. New York: Harper & Row.

Darnell, D. K. (1970). Clozentropy: A procedure for testing English language proficiency of foreign students. *Speech Monographs, 37*(1), 36–46.

Darnell, D. (1972). Information theory: An approach to human communication. In R. W. Budd & B. D. Ruben (Eds.), *Approaches to human communication* (pp. 156–169). New York: Spartan Books.

Davis, K. C. (1992). *Don't know much about geography: Everything you need to know about the world but never learned*. New York: Morrow.

Dennett, D. C. (1969). *Content and consciousness*. London: Routledge & Paul.

Dennett, D. C. (1991). *Consciousness explained*. Boston: Little, Brown and Company.

Dennison, P. E., & Dennison, G. E. (1986). *Brain gym: Simple activities for whole brain learning*. Ventura, CA: Edu-Kinesthetics.

Diener, C. I., & Dweck, C. S. (1978). An analysis of learned helplessness: Continuous changes in performance, strategy, and achievement cognitions following failure. *Journal of Personality and Social Psychology, 36*, 451–462.

Discover Magazine. (2010). Tree frogs shake their bums to send threatening vibes. *Discover Magazine*. Accessed at http://blogs.discovermagazine.com/notrocketscience/2010/05/20/tree-frogs-shake -their-bums-to-send-threatening-vibes/ on May 27, 2010.

DLTK. (2009). *American robin*. Accessed at www.kidzone.ws/animals/birds/american-robin.htm on March 12, 2010.

Dweck, C. S. (2000). *Self-theories: Their role in motivation, personality, and development*. Philadelphia: Psychology Press.

Dweck, C. S. (2006). *Mindset: The new psychology of success*. New York: Random House.

Dweck, C. S., & Master, A. (2009). Self-theories and motivation: Students' beliefs about intelligence. In K. R. Wentzel & A. Wigfield (Eds.), *Handbook of motivation at school* (pp. 123–140). New York: Routledge.

Dwyer, T., Blizzard, L., & Dean, K. (1996). Physical activity and performance in children. *Nutrition Review, 54*(4, Pt. 2), 27–31.

Dwyer, T., Sallis, J. F., Blizzard, L., Lazarus, R., & Dean, K. (2001). Relation of academic performance to physical activity and fitness in children. *Pediatric Exercise Science, 13*, 225–237.

Ebbinghaus, H. (1987). Regarding a new application of performance testing and its use with school children. *Journal of Psychology and Physiology, 13*, 225–237.

Emmer, E. T., & Gerwels, M. C. (2006). Classroom management in middle and high school classrooms. In C. M. Evertson & C. S. Weinstein (Eds.), *Handbook of classroom management: Research, practice, and contemporary issues* (pp. 407–437). Mahwah, NJ: Erlbaum.

Epstein, J. A., & Harackiewicz, J. (1992). Winning is not enough: The effects of competition and achievement orientation on intrinsic interest. *Personality and Social Psychology Bulletin, 18*, 128–138.

Ericsson, K. A. (Ed.). (1996). *The road to excellence: The acquisition of expert performance in the arts and sciences, sports, and games*. Mahwah, NJ: Erlbaum.

Erwin, J. C. (2004). *The classroom of choice: Giving students what they need and getting what you want*. Alexandria, VA: Association for Supervision and Curriculum Development.

Federal Reserve Bank of San Francisco. (2010). *Fun facts about money*. San Francisco: Author. Accessed at www.frbsf.org/federalreserve/money/funfacts.html on March 12, 2010.

Flatow, I. (1992). *They all laughed . . . from light bulbs to lasers: The fascinating stories behind the great inventions that have changed our lives*. New York: HarperCollins.

The Franklin Institute. (2010). *Blood vessels: Tubular circulation*. Philadelphia: Author. Accessed at www.fi.edu/learn/heart/vessels/vessels.html on March 12, 2010.

Gayle, B. M., Preiss, R. W., & Allen, M. (2006). How effective are teacher-initiated classroom questions in enhancing student learning? In B. M. Gayle, R. W. Preiss, N. Burrell, & M. Allen (Eds.), *Classroom communication and instructional processes: Advances through meta-analysis* (pp. 279–293). Mahwah, NJ: Erlbaum.

Gierasch, P. J., & Nicholson, P. D. (2004). Jupiter. In *World book online reference center*. Washington, DC: World Book at NASA. Accessed at www.nasa.gov/worldbook/jupiter_worldbook.html on March 12, 2010.

Gliessman, D. H., Pugh, R. C., Dowden, D. E., & Hutchins, T. F. (1988). Variables influencing the acquisition of a generic teaching skill. *Review of Educational Research, 58*, 25–46.

Good, C., Aronson, J., & Inzlicht, M. (2003). Improving adolescents' standardized test performance: An intervention to reduce the effects of stereotype threat. *Journal of Applied Developmental Psychology, 24*, 645–662.

Good, T. L., & Brophy, J. E. (2003). *Looking in classrooms* (9th ed.). Boston: Allyn & Bacon.

Goodenow, C. (1993). Classroom belonging among early adolescent students: Relationships to motivation and achievement. *Journal of Early Adolescence, 13*, 21–43.

Grant, A. (2009). Animal intelligence: Darwin plays game theory—and wins. *Discover Magazine*. Accessed at http://discovermagazine.com/2009/jun/04-game-theory-meets-darwin on March 12, 2010.

Grant, H., & Dweck, C. S. (2001). Cross-cultural response to failure: Considering outcome attributions with different goals. In F. Salili, C.-Y. Chiu, & Y.-Y. Hong (Eds.), *Student motivation: The culture and context of learning* (pp. 203–219). New York: Kluwer Academic.

Graseck, S. (2009). Teaching with controversy. *Educational Leadership, 67*(1), 45–49.

Hannaford, C. (1995). *Smart moves: Why learning is not all in your head*. Arlington, VA: Great Ocean.

Hattie, J. A. C. (2009). *Visible learning: A synthesis of over 800 meta-analyses relating to achievement*. New York: Routledge.

Hatty, M. (2003). *Interview: USA weekend*. Accessed at www.pilkey.com/int2.php on March 12, 2010.

Harter, S. (1982). The perceived competence scale for children. *Child Development, 53*, 218–235.

Haystead, M., & Marzano, R. J. (2009). *Meta-analytic synthesis of studies conducted at Marzano Research Laboratory on instructional strategies*. Englewood, CO: Marzano Research Laboratory.

Hess, D. E. (2009). *Controversy in the classroom: The democratic power of discussion*. New York: Routledge.

Hidi, S., & Baird, W. (1986). Interestingness—A neglected variable in discourse processing. *Cognitive Science, 10,* 179–194.

High-Tech Productions. (2010). *Fun science facts you didn't know.* Accessed at www.hightechscience .org/funfacts.htm on March 12, 2010.

Hoose, P. M. (1993). *It's our world, too! Stories of young people who are making a difference.* Boston: Joy Street Books.

Hosseini, K. (2009). Heroes & icons: Suraya Pakzad. *Time.* Accessed at www.time.com/time/specials/ packages/article/0,28804,1894410_1894289_1894277,00.html on March 12, 2010.

Hypatia. (2010). In *Encyclopædia Britannica.* Chicago: Encyclopædia Britannica Online. Accessed at www.britannica.com/EBchecked/topic/279463/Hypatia on March 10, 2010.

Ito, T. A., Larsen, J. T., Smith, N. K., & Cacioppo, J. T. (2002). Negative information weighs more heavily on the brain: The negativity bias in evaluative categorizations. In J. T. Cacioppo (Ed.), *Foundations in social neuroscience* (pp. 576–597). Cambridge, MA: MIT Press.

Jacobs, H. H. (2010). *Curriculum 21: Essential education for a changing world.* Alexandria, VA: Association for Supervision and Curriculum Development.

Jensen, E. (2005). *Teaching with the brain in mind* (2nd ed.). Alexandria, VA: Association for Supervision and Curriculum Development.

Johnson, D. W., & Johnson, R. (1979). Conflict in the classroom: Controversy and learning. *Review of Educational Research, 49*(1), 51–69.

Johnson, D. W., & Johnson, R. (1985). Classroom conflict: Controversy versus debate in learning groups. *American Education Research Journal, 22*(2), 237–256.

Jonas, P. M. (2010). *Laughing and learning: An alternative to shut up and listen.* Lanham, MD: Rowman & Littlefield Education.

Kay, K. (2010). 21st century skills: Why they matter, what they are, and how we get there. In J. Bellanca & R. Brandt (Eds.), *21st century skills: Rethinking how students learn.* Bloomington, IN: Solution Tree Press.

Kepner Middle School. (2010). *Kepner Education Excellence Program.* Accessed at www.keepdenver .org on March 15, 2010.

Kubesch, S., Walk, L., Spitzer, M., Kammer, T., Lainburg, A., Heim, R., et al. (2009). A 30-minute physical education program improves students' executive attention. *Mind, Brain, and Education, 3*(4), 235–242.

Ladd, G. W., Herald-Brown, S. L., & Kochel, K. P. (2009). Peers and motivation. In K. R. Wentzel & A. Wigfield (Eds.), *Handbook of motivation at school* (pp. 323–348). New York: Routledge.

Lagan, D. (2009). *The shortest war in history.* Accessed at www.militaryhistory.org/2009/09/the -shortest-war-in-history on March 12, 2010.

Land, M. L. (1980). *Joint effects of teacher structure and teacher enthusiasm on student achievement.* Paper presented at the annual meeting of the Southwest Educational Research Association, San Antonio, TX. (ERIC Document Reproduction Service No. ED182310)

Le Couteur, P., & Burreson, J. (2004). *Napoleon's buttons: 17 molecules that changed history.* New York: Tarcher/Penguin.

Lewis, B. A. (1992). *Kids with courage: True stories about young people making a difference.* Minneapolis, MN: Free Spirit.

Light. (2010). In *Encyclopædia Britannica.* Chicago: Encyclopædia Britannica Online. Accessed at www .britannica.com/EBchecked/topic/340440/light on March 18, 2010.

Loewenstein, G. (1994). The psychology of curiosity: A review and reinterpretation. *Psychological Bulletin, 116,* 75–98.

Lowry, N., & Johnson, D. W. (1981). Effects of controversy on epistemic curiosity, achievement, and attitudes. *Journal of Social Psychology, 115*(1), 31–43.

Markey, S. (2007). 20 things you didn't know about skin: Flesh-based ID tags, people with no fingerprints, and more. *Discover Magazine.* Accessed at http://discovermagazine.com/2007/feb/20 -things-skin on March 12, 2010.

Markus, H., & Nurius, P. (1986). Possible selves. *American Psychologist, 41,* 954–969.

Markus, H., & Ruvolo, A. (1989). Possible selves: Personalized representations of goals. In L. A. Pervin (Ed.), *Goal concepts in personality and social psychology* (pp. 211–241). Hillsdale, NJ: Erlbaum.

Marzano, R. J. (1992). *A different kind of classroom: Teaching with dimensions of learning.* Alexandria, VA: Association for Supervision and Curriculum Development.

Marzano, R. J. (2003). *Classroom management that works: Research-based strategies for every teacher.* Alexandria, VA: Association for Supervision and Curriculum Development.

Marzano, R. J. (2004). *Building background knowledge for academic achievement: Research on what works in schools.* Alexandria, VA: Association for Supervision and Curriculum Development.

Marzano, R. J. (2007). *The art and science of teaching: A comprehensive framework for effective instruction.* Alexandria, VA: Association for Supervision and Curriculum Development.

Marzano, R. J. (2009). *Designing and teaching learning goals and objectives.* Bloomington, IN: Marzano Research Laboratory.

Marzano, R. J. (2010). *Formative assessment and standards-based grading.* Bloomington, IN: Marzano Research Laboratory.

Marzano, R. J., & Brown, J. L. (2009). *A handbook for the art and science of teaching.* Alexandria, VA: Association for Supervision and Curriculum Development.

Marzano, R. J., Gaddy, B. B., Foseid, M. C., Foseid, M. P., & Marzano, J. S. (2005). *A handbook for classroom management that works.* Alexandria, VA: Association for Supervision and Curriculum Development.

Marzano, R. J., & Marzano, J. S. (2009). The inner game of teaching. In R. J. Marzano (Ed.), *On excellence in teaching* (pp. 345–368). Bloomington, IN: Solution Tree Press.

Marzano, R. J., Paynter, D. E., & Doty, J. K. (2003). *The pathfinder project: Exploring the power of one, teacher's manual.* Conifer, CO: Pathfinder Education.

Marzano, R. J., Pickering, D. J., & Pollock, J. E. (2001). *Classroom instruction that works: Research-based strategies for increasing student achievement.* Alexandria, VA: Association for Supervision and Curriculum Development.

Mastin, V. (1963). Teacher enthusiasm. *Journal of Educational Research, 56,* 385–386.

Mayer, H. (2010). The latest trend in aircraft: Really, really tiny. *Discover Magazine.* Accessed at http://discovermagazine.com/2010/mar/04-latest-trend-in-aircraft-really-tiny-microflier on March 12, 2010.

McCombs, B. (1984). Processes and skills underlying intrinsic motivation to learn: Toward a definition of motivational skills training intervention. *Educational Psychologist, 19,* 197–218.

McCombs, B. L. (1986). The role of the self-system in self-regulated learning. *Contemporary Educational Psychology, 11,* 314–332.

McCombs, B. L. (1989). Self-regulated learning and academic achievement: A phenomenological view. In B. J. Zimmerman & D. H. Schunk (Eds.), *Self-regulated learning and academic achievement: Theory, research, and practice* (pp. 51–82). New York: Springer-Verlag.

McCombs, B. L, & Marzano, R. J. (1990). Putting the self in self-regulated learning: The self as agent in integrating will and skill. *Educational Psychologist, 25,* 51–69.

McConnell, J. W. (1977). *Relationships between selected teacher behaviors and attitudes/achievements of algebra classes.* Paper presented at the annual meeting of the American Educational Research Association, New York, NY. (ERIC Document Reproduction Service No. ED141118)

McLeod Humphrey, S. (2005). *Dare to dream! 25 extraordinary lives.* Amherst, NY: Prometheus Books.

Miner, B. (2008). An urban farmer is rewarded for his dream. *New York Times.* Accessed at www.nytimes.com/2008/10/01dining/01genius.html on July 22, 2010.

Mitchell, M. (1992). *A multifaceted model of situational interest in the secondary mathematics classroom.* Unpublished doctoral dissertation, University of California, Santa Barbara.

Mitchell, M. (1993). Situational interest: Its multifaceted structure in the secondary school mathematics classroom. *Journal of Educational Psychology, 85,* 424–436.

Morehouse, L. (2009). Rural students reap academic gains from community service: In Fowler, California, one school district weaves farm-focused service learning throughout the curriculum. *Edutopia.* Accessed at www.edutopia.org/service-learning-fowler on February 4, 2010.

Moriarity, B., Douglas, G., Punch, K., & Hattie, J. (1995). The importance of self-efficacy as a mediating variable between learning environments and achievement. *British Journal of Educational Psychology, 65,* 73–84.

Moseman, A. (2010). How animals suck: 9 creatures that slurp creatively. *Discover Magazine.* Accessed at http://discovermagazine.com/photos/02-how-animals-suck-9-creatures-with-inventive-slurping-techniques on March 12, 2010.

Moursund, D. (2003). *Project-based learning using information technology* (2nd ed.). Eugene, OR: International Society for Technology in Education.

Multon, K. D., Brown, S. D., & Lent, R. W. (1991). Relation of self-efficacy beliefs to academic outcomes: A meta-analytic investigation. *Journal of Counseling Psychology, 38,* 30–38.

Murdock, T. B. (2009). Achievement motivation in racial and ethnic context. In K. R. Wentzel & A. Wigfield (Eds.), *Handbook of motivation at school* (pp. 433–462). New York: Routledge.

National Research Council, Committee on Increasing High School Students' Engagement and Motivation to Learn. (2004). *Engaging schools: Fostering high school students' motivation to learn.* Washington, DC: National Academies Press.

National Youth Violence Prevention Resource Center. (2010). *National Youth Violence Prevention Resource Center.* Accessed at www.safeyouth.org on March 15, 2010.

Ogg, A. (2009). Before-class exercise program at Allendale school aims to jump-start brainpower. *The Grand Rapids Press.* Accessed at www.mlive.com/news/grand-rapids/index.ssf/2009/11/before-class_exercise_program.html on February 4, 2010.

Osborne, J. F. (2009/2010). An argument for arguments in science class. *Phi Delta Kappan, 91*(4), 62–65.

Panati, C. (1987). *Extraordinary origins of everyday things.* New York: Perennial Library.

Pappas, T. (1989). *The joy of mathematics: Discovering mathematics all around you* (Rev. ed.). San Carlos, CA: Wide World/Tetra.

Pappas, T. (1997). *Mathematical scandals.* San Carlos, CA: Wide World/Tetra.

Patall, E. A., Cooper, H., & Robinson, J. C. (2008). The effects of choice on intrinsic motivation and related outcomes: A meta-analysis of research findings. *Psychological Bulletin, 134,* 270–300.

Pekrun, R. (2009). Emotions at school. In K. R. Wentzel & A. Wigfield (Eds.), *Handbook of motivation at school* (pp. 575–605). New York: Routledge.

Phosphorus (P). (2010). In *Encyclopædia Britannica.* Chicago: Encyclopædia Britannica Online. Accessed at www.britannica.com/EBchecked/topic/457568/phosphorus on March 12, 2010.

Platt, C. S. (2006). *Real cheesy facts about authors: Everything weird, dumb, and unbelievable you never learned in school.* Birmingham, AL: Crane Hill.

Pogash, C. (2009). A school-for-scribes program turns kids into novelists: Meet NaNoWriMo, a nationwide program that in which students write novels—for fun. *Edutopia.* Accessed at www.edutopia.org/arts-national-novel-writing-month on February 4, 2010.

Promislow, S. (2005). *Making the brain/body connection: A playful guide to releasing mental, physical and emotional blocks to success* (Rev. ed.). Ventura, CA: Edu-Kinesthetics.

Randolph, J. J. (2007). Meta-analysis of the research on response cards: Effects on test achievement, quiz achievement, participation, and off-task behavior. *Journal of Positive Behavior Interventions, 9,* 113–128.

Rapaport, R. (2008). Schools exercise fresh methods to keep kids active: Roll over, dodgeball—Bold new activities put the fizz back in phys ed. *Edutopia.* Accessed at www.edutopia.org/new-physical-education-movement on February 4, 2010.

Redfield, D. L., & Rousseau, E. W. (1981). A meta-analysis of experimental research on teacher questioning behavior. *Review of Educational Research, 51,* 237–245.

Reeve, J., & Deci, E. L. (1996). Elements of the competitive situation that affect intrinsic motivation. *Personality and Social Psychology Bulletin, 22,* 24–33.

Restak, R. (2009). *Think smart: A neuroscientist's prescription for improving your brain's performance.* New York: Riverhead Books.

Rhee, M. (2009). Scientists and thinkers: Roland Fryer. *Time.* Accessed at www.time.com/time/specials/packages/article/0,28804,1894410_1893209_1893465,00.html on March 12, 2010.

Roozendaal, B. (2003). Systems mediating acute glucocorticoid effects on memory consolidation and retrieval. *Progress in Neuro-Psychopharmacology and Biological Psychiatry, 27,* 1213–1223.

Rosenshine, B. (1970). Enthusiastic teaching: A research review. *School Review, 78,* 499–514.

Royte, E. (2009). Street farmer. *New York Times.* Accessed at www.nytimes.com/2009/07/05/magazine/05allen-t.html on July 22, 2010.

Ryan, R. M., & Deci, E. L. (2009). Promoting self-determined school engagement: Motivation, learning, and well-being. In K. R. Wentzel & A. Wigfield (Eds.), *Handbook of motivation at school* (pp. 171–198). New York: Routledge.

Samson, G. E., Strykowski, B., Weinstein, T., & Walberg, H. J. (1987). The effects of teacher questioning levels on student achievement: A quantitative synthesis. *Journal of Educational Research, 80*(5), 290–295.

Schiefele, U. (2009). Situational and individual interest. In K. R. Wentzel & A. Wigfield (Eds.), *Handbook of motivation at school* (pp. 197–222). New York: Routledge.

School of Mathematics and Statistics. (2005). *Arne Carl-August Beurling.* Accessed at www-history.mcs.st-and.ac.uk/Biographies/Beurling.html on March 18, 2010.

Schunk, D. H., & Pajares, F. (2009). Self-efficacy theory. In K. R. Wentzel & A. Wigfield (Eds.), *Handbook of motivation at school* (pp. 35–54). New York: Routledge.

Schwarcz, J. (2003). *Dr. Joe and what you didn't know: 177 fascinating questions and answers about the chemistry of everyday life.* Toronto, Ontario, Canada: ECW Press.

Shenkman, R. (1988). *Legends, lies, and cherished myths of American history.* New York: Harper Perennial.

Shenkman, R. (1993). *Legends, lies, and cherished myths of world history.* New York: HarperCollins.

Shors, T. J., Weiss, C., & Thompson, R. F. (1992). Stress induced facilitation of classical conditioning. *Science, 257,* 537–539.

Skinner, E. A., Kindermann, T. A., Connell, J. P., & Wellborn, J. G. (2009). Engagement and disaffection as organizational constructs in the dynamics of motivational development. In K. R. Wentzel & A. Wigfield (Eds.), *Handbook of motivation at school* (pp. 223–246). New York: Routledge.

Smith, H. A. (1985). The marking of transitions by more and less effective teachers. *Theory Into Practice, 24*(1), 57–62.

Smith, M. J. (1975). *When I say no, I feel guilty: Using the skills of systematic assertive therapy.* New York: Dial Press.

Smithsonian Center for Education and Museum Studies. (2010). *Secrets of the Smithsonian: Spiders in space.* Accessed at www.smithsonianeducation.org/students/secrets_of_the_Smithsonian/spiders _in_space.html on March 12, 2010.

Smithsonian National Museum of American History. (n.d.). *Gertrude Ederle: First woman to swim the English Channel.* Accessed at http://americanhistory.si.edu/sports/exhibit/firsts/ederle/index .cfm on March 10, 2010.

Smithsonian National Museum of American History. (2007). *On time: How America has learned to live by the clock.* Accessed at http://americanhistory.si.edu/ontime/marking/index.html on March 12, 2010.

Smithsonian National Zoological Park. (n.d.). *Goliath bird-eating tarantula.* Accessed at http:// nationalzoo.si.edu/Animals/PhotoGallery/Invertebrates/4.cfm on March 12, 2010.

Snyder, T. (2008). Barnum & Bailey clowns teach kids to be "circus fit": Kids learn to shape up, circus style. *Edutopia.* Accessed at www.edutopia.org/circusfit-circus-physical-education on February 4, 2010.

Stajkovic, A. D., & Luthans, F. (1998). Self-efficacy and work-related performance: A meta-analysis. *Psychological Bulletin, 124*(2), 240–261.

Stone, A. (2004). Fibonacci cactus. *Discover Magazine.* Accessed at http://discovermagazine.com/ 2004/jul/fibonacci-cactus0708 on May 27, 2010.

Styles, E. A. (1997). *The psychology of attention.* East Sussex, UK: Psychology Press.

Swearer, S. M., Espelage, D. L., & Napolitano, S. A. (2009). *Bullying prevention and intervention: Realistic strategies for schools.* New York: Guilford Press.

Szczurek, M. (1982). *Meta-analysis of simulation games effectiveness for cognitive learning.* Unpublished doctoral dissertation, Indiana University, Bloomington.

Taylor, W. (1953). Cloze procedure: A new tool for measuring readability. *Journalism Quarterly, 30,* 415–433.

Time. (2010). Person of the year: 1930s. *Time.* Accessed at www.time.com/time/personoftheyear/ archive/covers/1930.html on March 12, 2010.

The United States Mint, U.S. Department of the Treasury. (2010). *Historian's corner: Coin production.* Accessed at www.ustreas.gov/education/faq/coins/production.shtml on May 27, 2010.

Van Honk, J., Kessels, R. P. C., Putnam, P., Jager, G., Koppeschaar, H. P. F., & Postma, A. (2003). Attentionally modulated effects of cortisol and mood on memory for emotional faces in healthy young males. *Psychoneuroendocrinology, 28*(7), 941–948.

VanSickle, R. L. (1986). A quantitative review of research on instructional simulation gaming: A twenty-year perspective. *Theory and Research in Social Education, 14*(3), 245–264.

Vickers, D. (Executive Producer). (2010). *The tonight show with Jay Leno: Headlines* [Television show]. Accessed at www.nbc.com/the-tonight-show/photos/categories/headlines/1537 on March 5, 2010.

Walberg, H. J. (1999). Productive teaching. In H. C. Waxman & H. J. Walberg (Eds.), *New directions for teaching practice and research* (pp. 75–104). Berkeley, CA: McCutchan.

Weiner, N. (1954). *The human use of human beings.* Garden City, NY: Doubleday.

Wilford, J. N. (1981). 9 percent of everyone who ever lived is alive now. *New York Times.* Accessed at www.nytimes.com/1981/10/06/science/9-percent-of-everyone-who-ever-lived-is-alive-now.html on March 12, 2010.

Wise, K. C., & Okey, J. R. (1983). A meta-analysis of the effects of various science teaching strategies on achievement. *Journal of Research in Science Teaching, 20*(5), 415–435.

Wentzel, K. R. (2009). Students' relationships with teachers as motivational contexts. In K. R. Wentzel & A. Wigfield (Eds.), *Handbook of motivation at school* (pp. 301–322). New York: Routledge.

Williams, J., & Deal Reynolds, T. (1993). Courting controversy: How to build interdisciplinary units. *Educational Leadership, 50*(7), 13–15.

Williams, R. G., & Ware, J. E., Jr. (1976). Validity of student ratings of instruction under different incentive conditions: A further study of the Dr. Fox effect. *Journal of Educational Psychology, 68*(1), 48–56.

Williams, R. G., & Ware, J. E., Jr. (1977). An extended visit with Dr. Fox: Validity of student satisfaction with instruction ratings after repeated exposures to a lecturer. *American Educational Research Journal, 14*(4), 449–457.

Wyckoff, W. L. (1973). The effects of stimulus variation on learning from lecture. *Journal of Experimental Education, 41*(3), 85–96.

Xinzhen, L. (2008). The mother of invention: China's four great ancient inventions have left their mark on local and global development. *Beijing Review, 35*, 46–47. Accessed at http://media.web.britannica.com/ebsco/pdf/34/34233360.pdf on March 12, 2010.

Zimmer, C. (2009). The brain: Humanity's other basic instinct: Math. *Discover Magazine.* Accessed at http://discovermagazine.com/2009/nov/17-the-brain-humanity.s-other-basic-instinct-math on March 12, 2010.

INDEX

G

game-like activities, 9–10, 57–59, 80, 150–151, 168
Gerwels, M. C., 4
give one, get one, 26
goals, 12
    academic goals, setting personal, 119–121
    cognitively complex tasks, 14–15
    personal, 13–14
    providing choice of learning, 104
    self-system, 13
Goldsmith, M., 25
Good, C., 18
Good, T., 5, 10
Goodenow, C., 6
guest speakers, use of, 69

H

Handbook for Classroom Management That Works (Marzano), 37
Hands On: How to Use Brain Gym in the Classroom (Cohen and Goldsmith), 25
Hannaford, C., 25
Herald-Brown, S., 4
Hess, D. E., 61–62, 63
Hidi, S., 7
Hoose, P. M., 128
How do I feel? *See* emotions, assessment of
human graph, 26
humor, 6
    class symbol for, 34
    exercise, 35, 51–52, 163–164
    headlines or quotes, using funny, 32–34
    movie clips and media entertainment, 34
    planning, 150
    self-directed, 32
    websites, 33
Humphrey, S. M., 128

I

importance, perceived, 12–15
    connecting to students' life ambitions, 92–98
    connecting to students' lives, 88–91
    knowledge, encouraging application of, 99–109
incongruity theories, 9–10
inconsequential competition, 10, 57–59
individual interest, 7
information, presenting unusual, 11, 65

books for, 67–68
exercise, 70, 82, 170
guest speakers, use of, 69
to introduce a lesson, 68
online sources, 65–67
planning, 151
resources for, 67–68, 187–199
student research and collection of facts, 68–69
information about students, identify and use positive, 40
    class discussions, use of, 41–42
    class inventories, use of, 41
    fellow teachers, 43–44
    parents and guardians, 42–43
    structured activities, use of, 41–42
intensity, defined, 6
intensity and enthusiasm, demonstrating
    exercise, 35, 51, 163–164
    personal stories, 30
    planning, 148
    verbal and nonverbal signals, use of, 31
    zest for teaching, 31
interest
    research on role of, 7–12
    situational versus individual, 7
    triggered situation versus maintained situational, 7–8
interest, methods for maintaining situational
    competition, inconsequential, 10, 57–59, 80
    controversy, initiating friendly, 10–11, 59–65, 81
    game-like activities, 9–10, 57–59, 80
    information, presenting unusual, 11, 65–70, 82
    questioning strategies, 11–12, 70–78, 83–84
investigation, 100, 101
It's Our World, Too! Stories of Young People Who Are Making a Difference (Hoose), 128

J

Jacobs, H. H., 92
Jensen, E., 5
Jeopardy!, 58
Johnson, D., 10–11
Johnson, R., 10–11
Jonas, P., 6

K

Kay, K., 15
Kepner Educational Excellence Program, 106–107

MARZANO Research Laboratory

Powered by Solution Tree

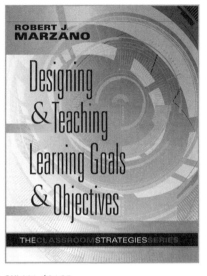
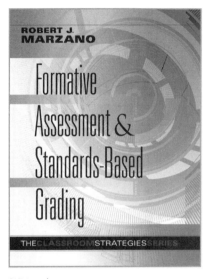

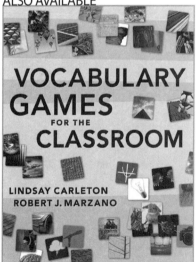